Praise for *Creating a Reading Culture in Primary and*

'Every educator engaged in promoting reading, school librarians, teachers, support staff and senio this book to their continuing professional development reading list. This comprehensive resource emphasises the cultivation of a reading culture within schools, with the ultimate goal of nurturing lifelong readers. The book extensively incorporates peer-reviewed research, not only from Western sources but also from other perspectives.

Establishing the significance and impact of fostering a comprehensive whole school reading culture, this book equips readers with the knowledge to comprehend and implement a diverse array of practical strategies, designed to be integrated into a well-managed approach that involves ethical evaluation and analysis. An invaluable tool for those wanting to foster a holistic culture of reading in both primary and secondary schools.'
Barbara Band, school library consultant and trainer, England

'Dr Merga has written a fantastic and valuable resource to help educators advocate for and develop a sound evidence-based reading culture that is an integral part of the school environment.

Having undertaken extensive research in this field, Dr Merga brings together her knowledge and insight to create the why and how for schools at all levels to create a reading culture, placing school libraries at the centre of the school community. This resource provides the data, evidence and the tools needed for schools to develop a healthy, positive and productive reading culture. With sections that include the why, the research, best practice, engaging stakeholders, implementation, evaluation and reporting, schools at any part of their journey to creating a reading culture will find just what they need in this resource. I can't wait to use this to help guide "my" school in our journey.'
Sasha Eastwood, Manchester Street School Librarian & Resource Manager, Manawatū, Aotearoa New Zealand

'More than anything, I wish to be a librarian in a school which embraces all the best practices which Dr Merga has recommended. This book provides a guide by which teacher librarians – along with fellow educators and leadership – can generate a whole school reading culture.

Supported by extensive research, Dr Merga outlines criteria and establishes priorities which directly result in students' increased opportunities to read and identify as readers. Our entire school community would immediately benefit by implementing the strategies which Dr Merga has set forth. Readers will appreciate the thoughtful and comprehensive approach to making real and impactful changes in how our schools foster a love of reading across all grade levels.'
Amy Hermon, High School Librarian, Michigan, USA and host of School Librarians United podcast

'This book is the WHY and the HOW of creating a reading culture in any school. Margaret provides robust confirmation for the importance and impact of reading for pleasure based on international evidence and her own rigorous research. The strength of the "why" makes it clear that this is a "must do" for all schools. The "how" is a highly practical and achievable guide which can be adapted and implemented in any context.

Educators are guided based on strong research evidence which draws upon a range of disciplines and industry expertise, including leadership, change management, educational and motivational psychology and research methodology. An essential book for all educators looking to improve the learning outcomes and wellbeing of their students.'
Hajnalka Molloy, Learning Resources Manager (Teacher Librarian), Concordia College, South Australia

'Supporting reading is rightly considered to be a main function and role for the contemporary school library/ian. If you're experiencing difficulties in embedding a reading culture or positioning the library as a major stakeholder in a school's strategy about reading, then *Creating a Reading Culture in Primary and Secondary Schools: A Practical Guide* by Margaret Merga is essential reading.

In an accessible and practical way, the author provides strategies, context, help and encouragement for librarians who identify the need to develop a school reading culture. As you would expect, the text is underpinned by research and evidence-based practice. Crucially, the book covers evaluating a reading culture and how to do it. Margaret's latest book offers dynamic, relevant insight for the school librarian to consider and ideas and strategies about how to implement this ever-important aspect of the school library/ian mission, which, as with other aspects of a school library programme, works best when in partnership with the school community.'
Dr Anthony Tilke, international school librarian, consultant, author and IB workshop leader, the Netherlands

'Margaret Merga's new book, *Creating a Reading Culture in Primary and Secondary Schools: A Practical Guide* is a hugely relevant read and coincides appositely with the Reading Schools accreditation programme in Scotland. She articulates all that I feel about the substantial role of school librarians in understanding pupils' reading habits and in establishing a reading culture in schools. She demonstrates with recent research that one of the most important things that schools can do to build a reading culture is to invest in a qualified school library professional.

Young people, more than ever, require literacy skill levels to participate in society and to access crucial information. Reading cultures must be a priority for schools. This is a vital book for our times and essential reading for all education professionals.'
Shelagh Toonen, Chair, School Libraries Group Scotland Committee, Scotland

Creating a Reading Culture in Primary and Secondary Schools

Every purchase of a Facet book helps to fund CILIP's advocacy,
awareness and accreditation programmes for
information professionals.

Creating a Reading Culture in Primary and Secondary Schools

A Practical Guide

Margaret K. Merga

© Margaret K. Merga 2023

Published by Facet Publishing,
c/o British Library, 96 Euston Road, London NW1 2DB
www.facetpublishing.co.uk

Facet Publishing is wholly owned by CILIP:
the Library and Information Association.

The author has asserted her right to be identified as author of this work. Except as otherwise permitted under the Copyright, Designs and Patents Act 1988 this publication may only be reproduced, stored or transmitted in any form or by any means, with the prior permission of the publisher, or, in the case of reprographic reproduction, in accordance with the terms of a licence issued by The Copyright Licensing Agency. Enquiries concerning reproduction outside those terms should be sent to Facet Publishing, c/o British Library, 96 Euston Road, London NW1 2DB.

Every effort has been made to contact the holders of copyright material reproduced in this text and thanks are due to them for permission to reproduce the material indicated. If there are any queries please contact the publisher.

British Library Cataloguing in Publication Data
A catalogue record for this book is available from the British Library.

ISBN 978-1-78330-638-1 (paperback)
ISBN 978-1-78330-639-8 (hardback)
ISBN 978-1-78330-640-4 (PDF)
ISBN 978-1-78330-641-1 (EPUB)

First published 2023

Typeset from author's files by Flagholme Publishing Services in
10/13 pt Palatino Linotype and Open Sans.
Printed and made in Great Britain by CPI Group (UK) Ltd, Croydon, CR0 4YY.

Contents

Figures and Tables	ix
About the Author	xi
Acknowledgements	xiii
Abbreviations	xv
Introduction	xvii

1. Why a Whole School Reading Culture? — 1
  Reading and social and environmental supports — 2
  Expired expectations and orphaned responsibility — 4
  Reading beyond testing — 4
  Benefits of reading engagement for literacy — 6
  Literacy and cross-curricular learning — 8
  Real-world advantages — 11
  The question of gender — 13
  Sliding literacy, reading interest and reading frequency — 15
  Read anything for literacy? — 19
  The ongoing importance of paper books — 20
  The importance of the school library — 22
  Recovering from COVID-19 related literacy learning loss — 23

2. Research-Supported Practices to Choose From — 25
  Opportunities for regular silent reading for pleasure — 26
  Supporting choice — 32
  Accessible and visible books — 36
  Investment in school libraries and collection building — 37
  Investment in qualified school library professionals — 39
  Teacher modelling — 43
  Engaging parental support — 48
  Talking about books — 53
  Creating and sustaining reading spaces — 56

	Reading aloud	59
	Professional development and laying the foundation	65
	Promising emerging possibilities	66
	Activities to be subject to measures of effectiveness	71
3.	**Stakeholder Engagement and Resourcing**	**73**
	Planning for initial and sustained educator and leader engagement	74
	Parents and guardians	77
	Grants for school-based research initiatives	81
4.	**Implementation Planning and Change Management**	**89**
	Change management	89
	Leading change in schools	90
	Step 1. Assess the opportunity for change and empower others to commit	92
	Step 2. Create and support a reading culture team	95
	Step 3. Formulate and communicate a powerful vision of the change	99
	Step 4. Plan for implementation	102
	Writing implementation plans	106
	Monitor and strengthen the change process over time	110
5.	**Evaluation**	**113**
	More about goals	114
	Introduction to basic quantitative, qualitative and mixed-methods analysis and data	118
	Getting quality evaluation data from children	121
	Quantitative analysis and data for schools	126
	Qualitative analysis and data for schools	138
	Mixed-methods analysis and data for schools	150
	Determining baseline data needs and evaluation planning	156
	Boosting quality with academic partnership	159
6.	**Reporting**	**167**
	Ethical reporting	167
	Professional outputs	171
	Media outputs	173
	Academic outputs	174
	Final points	178

Conclusions   **179**
    We need more research   180

References   **183**

Index   **205**

Figures and Tables

Figure
1	Smiley face rating scale	134

Tables
1	Percentage of children reporting enjoyment of reading books for pleasure by age group	17
2	Percentage of children who are frequent book readers (reading at least five times per week) by age group	17
3	Some possible distributed leadership roles on a whole school reading culture team	97
4	Differences in projected fruition of goals and evidence of success	105
5	Possible headings for implementation planning	107
6	Example of goals informing EQs and survey items (quantitative approach)	128
7	Joint display of reasons for agreement/disagreement on sufficient time	155
8	Joint display of influence of whole school reading culture implementation on students' enjoyment of reading	156
9	Possible headings for evaluation planning in Year 1 of implementation	158

About the Author

Dr Margaret Merga has written more than a hundred peer-reviewed and research-informed publications, with six non-fiction books on literacy, libraries, research methods and research communications. Margaret's research has been cited more than 2,600 times and translated into many languages.

Margaret is also an experienced educator who has taught in Australia, India, Thailand, Turkey and the US, across the age spectrum from kindergarten to adult education.

Recently, her 2022 book *School Libraries Supporting Literacy and Wellbeing* highlights her research on the relationship between libraries, reading and wellbeing.

Her 2023 book *Creating an Australian School Literacy Policy* details how to design and implement a whole school literacy policy.

Her most recent book *Creating a Reading Culture in Primary and Secondary Schools* explores building a whole school reading culture, including detailed content on the research in this area, as well as practical advice on how to evaluate such initiatives.

She runs Merga Consulting, working with schools, professional associations and government departments on a range of literacy-related projects. These engagements often involve developing or enhancing the schools' literacy culture.

Committed to sharing research knowledge beyond academia so that professionals can use research findings in practical ways, her work has been featured in the media, and she has won numerous awards for public engagement (see her LinkedIn profile).

Acknowledgements

First, I need to thank the schools and professional associations I have worked with over the years, both in a research and consulting capacity. I have learnt a lot from tailoring my work to your needs, and from the knowledge exchanges we have had.

Thanks to the wonderful team at Facet led by Pete Baker. As usual, you were responsive, supportive and enthusiastic, all an author can ask for. Thanks to Julie Rowbotham for applying your keen editorial eye, and to Michelle Lau for your diligence as Production Manager.

I also need to thank the Australian School Library Association for the ongoing encouragement and support I receive as your Patron. Your valuing of my work has motivated me to push through in challenging times. Thank you to the Western Australian School Library Association for also kindly making me your Patron.

I would also like to thank Professor Susan Ledger for appointing me as an Honorary Adjunct at the University of Newcastle, giving me access to the most current research in the field. Without this access, this book would not engage as deeply and directly with the current research evidence in reading engagement.

I would like to thank all of the co-authors I have worked with in the area of reading engagement, with a particular shoutout to my most regular collaborator in this research area, Dr Saiyidi Mat Roni. Thanks for also making yourself available for quick chats about the evaluation chapter, and for sharing your views on the validity of my assertions.

Finally, I want to thank my husband Marián for his support, and my sons Gabe and Sam for being consistently wonderful. Extra thanks to Gabe for the useful critical feedback on early drafts.

Abbreviations

ABS	Australian Bureau of Statistics
AISNSW	Association of Independent Schools of New South Wales
ASLA	Australian School Library Association
BUPA	British United Provident Association Limited
COVID-19	Coronavirus Disease of 2019
DoE	Department of Education Western Australia
EQ	Evaluation question
HDR	Higher degree by research
ISABR	International Study of Avid Book Readers project
NSW	New South Wales (in Australia)
OECD	Organisation for Economic Co-operation and Development
PIRLS	Progress in International Reading Literacy Study
PISA	Program for International Student Assessment
RCT	Randomised controlled trial
SHeLL	Sydney Health Literacy Lab
SLL	Struggling literacy learner
SMOG	Simple Measure of Gobbledygook
TLALAS	Teacher Librarians as Australian Literature Advocates in Schools project
UK	United Kingdom
UNESCO	United Nations Educational, Scientific and Cultural Organization
UNSW	University of New South Wales
US	United States of America
WASABR	West Australian Study in Adolescent Book Reading project
WASCBR	Western Australian Study in Children's Book Reading project
WASRA	Western Australian Study in Reading Aloud project
WHO	World Health Organization

WLR   We Love Reading project
WSLP   Whole school literacy policy

Introduction

Think back on your own time at school, and ask yourself the following questions:

1 Did your school encourage you to have a lifelong love of reading, or was it perhaps only concerned with reading for the purposes of assessment?
2 If you feel that your school encouraged you to have a lifelong love of reading, what was it about your school that led you to this conclusion?

Given that this book is focused on imagining and creating a reading culture, and fostering a lifelong reader identity in young people, critically reflecting on your own experiences as a student can be a good place to start.

Perhaps you found yourself within a richly supportive environment, where reading was celebrated, encouraged and supported. As explored in this book, and as you may recollect if this was your experience, schools can communicate valuing of reading in many diverse ways.

Alternatively, your school may have been a space where enjoyment of reading was positioned as peripheral and irrelevant. If this was you, and yet you are an avid reader, your love of reading may have been fostered at home, never nurtured within your school.

One of the key purposes of this book is to enable you to identify and harness the approaches, resources, and strategies that contribute to a school reading culture whether you had prior exposure to them or not. Even a thriving school reading culture can benefit from new insights that can make the culture even more effective, and help you to foster a love of reading in all of your students.

School culture is influential

Students spend so much time at school, it is vital that the activities, experiences and school cultures they are exposed to build their capacity as lifelong learners who will continue to develop their knowledge and skills in adulthood. Students in Organisation for Economic Co-operation and Development (OECD) countries spend an average of 7,590 hours of required instruction at primary and secondary school (OECD, 2019a), which is no small chunk of time. They are at a formative stage of their lives, and their schooling experiences can have a significant impact on their current and future trajectories. Unsurprisingly, the kinds of learning environments that students experience in their schools impact on their academic achievement (e.g. MacNeil et al., 2009), but students' experiences in school can also shape their behaviours and beliefs well beyond their schooling years.

What is a whole school reading culture?

Fostering a whole school reading culture can transform a school into a space where reading is supported, encouraged, normalised and valued. Reading cultures encompass environmental, skill and habit factors (Aslam et al., 2022), and the strategies and practices that underpin these kinds of cultures are directly linked to gains in reading engagement and related literacy performance (Merga, 2018a). Reading cultures seek to foster skills that have academic, vocational and social benefits, as well as conferring many other advantages as explored in this book. Given the ever-increasing literacy skill levels needed for active participation in society and capacity to access crucial information (United Nations Educational, Scientific and Cultural Organization (UNESCO), 2021), building reading skills through reading cultures should progressively emerge as a priority.

Motivation matters

It is the case that 'the activity of reading – with a focus on fiction reading – was and still is of primary importance for the development of children's and young adults' reading comprehension' (Pfost & Heyne, 2022, p. 2), as well as a range of additional benefits explored in this book.

When children begin to identify as readers, and they choose to read for enjoyment as one of their leisure pursuits, they are making an ongoing investment in both building and maintaining their literacy and cognitive skills, given that research has linked reading for pleasure and cognitive development in childhood (Sullivan & Brown, 2013), as well as cognitive function later in life (Chang et al., 2021). Despite these advantages, while researchers generally agree that motivation has an impact on student achievement, 'models of reading development generally fail to consider motivation or other social-emotional processes' (Toste et al., 2020, p. 442).

Motivation to read matters, but poor understanding of its importance is a key reason why advocates for reading cultures that foster reading engagement may lack the support they need to institute change within their schools. Unfortunately, fostering reading engagement remains a peripheral consideration in many schools (Merga & Gardiner, 2018), though you will be able to draw upon the research presented in this book to increase appetite for change in your school if needed.

Why this book?

I decided to write a practical and research-informed guide on how to create a whole school reading culture in primary and secondary schools as it is something I am very passionate about. It is also one of the things I am commonly asked to speak about at conferences and advise on within schools. I have personally published a considerable body of peer-reviewed research in this area, and I have also applied this research on a practical level, helping schools to develop reading cultures and engage teachers and parents in supporting reading beyond school. The point of this book is to make myself pretty much redundant, as you'll have the guidance you need to launch a whole school reading culture right here.

After a diverse career in education across age groups and continents, I have led a number of research projects that focused closely on reading engagement and factors that promote a reading culture.

- This started with my 2012 doctoral project, *The West Australian Study in Adolescent Book Reading* (WASABR), which was funded by an Australian Postgraduate Award. This project explored social and environmental factors that influence adolescent recreational book reading.
- Then in my first year as an early career academic I conducted the 2015 *International Study of Avid Book Readers* (ISABR), sponsored by an internal grant at my institution. This project collected data from more than 1,000 avid readers worldwide, providing key insights into the influences and resources that had resulted in them becoming keen readers.
- During this year I was also successful in winning an Ian Potter Grant, which enabled me to conduct the *Western Australian Study in Children's Book Reading* (WASCBR), which covered similar objectives to the WASABR but had a primary school rather than secondary school focus.
- Turning my attention to the reading engagement supportive practice of reading aloud in primary school, I was then co-lead investigator with Susan Ledger on the 2016 *Western Australian Study in Reading Aloud* (WASRA), funded by the Collier Foundation.

- I then led the Copyright Agency funded 2018 *Teacher Librarians as Australian Literature Advocates in Schools* (TLALAS) project, which examined the role of teacher librarians fostering reading engagement among numerous other objectives.
- Finally, the 2020 British United Provident Association Limited (BUPA) Health Foundation funded *School libraries promoting wellbeing* project enabled me to explore the link between reading engagement, libraries and wellbeing, despite the project being significantly hindered by the pandemic.

I have also been involved in or led many other literacy-related projects (e.g. Merga, 2020b).

What you will gain

I am passionate about translating research into practice, given that research in reading-supportive practices is of little use if it does not have practical implications that can be harnessed for student gains. In my 2023 book *Creating an Australian school literacy policy*, I explored the link between a whole school reading culture and literacy. However, given the focus of this book, I was unable to go into detail about how to actually establish a whole school reading culture.

This book picks up this thread but also stands alone as it can support you to establish a whole school reading culture. It contains easy-to-follow and research-supported information so that your approach to establishing this culture is both evidence-supported and realistically achievable among the other competing workload, resourcing and curriculum demands in your school.

Readers will finish this book with strengthened capacity in the following areas:

- You will be able to argue for the importance of a whole school reading culture, drawing on the recent research in this field.
- You will be knowledgeable about many research-supported strategies underpinning a whole school reading culture, and you will be able to select from these strategies to tailor your school's approach according to resourcing and priorities.
- You will have a clear trajectory for building and sustaining stakeholder engagement and resourcing, including insights into how to secure external funding for related initiatives.
- You will be able to plan and manage a sustained and multifaceted approach to enable real change within your school.

- You will have a broadened understanding of evaluation and reporting processes to measure and promote the successes you experience, sustaining the whole school reading culture into the future.

Finally, this book is for every educator working in a primary and/or secondary school. While my previous work focuses on school library professionals and English teachers, this book will be of use to any school-based educator or leader looking to successfully transform their school culture. This noted, it may be of particular relevance to school library professionals, as in my experience, this transformative work is often led from the library.

As with my previous work (e.g. Merga, 2022b), I have sought to draw on research literature from a wide range of nations, including translated works so that the knowledgeable insights of non-English speaking voices are not omitted, to ensure that my work has relevance that extends beyond the typically privileged Western perspectives (Mason et al., 2021). As a result, I hope the international reader will find that this book speaks to them, and that the recommended research-supported practical steps outlined within this book can be readily tailored to diverse learning contexts.

1
Why a Whole School Reading Culture?

Anyone who has ever set foot in a school will be able to tell you something about its school culture. As a former teacher, and as a researcher and consultant who has worked with schools in diverse capacities, it doesn't take me long to get a feel for what a school prioritises. Indeed, the more time we spend in a school, the more confident our perception will be, as we have increased exposure to the many tacit and explicit indicators of what it truly values.

Sometimes we may even see direct contradictions between what a school professes to value, and what they actually do in practice, as the shaping of a school culture is about what the school *both* believes and practises. Sometimes the tacit culture can subsume the explicit, approved culture. A school culture reveals itself in many ways, with students' academic results being just one of many indicators that those outside a school will draw upon to judge the merits of a school. A school culture relates to the values and norms of a school (MacNeil et al., 2009), and these are communicated by what occurs and is privileged within the school space, given the competing demands and differing resourcing schools experience, and the unique contexts contemporary schools are situated in.

The point of this book is to justify the transformation of school cultures into reading cultures, and to explain in practical terms how this can be done, drawing on the available research as well as my own experiences consulting with schools. A whole school reading culture cannot be achieved through making superficial or limited changes and commitments. In contrast, it

> provides children and young people the support, encouragement, role-models, resources and opportunity to read for pleasure. School leaders prioritise the development of the will to read, not just the skill, among students of all ages. They foster collaboration among staff, helping to weave reading for pleasure into every class, across the curriculum and into the daily life of the students.
> (National Library of New Zealand, n.d.-a, p. 1)

While there is limited research that has quantified the impact of a whole school reading culture on student reading engagement and achievement, there has been considerable research that has found positive effects of the *individual practices* featuring in a whole school reading culture, which are detailed and explored in the following chapter. Whole school reading cultures situate reading as important, enjoyable and valuable, and evidence suggests that young people who believe that reading remains important beyond learning to read are nearly twice as likely to read daily than those who do not hold this belief (Merga & Mat Roni, 2018a). A whole school reading culture can influence students' motivation to read, as well as providing valued opportunities to read, and access to reading-supportive environments and resources. As I explore in this chapter, a whole school reading culture can influence students' academic performance, but also offer a range of other advantages that are only just beginning to be fully realised in the research literature.

Reading and social and environmental supports

A school culture is shaped by its people as well as its physical environments and resources. Similarly, reading is a social practice that is absolutely influenced by both diverse social influences such as teachers, parents and friends (e.g. Merga, 2017a; Merga & Moon, 2016), as well as a wide range of other environmental elements (e.g. Merga, 2017d). Environments that communicate values and support beneficial behaviours can play a key role in sustaining young people's commitment to reading. Unfortunately, not all cultures, regions and nations celebrate the value of reading (Mahasneh et al., 2021), and as such, what is fostered in the culture of the school can play a key role in reinforcing the value of a practice that may not be encouraged beyond this space. However, this can be challenging when educational authorities and policymakers do not understand and support the need for whole school reading cultures (Margariti, 2022).

The strategies and practices promoted within a reading culture can emphasise the social acceptability of reading, influencing children's reading practices and identities. For example, a student described an exciting activity around reading which was held in her school library, explaining that

> we do a competition where we read (for) a certain amount of time, we record that time in minutes, and then we put that time into the library and they'll give it into points, and whoever has the most points wins at the end. We have it every year, and it's so much fun. And every day you get a sheet to fill it in, and it's so good . . . I'm so prepared.

Our class got first place out of the whole school for the first week, so we've got three very strong readers in the class, so that's not really a surprise.

(Merga, 2022b, p. 124)

As such, school cultures that value reading potential increase the social position of books and reading, providing extrinsic recognition not normally achieved by readers (Merga, 2022b). In the same way that schools celebrate their sporting victories, reading cultures celebrate reading and readers, situating reading as a socially desirable practice. This is a clear example of how whole school reading cultures are contexts where educators actively 'acknowledge the social practices connected with reading', and 'they build a sociocultural context that encourages the act' (Daniels & Steres, 2011, p. 3).

Becoming a reader is often a result of key social interactions with influential individuals and supportive environments. Findings from the ISABR project suggest that:

- most respondents became self-identified avid readers having been supported either directly or indirectly by key social influences (Merga, 2017a), and
- even avid readers need environments conducive to reading, that provide time, resources and space to make this possible (Merga, 2017d).

Paying attention to the social and environmental factors that influence the development of reader orientation is important given that we want children to have positive attitudes towards books and reading, as research suggests that young people who view books to be socially acceptable are more likely to read books in their free time, and to enjoy reading books for pleasure (Merga, 2014d). Whole school reading cultures set about creating spaces where reading is positioned as a valued social practice, and it cannot be taken for granted that students are already perceiving encouragement and support from influential individuals. In the WASABR, 29% of teenagers had no one encouraging them to read (Merga, 2014d). School cultures that value reading recognise the power of social and environmental influences, and take responsibility for ensuring that all students are being socialised to be readers.

Furthermore, when exploring reading as a social practice, we cannot ignore the potential impact of socio-economic status on young people's reading engagement. For example, in China, 'fewer children in lower-income households (<¥8,000) think reading books for fun is important compared to those in higher-income households (¥25,000+)' (Scholastic, 2020, p. 4), and there may be many reasons for this disparity, as explored further later in this book.

Expired expectations and orphaned responsibility

Reading remains important beyond the early years of school, and if we want young people to continue to read throughout the years of schooling, young people need to be *continually* socialised as readers, with social influences sustaining rather than withdrawing support as students move through the years of schooling. This can be related to two concepts that I have explored extensively in my previous work. These particularly come into effect once young people have acquired independent reading skills and focus may shift from learning to read to reading to learn within schools. Internationally, this is expected to occur by the fourth year of schooling (Mullis et al., 2023), though of course, this is not always the case for all students.

First is the concept of *expired expectations*. This relates to research findings that students may perceive a withdrawal of expectations that they read for pleasure once they learn how to read independently, which leads them to conclude that reading is no longer an important practice (Merga, 2023b). Second, encouraging children to read beyond the point of independent reading skill acquisition may become an *orphaned responsibility*, where parents view this as the responsibility of teachers, and teachers expect it to be the responsibility of parents, making it no one's role (Merga, 2023b).

It is vital that encouragement of young people is sustained beyond the period of independent reading acquisition, and that as far as possible, both home and school influences maintain their support and encouragement.

Reading beyond testing

One of the biggest challenges to schools' effective promotion of reading for pleasure relates to how literacy, and reading in particular, is situated within students' daily learning experiences. While the academic benefits of reading are clear, schools may inadvertently transmit the perception that reading is something done solely for the purposes of testing and learning, and not for enjoyment. Research findings from the WASCBR indicate that this conceptualisation of reading may not be uncommon, and that teachers' focus on reading for learning rather than enjoyment may play a role in cementing the divorce between reading and enjoyment (Merga, 2016b).

High-stakes testing in particular may influence how students view reading. It has been argued that

> perhaps no single educational policy change over the past fifty years has had as great an impact on the work lives of teachers in public schools in the United States and other developed nations as the movement to impose high stakes testing requirements.
>
> (Natriello, 2009, p. 1101)

Concerns have been raised across many nations about the amount of time spent teaching to the test in schools (e.g. Reeves et al., 2018), and recent media attention in the UK on the high-stakes testing of reading captured concerned parental comment, including a mother noting that 'it kind of feels like they're being taught how to pass the test, as opposed to being taught, and then the test is an addition' (Shearing, 2023, para. 12).

The media may play a significant role in amplifying the importance of literacy testing. High public interest in literacy means that slides in literacy performance at a national level rarely go unnoticed by the media. For example, recent declines in literacy performance in Year 6 students in the UK (in the first round of testing after the onset of the pandemic led to the cancellation of national curriculum tests in 2020 and 2021) were reported with the headline 'Sats results: Standards slip in Year 6 tests' (Shearing, 2022). On one hand, sustained focus on literacy learning is important, as literacy involves a complex skillset that needs to be developed across the lifespan. On the other, much has been written about the flaws of high-stakes testing: 'most types of assessments are very limited as student learning opportunities, and weighing the pig does not make it fatter' (Merga, 2023b, p. 133). It would be good to see greater understanding of this in the media, as well as greater understanding of the potential negative influence that these tests, and excessive *focus* on these tests, can have on students' attitudes towards reading.

If we want students to have a positive attitude towards reading, and see its value for life beyond high-stakes testing, we need to show its broader uses, and importantly, demonstrate how reading can be an enjoyable practice worth dedicating time to. I have recently explored how whole school literacy policies in Australia often place a disproportionate emphasis on high-stakes testing, noting that many of these policies rely solely on gains in high-stakes testing performance to demonstrate literacy improvement, as though literacy is limited to the narrow subset assessed in such tests (Merga, 2023b).

While this can be changed at a school level, resetting this positioning may need top-down support to give schools the freedom to prioritise reading for enjoyment. In some countries such as England, 'reading for pleasure has been mandated' (Cremin & Hendry, 2022, p. 214). In their statutory guidance, the Department for Education (2014) explicitly specifies in the *National curriculum in England: framework for key stages 1 to 4* that students should be 'encouraged to read for pleasure', and that 'schools should do everything to promote wider reading', providing 'library facilities' and setting 'ambitious expectations for reading at home' (p. 13). Despite these clearly articulated expectations, challenges to the effective implementation of these opportunities within schools remain (Cremin & Hendry, 2022), and schools may need explicit guidance on how to encourage reading for pleasure in research-supported ways. Nonetheless, in England there is a clear expectation that reading for pleasure be fostered in young people, whereas in many other countries such as Australia, reading for enjoyment is peripheral, sitting outside the expectations of a crowded curriculum (Merga & Gardiner, 2018).

The establishment of a whole school reading culture can broaden students' perceptions of the possible value of reading for pleasure, and encourage them to engage in the practice. For example, one of the positive effects of a US school's implementation of a whole school reading culture was a repositioning of reading: 'as one student said, "For the first time I feel that reading is valued for itself, not as a way to write a report or earn some points"' (Daniels & Steres, 2011, p. 9).

Benefits of reading engagement for literacy

Reading engagement has been conceptualised in many different ways, but it can be simplistically understood as relating to *attitudes towards reading* and *frequency of reading*, which may be reciprocally related to the development of *literacy skills* (e.g. Merga & Gardiner, 2018).

While frequency of reading is self-explanatory, attitudes toward reading should be understood in relation to the research on reading motivation. In their recent meta-analysis, van der Sande, van Steensel et al. (2023) differentiate between different types of reading motivation. They categorise motivational outcomes into three groups: '*affirming* (e.g. intrinsic motivation and reading self-efficacy), *extrinsic* (e.g. reading for competition and recognition), or *undermining* (e.g. avoidance goals and perceived difficulty of reading)' (p. 3).

Reflecting on the extant research findings that they analysed for this work, they note that 'affirming motivations are found to be most favourable for students' reading achievement, whereas undermining motivations are unfavourable', with findings on extrinsic motivations having varied effects on reading achievement (p. 3). Attitudes towards and enjoyment of reading as explored within this book typically relate to the building of affirming motivation as it is concerned with fostering a lifelong reading orientation, rather than satisfying short-term extrinsic goals. This position is taken given that 'investing in reading motivation can positively affect students' reading motivation and reading comprehension' (p. 18):

> reading motivation can be fostered by educational interventions and that, by promoting reading motivation, students' reading achievement can be increased. Apparently, increased motivation as an outcome of program participation results in students reading more frequently, which enables them to more effectively

practice their reading comprehension skills. Students might then enter a process of reciprocal causation, where increased motivation and proficiency mutually influence each other, eventually leading to long-term benefits. (p. 18)

As such, attention needs to be given to fostering affirming motivation. The mixed findings on extrinsic motivation mean that strategies and activities fostering this kind of motivation should be carefully considered, though I believe that when judiciously used, they can be very motivating. As I found in the *School libraries promoting wellbeing* project and the WASRA project, while the use of extrinsic motivators to encourage reading remains contentious, certain kinds of reward systems appear to have the power to motivate and encourage some students (such as the aforementioned school-wide reading competition that was so appealing to the student cited earlier in this book), and enhance the social positioning of books and reading (Merga, 2015c; Merga, 2022b).

Reading for pleasure offers benefits for students' vocabulary (Sullivan & Brown, 2015), and literacy benefits of reading are also particularly associated with reading comprehension (e.g. Torppa et al., 2020), which can be understood as an individual's capacity to understand and derive meaning from written text (Pfost & Heyne, 2022). Once children learn how to read, the volume of reading they achieve has a positive influence on their reading achievement, becoming a predictor of their gains in this key skill (Allington & McGill-Franzen, 2021). Pfost and Heyne (2022) explore how regular reading supports the development of reading comprehension in relation to the extant research, noting that regular reading:

- improves students' decoding skills, with repetition allowing students to develop 'their orthographic lexicon, which finally allows words to be read directly through a process of visual word recognition' (p. 3)
- exposes students to new words, supporting their vocabulary acquisition and knowledge
- fosters the building of prior knowledge, supporting text comprehension and leading to enhanced knowledge of narrative structures and concepts.

(Pfost & Heyne, 2022)

As such, building the habit of regular reading for enjoyment supports the development and maintenance of a diverse array of beneficial literacy skills.

While the importance of reading engagement for building and maintaining students' literacy skills may be poorly understood within schools, research has found that reading enjoyment contributes to reading achievement (e.g.

Retelsdorf et al., 2011). In one of the first longitudinal studies of the link between reading motivation and reading efficiency (as determined by eye-tracking), Rettig and Schiefele (2023) found that intrinsic reading motivation 'facilitates reading comprehension through its effect on reading efficiency, independent of variations in reading amount' (p. 1). A US study of more than 4,000 children in elementary school found positive associations between reading motivation, amount of reading and reading comprehension (Troyer et al., 2019), and international research across 65 countries contends that 'enjoyment of reading can predict as much as 18% of the variation in reading literacy on its own after controlling for other predictors' (Cheema, 2018, p. S150). A recent meta-analytic review of the relationship between motivation and reading achievement for school-age students, which included 132 research articles, found 'a significant, moderate relation between motivation and reading' (Toste et al., 2020, p. 420), also finding 'evidence to support the bidirectional nature of the relation between motivation and reading based on analysis of effects from longitudinal studies' (p. 442). This means that motivated readers show higher levels of reading achievement, with motivation influencing reading and vice versa. While further research is needed to explore how motivation shapes reading volume as well as reading performance, the growing body of research in this area highlights the importance of focusing on improving students' attitudes towards reading when seeking to improve their reading performance (Merga, 2023a).

Literacy and cross-curricular learning

Literacy skills have transferable value. Strong literacy skills developed in relation to reading motivation and frequency confer a significant advantage to students across the curriculum, given that literacy skills are drawn on both to learn and to communicate learning (Merga, 2023b). Students are assessed on their ability to demonstrate their learning, and this is mediated by their capacity to express this learning typically through writing and speaking. Literacy skills confer advantages across all learning areas, so a whole school reading culture can be expected to support improvements across these learning areas. Far more attention in schools needs to be given to the benefits of reading engagement for improving cross-curricular literacy (Merga, 2023b). Given the importance of the literacy skills being fostered by regular reading practice, schools that claim to support evidence-based practice should prioritise promoting positive attitudes towards reading and frequency of engagement in the practice in their students, and this goal should be supported by educators across the curriculum, as I explore further herein.

To further build understanding of the benefits of literacy skills strengthened by reading engagement across subject areas, given the current interest in enhancing whole school literacy, it is useful to consider these benefits in relation to *content area* and *disciplinary literacy* (Merga, 2023b). First, as previously contended, students who read regularly have stronger reading comprehension skills, and these general literacy skills are known as *content area literacy*, examples of transferable skills that support students' performance across *all* subjects. Building students' general literacy skills yields improvement across the curriculum. For example, literacy-supportive activities such as leisure reading are also related to stronger progress in mathematics (Sullivan & Brown, 2015), as previously highlighted.

Second, there are also *disciplinary literacy* skills which relate to literacy skills uniquely needed in a learning area, and these are also related to student attainment. For example, in relation to the subject history, recent research notes a link between subject-specific reading skills and students' historical knowledge and reasoning ability, and more generally in history, 'research has shown that both general reading skills and disciplinary literacy skills can contribute to students' understanding of the text and their content knowledge' (Beek et al., 2022, p. 5).

Reading skills also lead to advantages across the range of additional and valuable literacies with which they intersect. For example, 'basic reading comprehension literacy skills are needed to support health literacy so that meaning can be discerned from written information online' (Merga, 2023d, p. 295). As I explore in detail elsewhere, several nations include the building of health literacy in their curriculum (Merga, 2023d). Health literacy is a very important adjunct literacy skill that overlaps with traditional literacy skills, and given that health literacy is associated with improved health outcomes including longevity, it is literally a life-saving skill (Merga, 2023d).

Schools may stress the need for progressive digital literacy skills to equip students with the proficiencies needed to operate successfully in digitised workspaces, without necessarily considering the role of traditional literacy skills such as reading comprehension in underpinning these newer and evolving skills. The idea of being *future-ready* is pervasive and is promoted across the strategies and goals of many sectors, including education (e.g. Office of Educational Technology, 2016), but it may seem to ignore or even deliberately distance itself from persistent fundamental skills that continue to be needed for students to engage effectively with emerging technologies and applications.

For example, recent research has begun to pin down the advantages literacy proficiency offer students' digital literacy, which is increasingly essential to support students' academic performance in school. Findings suggest a strong link between reading achievement and quantity and quality of online navigation; as reading proficiency increases, the number of online pages visited also grows, with decreasing reading performance scores consistently related to lower activeness in navigation in most countries (OECD, 2021). It is important to also note that both the quantity and the quality of navigation are strongly related to students' reading performance (OECD, 2021), suggesting that better readers are more proficient at accessing information online. When you develop a literacy-supportive reading culture that encourages and provides opportunities for students to read deeply and often, and view reading in a positive light, you are also supporting students to build a skillset needed to remain abreast of online information needed to navigate increasingly diverse and complex digital data sources to meet academic requirements, also offering benefits beyond school. Genuinely 'future-ready' students will need old-school literacy skills applicable in new contexts, perhaps more now than ever.

Research into the specific benefits that reading skills confer across the curriculum has grown significantly in recent times. For example, there has been a recent 'growing expansion and maturity in the research on science and mathematics reading' (Tang et al., 2022, p. S11).

Neri et al. (2021) built on

> previous research, demonstrating that students' reading comprehension and item word count as one linguistic feature affect science performance. Our results indicate that with increased reading comprehension and word count, students' science performance increases as well. Particularly good readers seem to be able to extract the substance of written text from more extensive tasks and utilize it to solve items correctly. To ensure that weak readers do not suffer from a lack of competence in one area in other domains, enhancing reading comprehension in schools should be seen as a task not only for language education but also for science education or even across all subjects. (pp. 56–57)

If you are working in a secondary (high) school, your science teacher colleagues might be interested to learn that recent analyses suggest 'that the total effects of reading on science were much more than those of mathematics' (Zhu, 2022, p. 10), given that cross-curricular prerequisites for high-level science subjects are typically related to mathematics attainment rather than reading attainment.

Reading performance has also been found to have a significant influence on mathematics performance, with students with high reading performance also achieving high performance in mathematics (Ding & Homer, 2020). This relationship between reading and mathematics achievement may be particularly implicated in relation to mathematics word problems which require reading comprehension skills to be understood (Ding & Homer, 2020), placing reading comprehension as a gatekeeper skill for learning and performance in mathematics. In earlier research, the largest effects of reading skills for performance in mathematics have also been found in relation to 'Problem Solving and Data Interpretation skills', which are 'focused on the applications of mathematics knowledge', as well as 'Mathematical Concepts and Estimation' skills, with early reading comprehension related to a conceptual understanding of mathematics and the application of mathematics knowledge (Grimm, 2008, p. 410). As such, where students are struggling in mathematics, a focus on enhancing their reading skills can play a key role in improving their performance in this subject area (Merga, 2023e).

Real-world advantages

Linking in with the previous section, it should already be clear that the literacy capacities enhanced by a whole school reading culture confer real-world advantages beyond school. For example, knowledge of reading strategies to assess the credibility of sources has strong relevance for digital, information and health literacy (Merga, 2023d). Young people may need to assess the credibility of online sources on a regular basis for a wide range of academic and real-world requirements, and to do this effectively, they need to draw upon related traditional literacy skills in reading.

While young people are often confident users of technology, this does not necessarily mean that they have protective digital literacy skills which are related to reading comprehension. In a recent assessment of students' susceptibility to phishing, around 40% of students in OECD countries agreed that filling out a phishing form was somewhat appropriate or very appropriate, with less than a third of students agreeing that 'deleting the email without clicking on the link would be very appropriate' (OECD, 2021, p. 108). Unsurprisingly given this skill deficit, the US Federal Bureau of Investigation's (2022) *Internet Crime Report 2021* found that people under the age of 20 lost a stunning $101.4 million US dollars to online scams in 2021 alone. This highlights the intersection between reading skills and digital literacy, but also the valuable protective effect of these skills in online environments that students encounter beyond school.

Other real-world advantages of a whole school reading culture relate to the development of prosocial skills such as empathy and perspective-taking. As noted by Kozak and Recchia (2019), while 'extant research literature has focused primarily on the cognitive benefits of reading, such as spelling, vocabulary size, and general knowledge', 'recent empirical research provided exciting clues that the benefits of reading may extend to other abilities more directly reflected in social competence; namely, the ability to understand and sympathize with others' emotions, cognitions, and motivations', which can be known collectively as *social understanding* (p. 569). Exposure to fiction is associated with higher empathy levels, and some research suggests that exposure to fiction 'predicts performance on an empathy task', even after controlling for gender, age, English fluency and some related personality traits (Mar et al., 2009, p. 420). Other research in this space suggests that the extent to which readers are transported within a story may influence its capacity to foster empathy (Bal & Veltkamp, 2013), underpinning the importance that reading cultures facilitate young people's access to transportive fiction and spaces for immersive reading, to build the sustained attention needed to truly escape into a book.

More recent research seeking to understand the impacts of cumulative reading of fiction proposes that reading fiction can involve both exploring and experiencing complex emotions, highlighting an emerging relationship between fiction exposure and the capacity for moral judgement. The authors concluded that 'fiction exposure is a malleable intervention technique that cultivates one's ability to empathize, which in turn supports the experience of inferring and prioritizing actors' moral intention' (Xu et al., 2022, p. 278). This illustrates how a reading culture can do much more than strengthen students' skills across a range of literacies; it can also foster characteristics integral to compassionate citizenship.

On a related note, reading cultures can also make a powerful contribution to student wellbeing, with research associating opportunities for sustained and immersive reading with enjoyment, relaxation and an escape from stressors (e.g. Clark & Picton, 2020; Clark & Teravainen-Goff, 2018; Levine et al., 2022; Merga, 2017e). Regular reading is positively associated with young people's adoption of health-related behaviours (Mak & Fancourt, 2020b), and daily reading for pleasure may support the development of prosocial capacities, and lower levels of hyperactivity and related attentional issues (Mak & Fancourt, 2020a).

US surveys suggest that children may receive emotional support from the books they read, with:

- 74% agreeing that 'reading fiction and nonfiction is a way to help them understand the world'.
- 53% agreeing that a book has helped them through a difficult time.
- 52% looking for books that enhance their mood by making them laugh.

(Scholastic, 2019a, p. 6)

For an in-depth look at how libraries and reading can support wellbeing, my recent book *School Libraries Supporting Literacy and Wellbeing* (2022b) comprehensively covers the research in this area. School library staff see provision of a safe space for students as a key part of their role (Dix et al., 2020; Merga, 2022b). Furthermore, the World Health Organization (WHO, 2022) has included some of my research on libraries, reading and wellbeing in their WHO COVID-19 research database, highlighting the increasing recognition of the importance of libraries and reading-supportive cultures for young people. Other recent research with children in second grade in Israel has found 'reading motivation, wellbeing and literacy achievement were positively correlated' (Vaknin-Nusbaum & Tuckwiller, 2022, p. 17), warranting further investigation so that these interactions can be better understood.

The question of gender

When the subject of reading is raised, a focus on boys may be warranted, as in most nations, girls continue to typically outperform boys in high-stakes literacy testing of reading performance. In the recent Progress in International Reading Literacy Study (PIRLS) data that measured reading performance in students in Years 4 and 5, results indicate a general 'pervasive advantage in reading achievement' for girls in comparison with boys (Mullis et al., 2023, p. 29), though this was not found in all countries, and 'across countries in general, higher percentages of girls than boys responded that they "very much like reading", on average – 46 percent of girls vs. 37 percent of boys' (p. 118).

In the results for the Programme for International Student Assessment (PISA) 2018, which assesses older students at around 15 years of age (OECD, n.d.), 'girls outperformed boys in reading by 25 points after accounting for students' socio-economic backgrounds', though interestingly, boys typically felt that the test was easier (OECD, 2021, p. 106), indicating that confidence is not always strongly related to performance. Whole school reading cultures may play a key role in encouraging boys to adopt lifelong reader identities which can support their literacy skill development and counter some of the differences in ways that boys and girls are socialised as readers.

Socialising boys to be readers is important, as nurture is more important than nature when it comes to reading engagement and related literacy performance. While many have sought to attribute the difference in literacy performance between boys and girls to immutable differences with a presumably biological basis, boys can be avid readers (e.g. Merga, 2017b; Scholes et al., 2021), bringing this possibility into question.

The different socialisation practices of boys and girls and the resultant differences in participation in literacy-supportive activities can go a long way towards explaining why girls typically outperform boys. Loh and Sun (2020) describe how 'habitus' can shape young people's attitudes towards reading, drawing on a Bourdieuan definition of habitus as 'the embodied mental perceptions and attitudes of an individual which is developed through years of socialisation, often through one's early upbringing' (p. 235). They note that 'home socialisation practices that focus on cultivating independent and wide reading habits are key to the acquisition of school-valued ways of reading' (p. 247). This socialisation matters, and from the early years, it differs for boys and girls, as 'children come to schools differently resourced, not just in terms of the number of books but in terms of reading dispositions' (p. 247). The limited research we have on the socialisation of readers from Canada, the UK and the US indicates that parents spend more time reading with daughters than sons (Baker & Milligan, 2016), suggesting early differences in how we socialise young children as readers. Similarly, Australian research with children in primary school found that girls in primary school perceived more parental encouragement to read than boys, even though girls read more, so boys were in greater need of this encouragement (Merga & Mat Roni, 2018c).

Motivation and reading frequency matter when it comes to the gender gap, with research finding that girls have higher reading performance than boys, even when controlling for earlier literacy performance, and they also have 'higher intrinsic motivation than boys' (Kanonire et al., 2022, p. 8), and this more positive attitude towards reading has also been found by others (e.g. McGeown et al., 2012; Mullis et al., 2023). In Canada, 'girls (38%) are more likely than boys (30%) to be frequent readers' (Scholastic, 2017). In the US the difference is greater (26% of boys and 37% of girls) (Scholastic, 2019b). In general, international research supports the contention that girls read more often than boys:

> When asked how much time they usually spend reading for enjoyment, more than 75% of boys reported either none at all or less than 30 minutes a day; less than 3% reported that they read more than two hours a day. By contrast, 43% of girls reported that they read at least 30 minutes a day, and 8% of them reported reading more than 2 hours a day.
>
> (Schleicher, 2019, p. 32)

Reading cultures that support the development of positive attitudes towards reading can help to close the reading frequency and related reading performance gap between girls and boys.

However, while there is a lot of media attention on the gender gap, it is important to note that socio-economic status can be a more influential factor in shaping students' literacy performance (e.g. Medina & McGregor, 2019), and that in some countries there have been concerning declines in the reading performance of girls (Schleicher, 2019). Indeed,

> in 11 countries, namely Bulgaria, Hungary, Indonesia, Italy, Japan, Kazakhstan, Latvia, Mexico, New Zealand, the Slovak Republic and Switzerland, the narrowing of the gender gap in reading performance was due not to an improvement in boys' performance but to a decline in girls' performance. (p. 32)

Closing the gender-related performance gap should occur as a result of improving the performance of boys, not the declining performance of girls. The current reality is that 'on average across OECD countries, the gender gap in reading in favour of girls narrowed by 12 points between 2009 and 2015: boys' performance improved, particularly among the highest-achieving boys, while girls' performance deteriorated, particularly among the lowest-achieving girls' (OECD, 2016, p. 18).

As such, it is important that any gender-related consideration of literacy performance does not lose sight of struggling girls. Reading cultures should foster reading engagement and improve the literacy performance of all students. However, the impact of differences in socialisation in relation to gender may need to be taken into account, with emphasis given to the social acceptability of books and reading where cultural factors may position boys to believe that reading is not for them.

Sliding literacy, reading interest and reading frequency

Literacy performance is constantly being captured at individual, classroom, school, district/state and national levels, with sustained attention on improving performance to enhance students' learning outcomes.

At an international level, where literacy is measured through the somewhat limited Programme for International Student Assessment (PISA; for more on limitations, see Conclusions), nations seem to be locked into a relentless game of snakes and ladders, that given its system of ranking, can be viewed as a zero-sum game. In the last PISA capture of the limited subset of literacy skills tested, seven countries improved their reading, science and mathematics scores (Albania, Colombia, Macao (China), the Republic of Moldova, Peru, Portugal and Qatar), while seven countries saw declines in performance across these subjects (Australia, Finland, Iceland, Korea, the Netherlands, New Zealand and the Slovak Republic) (OECD, 2019b). While these assessments are useful for generating interest in enhancing student literacy, poor understanding of their limitations can lead to overestimation of their significance.

Nonetheless, they also have utility for drawing attention to dramatic differences experienced in underprivileged nations, highlighting the need for greater resourcing in these contexts:

> Around the world, the share of 15-year-old students, in grade 7 and above, who reached a minimum level of proficiency in reading (at least Level 2 on the PISA scale) ranged from close to 90% in Beijing, Shanghai, Jiangsu and Zhejiang (China), Estonia, Macao (China) and Singapore, to less than 10% in Cambodia, Senegal and Zambia (countries that participated in the PISA for Development assessment in 2017).
>
> (OECD, 2019b, p. 17)

Furthermore, 'on average across OECD countries, around one in four 15-year-olds did not attain a minimum level of proficiency in reading or mathematics' (p. 17), emphasising a need to identify and redouble efforts to support struggling literacy learners to attain functional literacy, and therefore optimise their academic, vocational and social goal attainment. Struggling literacy learners exist in every nation in varying concentrations, and they deserve attention and support that may in some contexts currently be inadequate (e.g. Merga, Mat Roni et al., 2021a).

Just as literacy performance sees fluctuations, young people's attitudes towards and frequency of engagement in reading for pleasure change over time. International data suggest that there has been a decline in reading interest; around half of students across OECD countries 'agreed or strongly agreed with the statement "I read only if I have to"', and this is a 13% increase in reluctance when compared with PISA 2000 (OECD, 2021, p. 78), and

> students seem to read less for leisure and to read fewer books of fiction, magazines or newspapers because they want to (as opposed to because they have to). Instead, they read more to fulfil practical needs, and they read more in online formats, such as chats, online news or websites containing practical information.
>
> (Schleicher, 2019, p. 14)

Recent international PIRLS data suggest that nearly 1 in 5 students in years 4 and 5 already report that they don't enjoy reading, and 'students who responded that they "do not like reading" had lower average reading achievement (491) than students who "very much like reading" (513) and students who "somewhat like reading" (501)' (Mullis et al., 2023, p. 115).

In Australia, 54% of 15-year-old students read 'only if they had to (38% in 2000, 42% in 2009 and 54% in 2018)' (Darmawan, 2020, p. 312), and a recent report from the Australian Bureau of Statistics (ABS) on cultural and creative activities in Australia found that children's participation in reading for pleasure had declined from 79% (2017–18) to 72% (2021–2) (ABS, 2023b). While 'around one third of these children read for two hours or less a week', 90% of children spent 'at least one hour a week on screen-based activities, with a rise in children spending more than 20 hours a week' (ABS, 2023a, p.1).

Similarly, research capturing trends in US adolescents' use of various media found that as contemporary adolescents increased their time spent on digital media, reading of books has shown a significant decline (Twenge et al., 2019), suggesting that modern affordances for competing media consumption may have played a role in the decline in reading engagement.

While these are not longitudinal data, and they are not captured at the same point in time, Scholastic surveys have attempted to quantify differences in book reading frequency and enjoyment between older and younger readers (see Tables 1 and 2).

Table 1 *Percentage of children reporting enjoyment of reading books for pleasure by age group*

	6–8	9–11	12–14	15–17
Australia	74	67	52	49
Canada	71	77	59	66
China	85	80	85	82
India	83	81	79	80
UK	80	65	46	43
US	70	66	52	42

(data from Scholastic 2016a; 2016b; 2016c; 2017; 2019b; 2020)

Table 2 *Percentage of children who are frequent book readers (reading at least five times per week) by age group*

	6–8	9–11	12–14	15–17
Australia	61	43	27	17
Canada	50	37	24	25
China	51	51	48	40
India	34	30	38	27
UK	54	43	24	17
US	55	35	24	11

(data from Scholastic 2016a; 2016b; 2016c; 2017; 2019b; 2020)

Due to the comparative stability of their (not longitudinal) data, China and India seem to challenge the trends seen in the rest of the countries in Tables 1 and 2, warranting research attention. This noted, in China and India, like the other countries, older children appear to be reading less than younger children. However, in China the oldest age group still reads books more often than in any of the other countries. The data from Canada were also interesting, as while comparison between the youngest and oldest age groups showed that the younger cohort read more often and had a more positive attitude towards reading, there was more variation in trends across the year groups than in Australia, the US and the UK.

There may also be a generalisable decline in relation to students' age in many cases, though more longitudinal research is needed that tracks the same cohort over time. Research suggests that 'in the upper half of primary school, students' interest in reading books and other long stretches of text begins to decline – a decline that continues into secondary education' (van der Sande et al., 2022, p. 2). US findings indicate 'a striking downward trend as children grow up' (Scholastic, 2019a, p. 6), and there is a decline in children's reading frequency in China that begins after age 12 (Scholastic, 2020). Similarly, researchers in Sweden recently found that typically, Grade 6 students held significantly more positive attitudes towards 'non-school-related reading' of both non-fiction and fiction than students in Grade 9 (Winberg et al., 2022, p. 14). Recent US research suggests that it is not uncommon for students to enter into higher education without having developed motivation to read, or confidence in their reading skills (Baldwin & Nadelson, 2022).

The causes of sliding interest and decline in recreational reading frequency may be complex. Research suggests that competing leisure pursuits may play a role (Scholastic, 2016a). There is a tendency for the decline in reading frequency to be explained away as a natural preference for other activities as young people mature. However, it is not that simple. Research findings from the subset of infrequent adolescent readers who took part in the WASABR suggest that while 'most respondents chose not to engage in recreational book reading because they preferred to do other things in their free time' (Merga, 2014e, p. 64), in many cases students reported 'physical and cognitive factors, a skill barrier, issues with access and choice and limited time availability' that also influenced this choice, so to simplistically attribute reader reluctance to a single cause can be problematic (p. 65). If we are serious about increasing young people's reading frequency in the later years of schooling, we will need to accept that there may be multiple factors that contribute to reader reluctance that will need to be given critical consideration in planning for a whole school reading culture.

Interestingly, young people have also reported changes in levels of encouragement received from their parents and teachers over time, with more support received in the earlier years of schooling than in the later years

(Merga, 2018a). For example, as part of the WASABR project, adolescents 'were asked to compare levels of encouragement to read books for pleasure at primary and secondary schools', and findings suggested that 'while many high school teachers were encouraging, most were not as encouraging as primary school teachers' (Merga, 2015c, p. 39). As such, I believe that at least to some extent, sliding literacy, reading interest and reading frequency can be related to the previously defined *expired expectations* and *orphaned responsibility*. We cannot, and should not ignore the impact of social influences on young people's attitudes towards reading, and, indeed, this book is very much concerned with fostering a culture in which social influences can combine to counter these two issues.

Read anything for literacy?

So can young people read anything in order to enhance their traditional literacy skills? As I have also covered extensively in my previous work, and I update here with reference to current literature, at this stage, all reading is not equally beneficial according to the extant research on the literacy-specific benefits associated with reading different text types.

Previous research has found that the reading of comic books is associated with minimal literacy benefit (OECD, 2010), whereas the reading of books, and fiction books in particular offer notable benefit (Jerrim & Moss, 2019). Book reading offers benefits for reading comprehension and vocabulary development, though reading e-mails, Internet-based information, social networking posts and text messages do not yield the same benefits (Baer et al., 2007; Pfost et al., 2013; Torppa et al., 2020; Zebroff & Kaufman, 2016). OECD (2011) research has found that while reading newspapers, magazines, and non-fiction books may offer some literacy benefit, 'the effect of these materials on reading performance is not as much pronounced as the effect of fiction books' (p. 100), and analysis of more recent PISA data also found that the reading of magazines, newspapers and comics 'seemed to negatively impact the reading performance of both female and male students' (Hu et al., 2023, p. 21).

However, this more recent research analysis of PISA data did yield new findings. In contrast to some previous studies (e.g. Mar & Rain, 2015) including those also using older PISA data (e.g. OECD, 2010), like the reading of fiction books, 'the frequent leisure reading of nonfiction books (e.g. informational, documentary), was also associated with high reading performance, especially among the male students' (Hu et al., 2023, p. 20). This new research is very welcome given the additional educative benefits that can be conferred in reading non-fiction books. For example, as I have explored in greater detail in my recent book, students can learn important health information from reading non-fiction books, and for some students, non-fiction books are the preferred text type for learning vital skills and knowledge in areas such as health literacy (Merga, 2022b).

One of the reasons that fiction books have been consistently associated with literacy benefits may be related to the richness of the vocabulary often used in fiction books. The reading of fiction books plays a key role in vocabulary growth, as 'compared to spoken language, fiction texts typically contain a greater number of word types, which appear in more diverse, meaningful contexts' (van der Kleij et al., 2022, p. 514). Children's leisure reading contributes 'to vocabulary knowledge, supporting the hypothesis that regular leisure reading promotes vocabulary development' (p. 521). Indeed, 'what is established beyond any reasonable doubt in research is the robust contribution of long-form, print reading – of books; often narrative – in the development and honing of a range of important reading skills' (van der Weel & Mangen, 2022, p. 6). As such, sliding interest in book reading may be of most concern for educators seeking to foster reading for literacy benefits.

This section should not be construed to mean that I think that young people should not be allowed to read comics, or that I think they should be banned from the Internet or prevented from sending text messages! Developing proficiency in different text types is a key component of literacy, and different kinds of skills can be built through engaging with multimodal texts. Indeed, my own research looks at how engaging with online texts could promote reading (Merga, 2021b). However, given the research on the impact of different text types on the fostering of traditional literacy skills, fiction and (as recent research suggests) non-fiction book reading should be encouraged and not excluded from a reading diet.

The ongoing importance of paper books

This is another area where opinions are strong, but not necessarily supported by research evidence. As noted previously, books may be a uniquely beneficial reading material (Merga, 2018a). Unfortunately, given their benefits, approximately a third of students rarely or never read books (OECD, 2021). However, in our push to be 'future ready' and responsive to students' preferences, should eBooks replace paper books?

Most children grow up in digitally saturated environments, with around 88% of students having home Internet and access to a computer for schoolwork (OECD, 2021). This ready availability, combined with the fact that young people are often broadly characterised as digital natives with uniform preferences for high levels of technology use, can lead to the assumption that they might prefer to read books in digital formats (as explored in Merga, 2015b).

However, research suggests that young people still enjoy reading paper books. Avid readers in Australia typically read paper books even where they have access to eBooks (Merga, 2014a; Merga & Mat Roni, 2017a), and a recent survey with children in China found that 83% 'would always choose to read books printed on paper even though there are eBooks available' (Scholastic, 2020, p. ii).

Is reading on devices the same as reading on paper? Recent research suggests that students who mostly read books on devices enjoy reading less, and score lower on reading, than students who read mostly paper books, or who read roughly equal amounts of both modes, even where gender and students' and schools' socio-economic profiles are taken into account (Ikeda & Rech, 2022). Unsurprisingly, there is also a clear link to student advantage in reading mode choice:

> On average across OECD countries, students who reported reading books 'more often in paper format' or 'equally often in paper format and on digital devices' tend to have more books at home than students who did not report the same. (p. 4)

I discuss issues around access and advantage further in the next chapter of this book.

International research has also found that students who read books in paper format more often than in a digital format 'perform better in reading and spend more time reading for enjoyment in all participating countries/economies in PISA 2018' (OECD, 2021, p. 14). Furthermore, the association between reading performance and time spent on digital devices for schoolwork was negative for most countries, even after accounting for the socio-economic status of both students and schools (OECD, 2021). Hu et al. (2023) also analysed PISA data, finding that 'students who read more often in paper format, regardless of their gender, tended to perform better in the reading assessment' (p. 18).

This is possibly due to differences in reading comprehension that have been noted between paper and digital text formats, with research finding that 'studying from digitally displayed text does lead to inferior understanding, as compared to studying from print' (Ben-Yehudah & Eshet-Alkalai, 2021, p. 427). A small study focused on children found that consistent with previous findings, children understand texts better when read on paper than on screen (Halamish & Elbaz, 2020). Furthermore, while further research is needed, recent research with adolescent boys in Italy also noted reading on paper related to better reading comprehension 'at the level of the main idea'

(Ronconi et al., 2022, p. 12). One of the most recent projects in this area (with 144 undergraduate student participants) found that while skilled readers had relatively similar recall of expository texts read in print and digital formats, researchers found 'a screen inferiority effect in less-skilled comprehenders' in both iPad and computer reading 'when compared to the paper condition' (Stiegler-Balfour et al., 2023, p. 8). As such, while further research is needed given the small sample size, it may be students with lower reading comprehension who are most negatively affected by shifts from paper to screen-based reading.

Furthermore, while there have been some contradictory findings, meta-analyses of reading comprehension between paper and digital formats have typically found that reading on paper is superior to reading on screen in terms of reading comprehension (e.g. Delgado et al., 2018; Kong et al., 2018), suggesting that at this stage, replacing paper books en masse with their digital equivalents without taking student preferences and differences in reading comprehension into account could have a negative impact on young people's reading attitudes, frequency and experience.

Recent research has been trying to find out why reading comprehension appears to be affected across modes. A study that found better comprehension in print format also noted that text format also 'affects the cognitive strategies employed, and that readers who read in print show more selective and intentional reading behaviours, likely reflecting self-regulation and metacognition to ensure better comprehension' (Jian, 2022, p. 1563). This suggests that people may approach reading paper and digital texts differently, using cognitive approaches that are not interchangeable, and therefore the differences in comprehension between text types should not be dismissed.

The importance of the school library

As I have explored extensively in my previous works (e.g. Merga, 2022b), a well-resourced and sufficiently staffed school library needs to sit at the heart of a whole school reading culture. Research examining the influence of diverse variables on children's reading has found that library visitation was a strong indicator of children's attitudes and frequency of recreational book reading, a more robust determinant than many diverse factors including but not limited to gender, age, and early literacy experiences (Mat Roni & Merga, 2019). Providing students with regular opportunities for library visits may be a valuable intervention for educators and parents seeking to enhance children's reading frequency and attitudes.

Many of the practices, strategies and resources explored in this book that underpin a whole school reading culture are available or facilitated through the school library. For example, school library professionals often play a key role in increasing staff reading engagement so that staff can be avid reader models for their students (Merga & Mason, 2019). However, the importance of these resources may be poorly understood, as I explore further in the following chapter.

Children need regular opportunities to visit well-resourced school libraries during class time in order to build and sustain a regular reading habit, and this is particularly important when children come from homes and communities that are not richly resourced in reading materials (Loh et al., 2022). Just because a school has a library, there is no guarantee that students will access it regularly, which is why facilitating access during class time is so vital:

> Levels of access to libraries to choose books during class time are concerning. Nearly a third of children with school libraries did not use them in class time to select books. In addition, it is surprising that 8.6% of students in school equipped with school libraries 'never' visit a school or public library to choose books. This suggests that schools are underutilizing libraries as a valuable resource and assuming that children have sufficient motivation to read to access books in their own limited free time. This places children in the position of having to choose between library visits, sports, and play, and therefore likely to predispose students who are not avid readers, or who do not have friends who are avid readers, to be infrequent library visitors for this purpose.
>
> (Merga & Mat Roni, 2017b, p. 623)

As children move through the years of schooling, library visitation 'during free time decreases compared to class time, highlighting the value of maintaining or even increasing library visits during class time' (p. 623). Reducing library visits during class time can communicate to children that reading for pleasure and books are no longer important, and it can seriously curb young people's access to (and motivation to access) reading materials, also limiting their access to a reading-conducive space.

Recovering from COVID-19 related literacy learning loss

Establishing a whole school reading culture can be a core part of a suite of strategies implemented to recover from COVID-19 related literacy learning loss, reinvigorating the school learning environment while clawing back lost learning in literacy. Impacts on normal operations varied widely:

> On average, across countries, only 14 percent of the fourth grade students attended schools where normal operations were 'not affected' by the COVID-19 pandemic during the 2020–2021 school year. In contrast, 47 percent attended schools where normal operations were affected by the COVID-19 pandemic for 'more than 8 weeks' of instruction. The remaining students experienced more moderate disruptions; 10 percent of students attended schools where 'less than 2 weeks' of instruction were affected by the COVID-19 pandemic, 15 percent where '2 to 4 weeks' of instruction were affected, and 13 percent where '5 to 8 weeks' of instruction were affected.
>
> (Mullis et al., 2023, p. 13)

Researchers are still scrambling to quantify the degree of learning loss experienced by students during COVID-19 related school closures, and while causation cannot be established, 'in general there are downward trends in PIRLS 2021 that likely are evidence of the assessment taking place during the COVID-19 pandemic' (p. 18). While ongoing effects are currently being measured, some findings indicate negative impacts on students' literacy learning, with declines in primary school reading comprehension (e.g. Lerkkanen et al., 2022) among recent findings. US research suggests that many students experienced a reading achievement gap, struggling to reach achievement gains typical in pre-pandemic conditions, and students from disadvantaged backgrounds face a longer recovery time than their more advantaged peers (Lewis & Kuhfeld, 2022).

Similarly, a longitudinal study conducted in the UK found that children in Year 2 have caught up with their expected attainment in maths, 'but are behind where they would be expected to be in reading' (Wheater et al., 2022, p. 5), and

> the proportion of very low attaining pupils has increased. In Year 2 reading, the proportion rose from 2.6% to 9.1% and for maths, from 2.6% to 5.5% compared with before the pandemic. In Year 3 reading, the proportion rose from 2.5% to 6.5% and for maths, from 2.4% to 3.9% compared with before the pandemic. (p. 5)

Once foundational independent reading skills have been attained, providing opportunities for reading in a reading-supportive environment can help to address these persistent literacy performance gaps.

2
Research-Supported Practices to Choose From

As I explore in this chapter, there is a wealth of research exploring the benefits of a range of socially and environmentally mediated practices designed to build reading engagement and a reading culture in a school. Simply, reading engagement cannot continue to be ignored as a crucial support for enhancing students' literacy performance. We need to foster whole school reading cultures that seek to improve students' attitudes towards and frequency of engagement in literacy-supportive practices such as reading, and do this alongside the explicit literacy skills instruction that ideally should be occurring across subject areas (e.g. Merga, 2023b).

As previously noted, young people who believe that reading remains important beyond learning to read are nearly twice as likely to read daily than those who did not share this view (Merga & Mat Roni, 2018a), and we cannot take for granted that students understand the importance of an ongoing commitment to reading. A survey of Australian children aged 6–17 found that only 58% of children understood that reading books for fun is highly important, and children's views on the importance of reading may decline dramatically by age (Scholastic, 2016a).

But how can we effectively encourage students to enjoy and value reading according to the research? What are evidence-supported practices when it comes to building reading engagement?

I explore research-supported practices that can feature in a whole school reading culture here, drawing on key research findings, and making reference to current research that has been released since my earlier book in this space (e.g. as reported in Merga, 2018a). While there are some good auditing tools that have been created around fostering a whole school reading culture (e.g. National Library of New Zealand, n.d.-a; n.d.-c), the links to the extant research in such tools can often be cursory, so reading this chapter will equip you to make a strong argument to support the implementation of any of the strategies detailed herein.

Opportunities for regular silent reading for pleasure

If we want young people to be readers, we need to provide opportunities for them to read. With research 'linking volume of reading to reading achievement and oral reading fluency', it is surprising that this educational practice is peripheral in many contemporary schools (Allington, 2014, p. 22). As such, enabling regular silent reading for pleasure can be one of the most potent strategies underpinning a push to see literacy gains, and to develop a whole school reading culture (Merga & Mason, 2019).

Recent analysis of PISA data of 439,847 15-year-old students from 61 countries/regions suggests that students should aim to read for pleasure for two hours per day to see optimal benefits for reading performance (Hu et al., 2023). While this may not be practical for all students to maintain daily given their many competing commitments, I am often asked by schools to provide a research-supported target amount that we can strive for. Students who read for less time than this, but still have reading opportunities, will still experience growth in their reading skills that may not be achieved where there is *no* time spent reading for pleasure. This study also found 'a positive relationship' between 'school-related reading of fiction and both female and male students' reading performance, extending previous research that highlighted the importance of the leisure reading of fiction' (p. 19), and highlighting the importance of providing opportunities for reading for pleasure at school.

If sustained opportunities for reading for pleasure are not provided at school, there is no guarantee that it is happening at home, so schools can never relinquish this responsibility. Children are not equally well-resourced in their home spaces, and adults do not always understand the time constraints faced by young people beyond school, some of which emerged in the WASABR research with adolescents:

> Some students were genuinely unable to read books for recreation due to heavy non-recreational commitments, including paid work, sibling care and a substantial load of schoolwork. One student commented that she was always 'either working, or I've got school, or school homework or exams or something like that. There's always something, so I hardly ever have time to do it'. She was balancing three casual jobs with widely varying working hours, and found herself unable to immerse herself in a book for a sustained period of time because of these distractions.
>
> (Merga, 2016c, p. 417)

This same student did often purchase books to read; she just rarely had time to read them. This scenario may resonate with some of the time-poor adults reading this book, who have 'to be read' piles next to their beds that are growing precariously tall.

For some students, the only sustained reading for pleasure that they do happens at school for many reasons, some of which relate to individual preferences for leisure time, as explained by an eleven-year-old boy that I interviewed. He explained that

> at school, I like to read a bit better, because like at home, 'cos at school I'm not really allowed to do, like, play on my video games as well at school, so then when I go home, I have the opportunity to play them, and then I also have martial arts and stuff that I do, so I have to go to those, and I have all these after school clubs, and stuff. So I prefer reading more at school.
>
> (Merga, 2018b, p. 75)

Students who do not choose to read at home, or who cannot read at home, have reported finding enjoyment and relaxation in reading at school:

> While speaking with a Year 10 male, who claimed to rarely read for pleasure, it became apparent that the silent reading session was the only time he read books. Even though he characterised himself as a staunch non-book reader, when I asked him if he enjoyed his silent reading time, he responded, 'Yeah, I do. I just like . . . sitting there for an hour, and just chillin'. He did actually read during this time, and was able to provide an account of books that he had slowly worked his way through.
>
> (Merga, 2013, p. 235)

I argue that 'one of the most significant indicators in favour of the continuance of silent reading into the secondary years was the number of students for whom this was the only book reading they did' (p. 242). Given the clearly detailed associations between reading opportunities and literacy growth outlined already in this book, curtailing these opportunities can be problematic. However, my research found that while 65% of Year 8s reported experiencing silent reading, only 13% of Year 10s still had a regular opportunity to read for pleasure at school (Merga, 2013), demonstrating how opportunities for silent reading in school may significantly drop as students progress through the years of schooling.

Without the encouragement and support of leadership, reading for pleasure can be viewed as peripheral pedagogy. Teachers may need to 'fight or be sneaky to allocate any meaningful time to actual reading' (Daniels & Steres, 2011, p. 6). This may in part be because of the crowded curriculums and priorities that many schools must be responsive to, but can also be attributed to the unfortunate reality that the educational benefits of reading opportunities already outlined in this book may be poorly understood in schools. The merits of commercial education products as literacy fixes may in many cases lack the research evidence underpinning sustained reading, but they have good salespeople.

As such, Vanden Dool and Simpson (2021) contend that reading for pleasure 'is a somewhat "fluffy" pedagogy', uncomfortably parallel to a didactic notion of literacy 'tied to economic rationalist motivations and generation of human capital' (p. 121). Opportunities for regular silent reading for pleasure may be situated as a waste of time where the diverse and significant benefits of the practice are not known, with time instead given to literacy practices and products that offer fewer benefits but fit the didactic model of learning. Once students have acquired foundational independent reading skills, readers of all ability levels benefit from the opportunity to extend their literacy skills through immersive and sustained exposure to reading. However, the WASCBR research has found that 'silent reading was positioned as an optional extra in some contexts, which made it vulnerable to inconsistent delivery', and 'where silent reading was not privileged', it was easily ignored or replaced by other competing demands, ironically often associated with less educative benefit (Merga, 2018b, p. 78). We will now turn our attention to how to ensure that students have a high-quality experience when engaging in silent reading for pleasure within our school.

Self-selection: preferable but not always viable

Self-selection of reading materials has long been positioned as an important component of silent reading for pleasure, with Krashen (2011) listing 'let students select their own material' as one of 15 guidelines on sustained silent reading (p. 9). My research also found that 'one of the favoured aspects of silent reading was the possibility for choice, with access to books closely related to enjoyment of the activity' (Merga, 2018b, p. 74). One young girl explained that

> we get to choose different books, and we don't have to . . . well when we feel like we don't want to read this book we can go put it back, and sometimes if like you're really stuck into it, they might give you five more minutes of extra time. That's really cool. (p. 74)

However, more recently researchers have contended that where students lack the skills to select books that meet their interests and ability levels, self-selection can actually have a dampening effect on reading engagement (van der Sande et al., 2022). While I explore this issue further in the subsequent section on supporting choice, it is important to note here that self-selection only works if students know *how* to do it, and if the collection is reflective of the interests of all students. It also fails to reflect the vital role that library professionals in school and public libraries can play in meaningfully connecting students with reading materials that meet their unique interests and needs.

Reinforcing the importance of reading

Silent reading at home may offer greater educational benefit than some of the tasks assigned (Merga, 2018a), and when teachers allow students to replace homework time with reading time at home, it can be an effective way of communicating the continued importance of the practice. Having expectations that students read, coupled with supportive encouragement and provision of opportunities to read at school can be particularly effective. For example,

Craig reflected that his teacher last year really encouraged the students

> because we had this holiday reading challenge thing, and you had – it was compulsory. So you had to read, but, yeah, last year, our teacher was more, like, 'You should read, you should read,' more than our teacher this year.

This teacher's expectations that students read at home were coupled with regular encouragement to read. Craig believed her to be considerably more encouraging compared with his Year 8 teacher, who also had high expectations of him to engage in regular reading, but without the same level of supportive encouragement.

(Merga, 2015c, p. 44).

In a similar vein, making time for silent reading at school, and taking students to the library to optimise the reading experience, demonstrates teacher valuing of reading, as described by this adolescent student:

Richard viewed the amount of time his teacher devoted to silent reading in the library as an indicator of his teacher's love of reading. When asked how his teacher felt about reading books, he stated, 'She loves reading. She's always going on about it. That's why we go to the library, I don't think any of the other classes do.' Providing an environment conducive to reading, such as a school library, was perceived as encouraging.

(Merga, 2015c, p. 44)

Given the many competing demands for student time, teacher investment of time in fostering this activity is perceived by students as reinforcing the continued importance of the activity.

Influencing the social positioning of reading

Some schools have risen to the challenge of making silent reading a whole school priority. For example, I recently worked with a dynamic team who implemented a sustained, whole school approach to silent reading across their school which generated a wealth of positive outcomes for students (Collins et al., 2022):

> The project saw an increase in staff and students reading more for enjoyment as reading fiction became a habit and books became less 'nerdy'. This has been one of the greatest achievements of the *Just Read* project. Some staff and students have begun enjoying books of fiction for the first time in their lives and others have rekindled a love of reading.
>
> (Queenwood, n.d.)

As such, improving the regularity of exposure to silent reading can be an effective strategy that builds students' literacy skills, while also enhancing the social positioning of books and reading within a school.

Best practice

However, for silent reading to succeed, some conditions should ideally be met. Here are ten important things we need to do to make the most of silent reading in our schools which I published in my explainer *10 ways to get the most out of silent reading in schools* (Merga, 2019a), and I have adapted this below for print format.

1. **Enjoyment is the focus**
   Enjoyment of reading is associated with both reading achievement and regular reading (Merga, 2018a). If we want young people to choose to read more to experience the benefits of reading, then silent reading needs to be about pleasure and not just testing (Merga, 2016b).
2. **Students choose the books**
   Young people should not be prevented from choosing popular or high-interest books that are deemed too challenging. Books that are a bit too hard could motivate students to higher levels of achievement (Merga, 2014c). Students have reported enjoying and even being inspired by

reading books that were challenging for them, such as J. R. R. Tolkien's *The Lord of the Rings*. Silent reading of text books or required course materials should not be confused with silent reading for pleasure.

3. **The space is right**
   Like adults, children may struggle to read in a noisy or uncomfortable space (Merga, 2017d). Schools need to provide space that is comfortable for students to enjoy their silent reading. Children need space to enjoy silent reading.

4. **Opportunities to chat (before or after)**
   Discussion about books can give students recommendations about other books and even enhance reading comprehension (Merga, 2018b). But silent reading should be silent so all students can focus on reading.

5. **Inspired by keen readers**
   If students see their teachers and teacher librarians as keen readers this can play a powerful role in encouraging avid and sustained reading (Merga, 2016b). School principals can also be powerful reading models, with their support of silent reading shaping school culture (Merga & Mason, 2019).

6. **Students have access to a library**
   Even when schools have libraries the research shows students may be given less access to them during class time as they move through the years of schooling (Merga, 2019d). Not all students are given class time to select reading materials from the library (Merga & Mat Roni, 2017b). All students should be encouraged to access the school library.

7. **It happens often**
   This is particularly important for struggling readers who may find it hard to remember what they are reading if opportunities for silent reading are infrequent (Merga, 2018b). These students may also find it difficult to get absorbed in a book if time to read is too brief.

8. **Paper books are available**
   Reading comprehension is typically stronger when reading on paper rather than on a screen (Kong et al., 2018). Screen-based book reading is not preferred by most young people and can be associated with infrequent reading (Merga & Mat Roni, 2017a). Students can find reading on devices distracting.

9. **There is a school library and a school library professional**
   School library professionals can be particularly important in engaging struggling readers beyond the early years of schooling (Merga, 2019c). They may find it hard to find a book that interests them but which is also not too hard to read. Teacher librarians are also good at matching students with books based on movies they like, or computer games they

enjoy (Merga, 2019f). They play a key role in supporting the choices of students who are still developing this skill set.

10. **We need to make the school culture a reading culture**
    Reading engagement is typically neglected in plans to foster reading achievement in Australian schools (Merga & Gardiner, 2018). Practices such as silent reading should feature in the literacy planning documents of all schools. Allowing students to read for pleasure at school is a big step towards turning our school cultures into reading cultures. Students need opportunities to read, as regular reading can both build and sustain literacy skills.

Supporting choice

Where possible, free choice of reading material can be associated with reading engagement. For example, 98% of Chinese children in a recent survey indicated that they are more likely to complete a book if they have chosen it themselves (Scholastic, 2020).

The need for explicit instruction and modelling choice

However, as contended in the previous section, students may lack strategies to choose the right books for themselves (Kragler, 2000; Merga & Mat Roni, 2017b; Scholastic, 2020). In the WASABR research project, I asked teenagers at 20 schools in Western Australia what would make them read more, and I found that many of them lacked sound strategies for choice:

> Many students were not equipped with efficient strategies for selecting books and were unaware of currently existing tools to help support their search, with students commenting that 'I wish there was a site where you could find books and do a quiz to find a perfect book for you', and 'I find it hard to find a book that I like and I'm interested in'. One reluctant reader explained that he feared 'choosing and then getting stuck with the book that you don't really like'. This student no longer chose his own books, outsourcing the task to his mother. Another student commented that 'I barely ever find a book that I like' and that this was the main reason that she read infrequently.
>
> (Merga, 2016c, p. 411)

While where possible students should independently select their reading materials, they may need to be taught how to do so, and/or given some recommendations and guidance. Students who do not come from literate or literacy-supportive homes may have had less exposure to libraries and fewer discussions with parents about books and authors, leaving them less well equipped to make reading material selections that meet their needs (van der Sande et al., 2022). It is contended that 'these students may rely on superficial selection strategies, based, for example, on physical features such as cover or length, and, consequently, do not succeed in finding books that are attuned to their skills and interests', with silent reading becoming 'a frustrating endeavour, resulting in discouraging reading experiences, leading to a decreased reading attitude' (p. 3).

For example, I interviewed students in the upper primary school years about their book selection processes, and some students lacked sound strategies for choice that made them reliant on questionable indicators, such as the colour of the book:

> The aesthetic elements of the cover often were as significant in directing choice, with the colour of the book surprisingly influential in some cases. For example, Jason explained that 'I look at mainly the chapter books, and if I see something like a black or cool colour, kind of thing, that I like, then I look at it'. Bruce also used this as a key determinant, in that he would 'go for the ones with good colours that look nice'; however, he also confirmed that this led to the selection of a good book only around half the time, a relatively low success strategy in his case.
>
> (Merga & Mat Roni, 2017b, p. 618)

Unsurprisingly, reading books that are poorly aligned with students' abilities and interests can result in negative reading experiences that can have a detrimental impact on students' attitudes towards reading, and subsequently, their reading skills (van der Sande et al., 2022). Recently researchers explored the impact of personalised expert guidance from a librarian on students' book choices in primary and secondary education. They found that 'guiding students' book selection appears to counter students' waning interest in reading and promote their further reading development' (van der Sande et al., 2022, p. 19). Students need explicit instruction from expert staff (such as school library professionals) on how to select books that are engaging, interesting and accessible to them at their current literacy level. This is not to say that books should be easy; some students thrive from being challenged by difficult books (Merga, 2017f). However, for struggling readers, finding books that are topically interesting but not frustratingly difficult is important. Students may need ongoing access to support for choice given that their tastes in reading materials may not remain consistent over time (Loh et al., 2022).

Gender and choice

When supporting choice, it is important that those professionals guiding choice do not fall back on outdated stereotypes related to gender. Many people believe that boys prefer to read non-fiction, and the stereotype has been persistent, despite being poorly supported by the extant research.

Research from Australian and substantial international samples found that both girls and boys typically prefer to read fiction rather than non-fiction, with only 8.6% of boys in my study of 997 primary school aged children preferring to read books about information and facts (Merga, 2017b). Almost half (48%) preferred fiction, with the remaining boys not having a distinct preference either way (Merga, 2017b). Boys can love reading fiction (Scholes et al., 2021).

The gender of the protagonist may matter to some readers, but this cannot be broadly assumed at this stage. While some readers may have this preference, this is not always the case, as can be seen in the popularity of books like *The Hunger Games* with male readers as reported in the media (Dodes & Jergensen, 2012). A recent study of children in Germany found that 'no statistically significant differences in text-based interest' related to protagonists' gender, with the researchers noting that 'other characteristics of protagonists, such as character traits, might outweigh the role of protagonists' gender' (Lepper et al., 2022, p. 548). When supporting choice, we need to keep an open mind and allow the student's interests to dictate how we guide their choices.

There are negative consequences of encouraging boys to choose non-fiction regardless of their interests and personal preferences. Boys may read less often if steered towards books with less appeal. The reading of fiction may offer unique benefits in that it can foster prosocial skills such as empathy and perspective-taking, which we want boys as well as girls to develop. For example, recent research has found associations between reading of Young Adult fiction and 'empathic concern, integrity, and moral agency' (Black & Barnes, 2021, p. 149). Furthermore, research with primary school aged children suggests that within fiction, different genres evoke different 'life-resonant' responses in the reader (Kuzmičová & Cremin, 2022, p. 38), with further research needed to explore these implications. Ultimately, when we make stereotypical assumptions about boys' reading preferences we can constrain students' perceptions of themselves as readers, and limit the scope of books they may select from (Scholes et al., 2021). We should always match books to the *individual*, rather than the gender, and we should encourage children to read a rich range of books that may appeal to them.

So how do we support choice?

We need to consider students' interests, ability level, degree of challenge preferences, and degree of accepted flexibility with authors and genres.

Some students really refuse to read outside their genre and author preferences, so with these students, steps to extend their interests may need to be very cautious with reference back to commonalities with works and authors they do like. After interviewing primary school aged children about their reading habits, we noted that

> children solely reliant on familiarity as a key factor in choice risk being confined to repeat reading of a small set of pre-experienced series, and they may experience periods of nonreading while waiting for the next installation of favoured series. However, the solution to the potential limitations raised was also in the data set; supported choice, in the form of recommendations from trusted and knowledgeable people familiar with their interests and skill, such as experienced by Rose, can help to extend the scope of 'familiar' texts while still acknowledging children's desire for the security of the known to some extent.
> (Merga & Mat Roni, 2017b, p. 625)

The relationships that school library professionals and classroom-based educators build with students are clearly crucial to inform and facilitate one-to-one matching.

While one-to-one matching, where a student is given a book that a library or classroom-based educator is confident meets their needs, can play a valuable role in matching young people with books tailored to their needs, students must also be taught the skillset needed to independently choose an appealing book. As we have noted elsewhere, 'while librarians, parents, friends, and other social agents can be valued agents of supported choice, there is a risk that children may entirely surrender their choosing to these agents' (p. 625).

This training should also include modelling the right to cease reading a book that doesn't interest them after first trying it. Some students will attempt to force themselves to read a book that initially seemed appealing but ultimately was a bad match, and such experiences can discourage them from reading, given that 'the perceived risk of wasted time was found to loom as a significant potential inhibitor to reading' (p. 625). Just as adults do not like to waste their time, children also dislike investing time in a book that does not appeal to them.

Accessible and visible books

Students in supportive school reading cultures have easy access to books and learn in book-rich environments. The link between access to books and student literacy attainment is logical. Access to books is related to students' academic achievement, and the number of books at home is a predictor of students' growth in reading (e.g. Retelsdorf at al., 2011).

Books in the home?

However book-rich our own homes may have been in our childhood, we cannot assume that students have access to books in the home, and unsurprisingly, household income is a notable determinant of this access (e.g. Scholastic, 2020). A recent US study of low-income elementary students found that 'students with a larger number of books in their home reported higher reading motivation', and that 'having a greater number of books was significantly predictive' of a greater amount of reading outside of school time, even after adjusting for motivation (Zucker et al., 2022, p. 268). This means that schools must help to ensure that homes are book-rich environments as an equity-related imperative. My research found that

> access to books in the home appears to confer benefit for students' attitudes toward, and frequency of engagement in, recreational book reading. There may have been a decline in access to books in the home in Western Australia since the 1990s, nearly a third of respondents now living in a household containing fewer than 50 books. While it could be supposed that trips to the library and access to eBook reading devices could provide alternative avenues for access to books, students did not seem to be utilising these avenues.
>
> (Merga, 2015a, p. 207)

International analysis also notes that the number of books available to students in the home significantly declined between 2000 and 2018 (Ikeda & Rech, 2022). Furthermore,

> during this 18-year period, not only was the socio-economic gap in terms of accessing books at home not reduced, disadvantaged students fell even further behind advantaged students. In 2000, advantaged students reported having access to 250 books while disadvantaged students reported having access to 133 books, which was over half of what advantaged students reported. In 2018, advantaged students reported having access to 215 books while disadvantaged students reported just half of this, at 107 books. (p. 3)

It is now more important than ever that schools shoulder responsibility for ensuring students have regular access to a high-quality collection of reading materials in their school library as part of their commitment to mitigating educational inequity related to relative advantage. Closing school libraries that service school communities in low socio-economic contexts is a discriminatory practice, as students who come from disadvantaged homes will be disproportionally affected by such decisions.

It may be the case that the size of the book collection in the school library 'may be less relevant than the kinds of books in the selection and the display strategies used to draw students' attention' (Loh et al., 2017, p. 342), so schools focusing on enhancing their book collections should focus on quality as well as quantity, and ensure that effective displays are used both within and beyond the library to attract readers. School library professionals have expertise in this area and are essential staff in maintaining, building and displaying a collection as well as facilitating regular access to books (Merga, 2020b; 2021d; Merga & Ferguson, 2021), as I will explore further in this chapter.

Investment in school libraries and collection building

For students of all ages to read for pleasure regularly, they need to be able to access enjoyable literature that resonates with their sometimes unique interests and preferences, and where feasible, all schools should have access to a well-stocked school library. Research suggests that currency of reading materials is also important, with adolescent students making comments such as 'I do like reading interesting books but libraries don't have interesting books. I would read more if the library had interesting and new books that we could borrow', and

> my closest library to my house is about 20 minutes away, and even then, the majority of the books are sub-par, 90s informational books that are not worth reading. I would read a lot more if I had access to a better library.
> (Merga, 2016c, p. 416)

As covered in the previous section, many students do not have access to a rich selection of books within the home, so ensuring that students have ready access to a regularly weeded and developed school library is crucial to support their reading.

Declining investment in a crucial literacy resource

I constantly reiterate the importance of school libraries throughout this book. However, in many contexts, school libraries are facing severe budget cuts (e.g. Lance et al., 2023; Merga, 2019d) leading to library closures. Insights from Greece suggest that 'there are still no functional libraries in most Greek state schools' (Margariti, 2022, p. 2):

> Specifically in secondary education, there is no culture of reading and the majority of existing libraries in state high schools are usually in bad condition or just being locked; rooms that receive little or no sunlight at all, unattractive places, with old, musty smelling books, left untouched and useless. (p. 2)

Where libraries exist, ongoing investment in resourcing is needed to ensure that the environment is appealing (Merga, 2022b), and that the collection continues to meet the needs and interests of an often diverse student body (Merga & Mason, 2019).

For more than 10 years Softlink has been collecting data on school libraries in Australia and New Zealand. The most recent report found that 'if you feel your library is understaffed and that budgets are not adequate, you're like most school libraries across the country' (Softlink, 2023, p. 4), with more Australian libraries reporting a decrease in budget (26%) than an increase (17%). The situation was even more concerning in New Zealand, where 3% of respondents saw an increase in their budgets compared with 39% who saw a decrease. Staffing is also of concern, with more Australian libraries reporting a decrease in staffing (29%) than an increase (9%), and in New Zealand, '3% reported it had increased, and 20% reported a decrease' (p. 6).

Under-resourcing of libraries is linked to broader inequities that play out within education systems, such as those related to socio-economic context, and it may vary significantly between geographic contexts even within the same nation. A recent report by Great School Libraries (2023) in the UK found that in England,

> it is clear there is a three-tier system in operation, with pupils in schools that have a high percentage of children eligible for Free School Meals least likely to have access to a library space and a dedicated librarian or library staff. Children from disadvantaged backgrounds have less access to fewer books than those in more affluent areas. (p. 4)

This report also found that in Scotland, two-thirds of school libraries have no library budget, with 'rural areas less likely to have access to a school library and librarian than urban areas' (p. 4). A quarter of schools in Wales do not have a school library, and lack professional staff where school libraries exist, and 'one third of schools in Northern Ireland have no designated library area on site' (p. 20). Adequate resourcing of libraries is an equity issue, particularly given that children in low socio-economic contexts are less likely to have a wealth of books at home, making them more dependent on school libraries than their affluent peers to have reading resources at hand (Heppt et al., 2022).

Quantity and quality in collection building

So in terms of volume, how many books are needed?

In their US context, Wilson et al. (2016) note that while a school library meeting resource recommendations will have 15 to 20 books per child, and around $12–$15 per student invested each year to have a positive contribution to student outcomes, many school libraries may be falling short of this mark.

Of course, quantity of collection is not everything; even where a collection is large, it may be outdated and lack diverse genre and thematic coverage. Stale and unappealing texts may predominate in some contexts, with 'textual hierarchies' persisting in some schools, 'with long novels and classics positioned as the gold standard in both primary and secondary education' (Cremin & Hendry, 2022, p. 214). Even for those who are in the fortunate position of having a large library with many books in it, an ongoing commitment to ensuring that these works cover the full breadth of evolving student interests is essential to maintain student reading frequency and related literacy attainment.

Furthermore, representation matters, and as the cultural composition of your school expands and evolves, the collection must become increasingly inclusive. Recent research found that the majority of students from age eight to adulthood believe that it is 'important for books to include characters or people from lots of different backgrounds' (Picton & Clark, 2022, p. 2). Your library needs to be reflective of and responsive to your school population so that your students can see themselves and their lives reflected in the texts they consume. However, young people also enjoy reading about people from different cultural backgrounds from their own (Picton & Clark, 2022), so even if you work in a relatively culturally homogenous context, books with diverse representation are a must.

Investment in qualified school library professionals

One of the most important things that schools can do to build a reading culture is to invest in qualified school library professionals. The role that school library professionals play in understanding students' reading interests matters, as research suggests that reading for interest can be a strong indicator of growth in reading skills; 'students who discover reading as an effective tool to satisfy their curiosity on certain topics gain higher levels of performance growth' (Retelsdorf et al., 2011, p. 555). This makes sense on a basic level, given that even as adults, we tend to invest our time (where we have a choice) in activities or engaging in texts that reflect our interests.

What do school library professionals do to promote reading engagement?

They are experts in building students' reading engagement and literacy learning, though their role may be poorly understood. For example, based on my research findings (and in no particular order),

> as part of their role in supporting literacy and literature learning, a teacher librarian may draw on the following practices which can be related to evidence of benefit in the research literature:
>
> 1. Endeavour to provide students with regular time in the library
> 2. Bring the library to the students through pop-up/mobile libraries
> 3. Enable generous access hours
> 4. Facilitate student purchases of books for the home
> 5. Provide access to a broad range of text types
> 6. Meet the access needs of diverse families to provide reading support at home
> 7. Facilitate peer recommendation
> 8. Convene book clubs
> 9. Facilitate and publish student book reviews
> 10. Promote students' knowledge of themselves as readers
> 11. Use student book recommendations to support collection development
> 12. Provide a one-to-one matching service
> 13. Read aloud (books and hooks)
> 14. Model reading strategies
> 15. Teach skill scaffolding for supporting choice
> 16. Undertake staff reading promotion
> 17. Facilitate silent reading
> 18. Encourage reading outside the library
> 19. Read widely, including Young Adult texts
> 20. Provide book talks
> 21. Create reading lists
> 22. Facilitate author exposure and visits

23	Facilitate participation in literature festivals and events
24	Undertake book promotional activities and displays
25	Act as an advocate of screen-free time
26	Support the implementation, creation and ongoing production of recreational reading logs/journals
27	Draw on and share research evidence
28	Provide promotional materials
29	Positively position books and reading as awards/rewards
30	Provide lessons on literacy and literature
31	Make explicit links with English curriculum
32	Prepare students for high stakes testing
33	Support intertextual and contemporary text connections, stimulating creativity and interest
34	Liaise with staff to influence the choice of class reading material
35	Support whole school literacy and broader policy planning
36	Target and support reluctant readers
37	Support reading adjustments for students struggling with dyslexia and other issues that can influence reading outcomes
38	Monitor borrowing and reading engagement data
39	Provide a balanced and diverse collection with age and skill level-appropriate choices
40	Design and facilitate targeted programs.

(Merga, 2019d, pp. 94–95)

Their contribution to a school's reading culture can be substantial, and I have seen them lead initiatives that have transformed a school culture into a reading culture (e.g. Mace & Lean, 2021a).

They can also be key social influences that lead young readers towards adopting a lifelong reader identity. Findings from the 2015 ISABR suggest that

> Librarians and teachers featured strongly in this context as key social influences that extended their role to connect respondents with books and genres that these readers subsequently enjoyed. A respondent from the U.S. described how her 'elementary school librarian made it a priority to help her students find books that interested them and helped them gain a love for reading.' Another respondent from the U.S. described how an elementary school librarian's support of a student ultimately determined his academic pathway:
>
> > My 5th grade librarian was the first person to explain the difference between fiction and non-fiction reading. She showed me the US history section of the

library and I fell in love. Ten years later I'm in college studying history and philosophy. It was one of the most defining moments of my lifetime and she has no idea what she did for me.

(Merga, 2017a, p. 11)

As such, the contributions of school library professionals can literally be life-changing for young people.

A profession in decline?

School library professionals may be part of a profession in decline, a greying demographic that may not always be well-supported within their schools (Merga, 2019b). They may often be marginalised 'as invisible workers who silently carry out necessary work in the background' (Centerwall, 2022, p. 10), and be poorly understood by colleagues and school leaders (Merga, 2019b).

This lack of collegial understanding may contribute to under-resourcing of library staff. Many schools fail to adequately invest in qualified school library professionals. In their school library perspectives from Singapore, Hong Kong and Japan, researchers noted that 'the invisibility of the school librarian's work remains a problem across the three countries' (Loh et al., 2019, p. 6), and this lack of recognition is also a well-documented issue in Australia and elsewhere (see Merga, 2019b). Recent US research found that, given shrinking numbers of school library professionals,

having a school librarian is becoming a privilege reserved for some students. Access to school librarians is strongly related to both race and ethnicity and either persists or is exacerbated when selected district characteristics – specifically poverty, locale, and enrolment – are considered. And certainly, the COVID-19 pandemic has diminished access to school librarians . . . inequities associated with race and ethnicity were exacerbated considerably for students living in extreme poverty, in more-isolated locales, and in the smallest districts.

(Lance et al., 2023, pp. 10–11)

Thus access to a school library professional is an equity issue, given the benefits they confer on student learning and the school environment, and disadvantaged children are most likely to miss out on having access to their professional support and knowledge.

In South Australia, while the vast majority of schools have a dedicated individual to manage the library collection, in less than a quarter of cases the person holding this position is a qualified teacher librarian, and more than half hold no library qualifications (Dix et al., 2020). This report also found that 'schools with a qualified teacher librarian in this role are more likely to have improved student literacy outcomes', drawing on students' performance on high-stakes literacy test scores and finding that 'students' reading, writing, spelling, grammar and punctuation outcomes at Years 3, 5, 7 and 9 were found to be significantly associated with the qualification-level of the person who manages the library' (Dix et al., 2020, p. 5).

Furthermore,

> students in schools with a qualified teacher librarian had up to two months' learning gain, compared to students in schools with no staff member managing the library, taking into account the effect of socio-economic status. The difference in Year 9 student literacy outcomes was particularly evident. (p. 5)

While more research is needed to capture the extent to which these findings are generalisable, these data are certainly very concerning and indicate that further research is needed. It is also important that a commitment to maintaining qualified school library staff in secondary (high school) libraries as well as in primary (elementary) context is made, given that deprofessionalisation is a serious challenge to the quality of learning provided in the school library resource (Merga, 2022b).

But how can schools know if their levels of staffing are sufficient? While this may vary from country to country, within Australia schools can use the Australian School Library Association (ASLA) and Australian Library and Information Association (2020) document *Recommended Minimum Information Services Staffing Levels*, which specifies optimal staffing levels for school libraries.

Teacher modelling

Students need exposure to reading models within and beyond school, and staff who read are a key pillar in the development and maintenance of a school reading culture (Merga & Mason, 2019). Findings from the ISABR suggest that teachers can play a vital role in connecting young people with reading resources and inspiring them to adopt reader identities (Merga, 2017a). For example, a

> young respondent from Estonia described receiving support from her teachers, 'who in many lessons show us books and ask if we have read them or they just talk about some cool books they have recently read', stating further that she always 'write(s) the books down to read them in the future'. (p. 12)

Recent research also found that even in adulthood, respondents recalled how their teachers influenced their early reading experiences, remembering 'what their teachers did (or did not do), reinforcing the push to encourage reading for pleasure in primary school classrooms', and calling 'into question the notion raised by some teachers that reading motivation cannot be taught' (Zare et al., 2023, p. 11). The WASABR research found that 'teacher excitement about books was viewed as highly encouraging', with a student describing 'how her English teachers' excitement about books elevated the social capital of books in her classroom' (Merga, 2015c, p. 41):

> When asked how her English teacher felt about reading books, she stated that, 'I think she gets really excited about it. She seems like a very excited person when it comes to books.' Stacy described how her teacher would get a 'big smile on her face' when books were discussed in class and how this attitude was conducive to encouraging discussion of books:
>
>> you see some kid mention it, and then someone overhears it, instantly gets excited, like, 'Yes, I've read that,' then, that person feels excited to read it and, then another person does, so yeah, just . . . I think it's really just excitement that gets people. You hear about it, like, 'Oh my God that sounds good', so you decide to do it, 'cos (if) it makes other people happy, it might make you happy too.
>
> (Merga, 2015c, p. 41)

This student illustrates how a teacher's demonstrated love for books and reading can influence the culture of her classroom, and the interests of her students.

These reading models can break stereotypes about what it means to be a reader, as described by Grace, a teacher librarian, who

> also noted that many of her staff members were readers, also explaining that 'and what I love is the fact that our physical education (PE) teachers love to read. Because we have a very strong sports ethic in the school, so the fact that our PE teachers read is really good'. With sport as a school priority, having PE teachers model positive attitudes toward reading could improve the social acceptability of the practice and demonstrate that reading can be part of a sporting identity.
>
> (Merga & Mason, 2019, p. 182)

When teachers from a range of learning areas model avid reading behaviours and actively promote books and reading, this helps students to see that many different kinds of people can be readers, challenging the nerdy bookish stereotype.

Are all teachers readers?

However, not all teachers are a source of inspiration for students when it comes to modelling positive attitudes towards reading. Some primary school teachers may not be effective models who are seen as readers by students (Merga, 2016b), and surprisingly, even some secondary school English teachers are not seen as readers by their students:

> Teachers who demonstrated interest in personal reading for pleasure were more likely to be viewed as both encouraging and knowledgeable. Many students were unable to confirm that their current secondary school English teachers actually liked reading books themselves. When asked how his teacher felt about reading books, Luke stated that, 'I'm not sure how he likes reading books, because I've never really heard him talk about reading books, other than the ones we read at school, so, I couldn't give you a true opinion on that'. A number of other students also indicated that they were unwilling to endorse a positive position towards reading in their English teacher, due to lack of evidence.
> (Merga, 2015c, p. 42)

Extensive research focus has further established that not all teachers and pre-service teachers are motivated to read (e.g. Applegate & Applegate, 2004; Benevides & Peterson, 2010; Cox & Schaetzel, 2007; Griffin & Mindrila, 2023; Nathanson et al., 2008). For example, in Norway, Skaar et al. (2018) found that both Norwegian pre-service and in-service primary school teachers had 'little interest in reading literature', and 'few teachers, and practically no teacher students, are eager readers of traditional literature' (p. 312). They conclude that while 'we assume teachers are likely to draw on their own literary experiences when introducing their students to literature in the classroom',

> our study indicates a downward trend in teachers' capability to create enthusiasm for literary fiction in class. Moreover, their own dwindling interest is likely to have a significant impact on the future life of literary fiction in primary school education altogether. (p. 320)

Similarly, Tovey (2022) contends that 'before teachers can intrinsically motivate their students to become avid readers, they need to, themselves, experience reading enjoyment' (p. 286), so pre-service education of teachers should foster their reading engagement rather than presume that they are already avid readers with the capacity to be effective models.

Boosting teacher and student reading

As part of efforts to build and sustain a whole school reading culture, collection of data on teachers' levels of reading motivation and engagement prior to implementation can be beneficial, so that you know if staff-focused interventions are needed. Motivating interventions can focus on boosting teachers' levels of reading engagement, as well as student levels.

School library professionals are often experienced in enhancing teachers' levels of reading engagement, as well as students' levels, using strategies such as one-to-one book matching with teachers as well as students, and organising teacher libraries, to enhance teacher borrowing and interest in reading. For example, one teacher librarian described taking the following approach:

> We also encourage the staff to read. In the staff room, we put books up there so that they don't have to come down to the library to borrow them, they can just borrow them from there. I make it easy, they just email us and say, 'I've got this book,' and they do. And it's interesting that the maths department are the heaviest borrowers.
>
> (Merga, 2019d, p. 108)

In this manner, staff in diverse subject areas may be 'encouraged to increase their reading frequency and engagement', with 'teacher librarians working to actively mitigate hurdles to staff reading' (p. 108), so that students can be exposed to avid reading models across the school.

Raising awareness of a valuable role

Teachers are not necessarily aware of the important role that they can play in this regard. Teachers are typically university-educated professionals whose own often comparatively privileged literacy-rich backgrounds may blind them to the 'inequalities of opportunity' experienced by their students (Cremin & Hendry, 2022, p. 210). The important role they can play as avid reader models may not be known or valued by them unless they consider that in the lives of some of their students, they may very well be the only avid reading models, and ponder the implications of this.

Research attempting to capture the extent to which teachers take responsibility for motivating students to read has found that in some cases, teachers do not see this as their responsibility at all (e.g. Garces-Bacsal et al., 2018). We can return here to the previously defined notion of orphaned responsibility, where once children have learnt to read, 'it is little surprise that the role of motivational support can become an orphaned responsibility, where both teachers and parents may perceive it as the role of the other party'

(Merga, 2018a, p. 30). However, some teachers may *never* see fostering reading motivation as part of their role.

Advocates for a school reading culture need to build teachers' understanding of their *ongoing* responsibility to act as keen reading models, and encourage teachers to commit to supporting their students' reading engagement. Recent research suggests that pre-service teachers with a low attitude towards reading 'were least likely to read and perceived themselves as least competent in reading', and importantly, 'they further appeared to be least willing to invest in reading promotion in their future school(s)' (Vansteelandt et al., 2022, p. 1). I cover the professional development implications of this finding later in this chapter, but here it is important to highlight that research is suggesting the existence of a notable and logical relationship between future teachers' attitudes towards their own reading and their willingness to play an active role in promoting the reading engagement of their students.

How to be a model

So what does a teacher who is a reading model do differently?

Cremin et al. (2009) contend that real 'Reading Teachers' established this status by positioning themselves as 'fellow readers in the classroom community, who talked about their practices, preferences, habits and histories and explored the dynamic between their own and the children's reading' (p. 15). More recently I explored this question in research with children in upper primary school. While many of these students did not feel that their current teacher was a reader, almost all described having had a previous teacher they were confident loved reading, and did not purely frame reading as something done for the purposes of testing and learning; 'students should be unequivocally aware that their teachers like reading and don't just view it as "an educational thing"' (Merga, 2016b, p. 265).

Specifically, children and adolescents from the WASCBR and WASABR projects described teachers as readers and encouraging role models when they do the following.

1 Talk about books in the context of pleasure
2 Instigate and support student-centred discussion around books
3 Visibly read independently whenever they can
4 Read aloud to the class with expression and emotional connection
5 Show a personal enjoyment of reading that is clearly apparent
6 Possess a broad knowledge of children's books, young adult texts and youth popular culture

7   Effectively communicate expectations that students will read at school and at home
8   Facilitate access to books to select for reading for pleasure during class time
9   Demonstrate knowledge of the interests and aspirations of the students
10 Frequently use in-class practices that encourage reading for pleasure, such as reading aloud to students and silent reading.

(Merga, 2015c; 2016b)

These characteristics may seem simple, but the children involved in my research have been sensitive to nuance and sincerity. For example, according to children in primary school,

> talking about books involves more than just being generally enthusiastic when the opportunity arises. Teachers need to show strong enjoyment of specific books, recommend books, and identify key features that are engaging, to invite children to see and enjoy these features. Children should also, where possible, be able to join in the conversation.
>
> (Merga, 2016b, p. 266)

It's also important to note that 'teachers beyond the early years of schooling need to do this as effectively as teachers in the early years', as 'fostering a lifelong love of reading is not a project limited to these early years' as it offers lifelong benefits (Merga, 2016b, p. 265).

Leaders who model

A school leader who models reading leads a reading culture from the top down. Loh et al. (2017) described how a focus on reading within a school was 'driven by the principal, an avid reader himself, and supported by the staff', noting that his encouraging attitude made him a model for the staff as well as the students. Similarly, Australian research found that 'school leadership can play a crucial role in the development and maintenance of a school reading culture that positions reading as both valuable and pleasurable' (Merga & Mason, 2019, p. 185), with the importance of leadership support covered further in the subsequent chapter.

Engaging parental support

Just as teachers can be valuable models, the reading parents and guardians do and the reading-supportive practices that they model and employ can have a significant impact on young people's attitudes and learning. For example, recent research found that young people's reading habits in Malaysia were strongly and positively associated with parental influence (Rasiah et al., 2022), with findings across diverse contexts suggesting that parents can play a powerful role in influencing their child's reading behaviours and attitudes (e.g. Merga & Mat Roni, 2018b). Findings from the recent PIRLS data support this link:

> The results indicate a positive association between parents' liking to read and their children having higher reading achievement at the fourth grade. Across the PIRLS 2021 countries, on average, 31 percent of students whose parents 'very much like' reading had higher average achievement than the 52 percent of the students whose parents only 'somewhat like' reading (526 vs. 498, respectively). In turn, 17 percent of students whose parents 'do not like' reading had the lowest average reading achievement (479).
>
> (Mullis et al., 2023, p. 92)

While these high-stakes testing data have notable limitations, they can be used to encourage parents to commit to supporting their child's reading engagement by showing how parental attitudes and practices can influence students' performance.

Do parents model reading?

One way that parents influence their children to read is through modelling keen reading. However, many parents are not readers, though there is great variation across nations and socio-economic contexts. US research suggests that more than a quarter of men in the US had not read a book in a year (Gelles-Watnick & Perrin, 2021), and the average Arab citizen in the Middle East may read less than their American and British counterparts (Al-Musalli, 2014). Chinese parents may read books far more frequently, though parents in higher-income households read books more frequently than those from lower-income households (Scholastic, 2020), highlighting the influence that both culture and socio-economic status can have on parental modelling of avid reading.

Children know if their parents are readers, and have reported perceiving their parents as non-readers in some cases; 'when parents expected their children to read but did not read themselves, children were sensitive to this contradiction' (Merga & Mat Roni, 2018b, p. 216).

The role of schools in supporting parents to model

Schools need to communicate to parents the benefits of their reading and literacy-related home support for both young and older children. School cultures that are reading cultures try to reach out to parents and engage them to be models to the best of their individual capacity (Merga & Mason, 2019).

Parents may not know what they can do to support their child's reading engagement, particularly beyond the early years, and schools can provide training and guidance. Where possible, schools should reach out to parents and make explicit the benefits of parents acting as avid reading models, with research suggesting that 'the presence of parents with enthusiasm for reading is a positive influence in the reading attitudes of their children', and 'the effect on the children could lead to a long-term change of habits for teenagers: once the student finishes his/her studies, he/she will still keep reading just for pleasure' (Clavel & Mediavilla, 2020, pp. 250–251).

Research has also explored the many ways that parents can foster an ongoing love of reading in their children beyond the early years, using a range of strategies and approaches. According to adolescent respondents,

> parents who continued to encourage their children's recreational book reading into adolescence were encouraging and responsive to their children's individual taste and preferences. They were active in modelling keen reading, providing informed recommendations for their children, and facilitating access to books.
> (Merga, 2014c, p. 161)

Parents can also help their children learn skills that support reading, such as choosing books. They may also provide valued recommendations.

Parents may also not understand that the role they play in supporting their child's reading engagement needs to be ongoing, sustained beyond the point where children can read by themselves, and even beyond the point where the child identifies as an avid reader. For example, parents should continue to read aloud to and with their children for as long as practicable (Merga, 2019e), and many parents are unaware of the ongoing benefits of this practice. The WASRA research found that while many parents enjoy reading to their children, finding time to do this can be a significant barrier, and more than one in five parents believed that reading with their child was no longer necessary after their child could read independently (Merga & Ledger, 2018). This is problematic because, as I explore in greater detail in the subsequent section on reading aloud, it is a practice that continues to offer both academic and social benefits for children beyond the early years. Schools need to communicate this effectively so that parents can make informed decisions about the levels of support and encouragement they provide in the home.

This support and encouragement needs to extend beyond gender stereotypes so that boys do not miss out due to a perception that they are less likely to become readers. Fathers may need to be specifically targeted, given that research suggests that according to children, their mothers are far more likely to model positive attitudes than their fathers, which can position reading as something that is a primarily feminine activity (Merga & Mat Roni, 2018b).

The 'summer slide'

Sadly, the 'summer slide' does not refer to a water park slide.

Instead, it refers to the outcome of periods of limited exposure to reading opportunities, where students' performance in literacy can stagnate and regress (Allington et al., 2010). However, research with US parents found that many are unaware of this phenomenon:

> At first glance, parents seem aware of the importance of summer reading, as 94% agree reading over the summer can help their child during the school year. And yet, nearly half of parents with school-age children are unaware of the 'summer slide' (47%), the loss of academic skills that occurs when school is not in session and which is attributed largely to the lack of reading. This is of critical importance as the effects of the summer slide are cumulative ... Lower-income families, as was the case in 2016, remain less likely to be aware ... This is of notable concern as the summer slide is a primary contributor to the reading achievement gap between lower- and higher-income students.
> (Scholastic, 2019d, p. 4)

Furthermore, this research found that children whose parents are aware of the summer slide viewed summer reading at home more positively (Scholastic, 2019d), highlighting how parental awareness might influence children's attitudes and behaviours, though further research is needed in this area. As such, schools need to be effective in communicating with parents about the importance of sustaining reading activities during the educational interruption associated with holiday periods, and provide students with access to reading materials over these periods. Again, there are equity implications associated with this vital communication.

Parents as public library access facilitators

Recent research has highlighted the value of joint library visits, where parents visit the library with their children, which can enhance students' reading frequency and therefore offer associated benefits for literacy skills. Pfost and

Heyne (2023) found joint library visits 'predicted students' self-reported time spent in leisure time reading as well as students' knowledge of specific children's fiction books (reading exposure)', with these associations remaining significant even 'after taking concurrently further control variables such as vocabulary into account' (p. 15). This led the authors to conclude that

> as public libraries are typically open to all families independent of their socio-economic status or migration background, this finding highlights the importance of public libraries within local communities. Besides possibilities of use and borrowing of books and further media, public libraries are engaged in providing further reading opportunities to children such as storytimes or summer reading clubs. (p. 15)

Schools should form strong relationships with local public libraries, and be active in encouraging parents to make the most of this resource.

What messages should schools promote?

Schools cannot afford to take a passive approach to engaging parental support. As part of fostering a whole school reading culture, maximising parental commitment to supporting young people's reading engagement beyond the early years of schooling is crucial. Planning to build capacity through parent-supported learning and defined roles for parents already features in some schools' whole school literacy policies; ideally, this should appear in *all* schools' literacy planning and activities (Merga, 2023b).

Schools in vulnerable communities need to be particularly effective at sharing key messages with the families of their students, given that US research indicates that lower-income families are less likely to receive information on reading engagement and literacy-supportive strategies such as reading aloud from the early years of schooling (Scholastic, 2019c).

So how should parents sustain encouragement of reading engagement?

- Talk about books and share book recommendations, keeping reading for pleasure in focus rather than academic testing
- Promote access to books in the home, visiting the public or school library with their child
- Share quality read-aloud experiences
- Model a love of reading, and encourage and expect children to devote regular time to reading for pleasure.

(adapted from Merga & Mat Roni, 2018b)

These and related messages should be shared with parents on a regular basis, with both research and its practical implications clearly explained, and practices such as reading aloud modelled for parents who have no prior experience of this.

Talking about books

For recreational reading to compete with other leisure pursuits, parents, teachers, school library professionals and indeed, any social influence seeking to promote young people's reading engagement need to talk about books. However, just reminding students and parents of the importance of reading may not achieve much in isolation. Recent research

> tested whether regularly sending reminders of reading might be helpful and prevent the dominance of other leisure time activities than reading. Sending reminders indeed made some students more positive about reading and more inclined to opt for reading as a pastime. However, for most students, sending reminders to parents or the students themselves was insufficient to move them toward more leisure time reading.
>
> (van der Sande, Wildeman et al., 2023, p. 13)

As such, while reminders can make a difference, more sustained and interactive discussion about books is more likely to trigger interest and engagement in reading.

Readers know that book recommendations and motivating discussions about books and reading can help them to sustain their habit as avid readers (Merga, 2017a). Even adults are motivated by book recommendations, as seen in the popularity of former US President Barack Obama's annual reading lists (Vershbow, 2023). In the same way, to stimulate interest in books and reading, students need to know what possibilities lie beyond their range of experience, and to be motivated to embark on an immersive journey between the pages of a book. Willingness to provide recommendations to students also influences students' perceptions of the provider of recommendations as a model.

For example, in the context of adolescent students,

> beyond talking about books and demonstrating a love for reading, some teachers were comfortable making recommendations for students. For Lisa, this was a clear indication that her teacher viewed reading favourably. She found that 'even just the books in class that we read, how she'll talk about them, and just having conversations with her about other books that are similar and stuff that she's

read and liked, and . . . things like that,' were all indicators that her teacher enjoyed reading.

(Merga, 2015c, p. 42)

As such, the benefits of talking about books in the classroom in the context of pleasure, of being seen to invest time and thought to this kind of guidance and encouragement, can influence students' perception of the social acceptability of books and reading, provide them with aligned reading materials, and enhance their sense of their teacher or other social influence as an avid reader.

While the educational benefits of book discussion may be poorly understood, research has linked discussion about books to benefits for young people's attitudes towards books and reading (Alvermann et al., 1999; Ivey & Johnston, 2013; Merga, 2018b), and 'harnessing book discussion to evoke student engagement enhances the social aspect of reading' (Merga, 2020c, p. 23). There are many engaging ways that educators can talk about books with students, and students can be encouraged to discuss books with each other. While as I have explained previously, reading can be seen as something purely done for the purposes of assessment, opportunities for book discussion 'can help to promote a culture of reading in a school, and act to counter some of the negative trends that threaten to subsume the significance of reading for pleasure in young people's lives' (p. 23). US research found that across learning areas, students exhibited higher levels of reading motivation in classrooms 'which included the most intimate and student-centred interactions between teachers and students about texts – specifically, classrooms where teachers discussed text one-on-one with students' (Neugebauer & Gilmour, 2020, p. 357). While this study was focused on reading for information rather than reading for pleasure, the benefits of dyadic teacher and student exchanges around reading for enhancing student motivation deserve attention.

Ways of talking about books to promote reading engagement

While talking about books in schools often aligns with skill and knowledge-based goals of the curriculum, books can also be discussed in the context of pleasure in many ways, and for a range of purposes, including, but not limited to the following:

Peer promotion and recommendations

Peer recommendations were encouraged and supported by respondents who linked these opportunities to surges in interest in particular texts, and such recommendations were felt to be effective in motivating disengaged readers.

Talking with authors
Book discussions could be generated by the authors of the books themselves, and teacher librarians often organised author visits.

One-to-one book matching and guiding choice
This process involves communicative exchanges between the teacher librarians and the students, which are essential to finding a book that is a good fit for students' interests and abilities.

Teacher or student-led book talks and discussions
Book talks could take multiple forms, with a number of teacher librarians describing a didactic form, where a teacher or student would deliver a book talk in front of a student audience. Unlike peer discussion, or shared discussion (with teacher librarian also as participant) around books, teacher or student-led book talks usually had a single primary presenter and were not characterised by fluidity of exchanges. They also typically had a specific purpose.

Student recommendations supporting collection building
Where students discuss and recommend books, they can support the teacher librarians' efforts in collection building to ensure a quality collection that is reflective of students' diverse and evolving reading interests.

Discussing reading for benefit
As aforementioned, there is an association between young people's understanding of reading as important, and their continued engagement in the practice. Exchanges around the benefits of reading could be both student and teacher initiated. They could lead to students' enhanced task valuing in relation to reading, which in turn can improve their reading engagement.

Modelling being a reader
Teacher librarians were also cognisant of the importance of modelling positive attitudes towards reading. Teacher librarians verbalised their reading strategies and explained how reading can be incorporated into daily practice so that students can achieve their reading frequency goals.

(adapted from Merga, 2020c)

While the above examples were generated from research concerning teacher librarians fostering discussions about books and reading, again I stress that classroom-based educators, parents and other social influences can also play an important role in talking about books, and the adolescents involved in the WASABR have shown appreciation when their classroom-based educators have taken the time to discuss books and reading with them (Merga, 2015c). Students identified 'a willingness to instigate and support student centred discussion around books' (p. 47) as a key supportive trait of teachers who encourage recreational book reading.

Creating and sustaining reading spaces

When you imagine yourself deeply immersed in enjoyable reading, where are you? Many people have personal preferences for the kinds of environments, furnishings, and surrounding noise levels and ambience that may influence their ability to truly lose themselves in a book. Wherever students are expected to read, the environment needs to be conducive to application of sustained attention. The deep attention required to read lengthy texts may pose a notable cognitive challenge, so controlling environmental factors to enhance this capacity is important.

How loud can it be?

Perhaps one of the most influential factors impacting on your ability to read may be surrounding noise. While there is a paucity of research that focuses on the environmental preferences that younger readers have, the limited available research suggests that at university level, readers using a library prefer a quiet environment so that they can apply sustained attention (Dryden & Goldstein, 2013; Massis, 2012). In the ISABR, more than two in five self-identified avid readers sometimes had difficulty concentrating when they read, and 'attempting to read in a noisy environment . . . affected more than half of respondents (56.4%) who reported difficulty concentrating while reading' (Merga, 2017d, p. 57). For struggling readers, particularly those experiencing attentional issues that impact on their ability to apply sustained attention, noisy environments can mitigate their best efforts to engage in the immersive practice of reading.

I am certainly not suggesting that it is desirable or practical that school libraries have a blanket total silence demand; indeed, some students 'simply do not feel welcome in a space that demands silence' (Layton & Love, 2021, p. 48). My own research has found that tolerance for background music widely varies (Merga, 2017c). Modern school reading spaces, whether they be classrooms, libraries or other areas, need to meet multiple student needs, and where possible libraries should include some space(s) for relatively quiet and undisturbed reading, as while those who prefer to read with background noise can wear headphones and listen to music, those who need silence in order to apply sustained attention may find it harder to regulate background noise, even with noise-reducing technology.

Varied spaces for varied preferences

It will be no surprise to you that just as adults may have varied preferences for reading environments, young people do too. This has implications for classroom-based reading, but also for the resourcing and organisation of the school library. Research by Loh et al. (2017) on promoting a strong reading culture through the school library noted that 'school libraries need to attend to students' need for comfortable and varied spaces in their design of space and organization of furniture' (p. 344). They described what this can look like:

> Since the school wanted to encourage reading through the school library, there was deliberate attempt to ensure multiple and varied kinds of spaces for reading. The armchair area situated beside the windows looking out to greenery and the car park space provided students interested in browsing or sustained reading with a comfortable spot to locate themselves. The beanbags and steps at the performance area provided additional seating. Students also colonized the study spaces for reading. (p. 344)

Similarly, my research with avid readers found that some had specific furnishing preferences that enhance their reading experience.

> The importance of a comfortable couch, chair, or bed was highlighted. For some, the furniture was specifically selected for its capacity to be conductive to reading, such as the respondent who stated that, 'I have a contoured chair I bought just for sitting to read'.
>
> (Merga, 2017d, p. 60)

It may not be practical for classrooms to contain the kinds of comfortable furnishings that are preferred by many readers, highlighting the importance that students have regular access to a school library that has a sustained budget for furnishing resources as well as other material resources such as books. Indeed, library managers put considerable effort into thoughtfully purchasing and arranging furniture, sometimes within severe budget constraints, so that students can read in comfort (Merga, 2021c). A quiet space with welcoming and comfortable furniture can make the library a safe space where students can escape into a book (Hughes et al., 2016).

Of course, silent reading will need to occur in classrooms as well as school libraries, so attention to allowing modified ways of using existing furniture and space in classrooms may be pertinent. In a recent study on the implementation of a whole school silent reading programme,

> some teachers commented on the lack of comfort for some students when reading. Reading in spaces not designed for reading, for example, science labs or art rooms with high stools meant that some teachers either supported, or were reluctant to allow students to read outside or on the floor.
> (Collins et al., 2022, p. 98)

As such, classroom teachers may need to show some flexibility when silent reading is being conducted in spaces and with furnishings that may constrain comfort, being open to allowing students to move to an alternative space, such as a grassed area, or by providing cushions so that students can move onto the ground. There are budgeting implications related to providing these affordances, which should be considered when planning whole school reading initiatives. This is one of the areas where the widely varied budgets that schools have access to again influence students' experiences and attainment, and a lack of reading-conducive space due to limited school budgets can further promote unequal learning opportunities for students when compared with more affluent schools.

Space invaders

As school libraries seek to accommodate the diverse needs of the school community, in some cases, reading spaces have been significantly encroached upon or even lost (Merga, 2019d).

It cannot be taken for granted that contemporary school libraries include spaces that are conducive to reading. Teacher librarians in Australia have raised concerns about 'the forced multipurpose space of the library' (Merga, 2019d, p. 163), where teaching and other needs for the space sometimes limited its use for reading. Indeed, the library itself was being incrementally lost in some cases; 'it was common for parts of the library to be appropriated or annexed for unrelated purposes', reducing 'the amount of space available for reading and literacy related activities' (p. 164). Library staff raised concerns about how activities undertaken in the library meant that the environment was not conducive to reading, and that in some contexts, there was a lack of available comfortable furniture, with one teacher librarian noting that they would 'like a reading pit, or a reading area where you can totally relax, rather than sitting in chairs, I'd like bean bags' (p. 164). However such furnishings could be beyond the often very modest budgets of school libraries. As such, 'space to read was not guaranteed in a contemporary school library' (p. 165), so when building a whole school reading culture, it is vital that attention be given to creating and sustaining reading spaces, with particular focus on adequately resourcing the school library.

Given that in my earlier research some adolescents expressed a keen preference for reading in the school library rather than the classroom, this investment is crucial (Merga, 2013). While it will rarely be practical for all reading for pleasure undertaken in school to occur in the school library, there should be at least some opportunities for students to read in this context, enabling them to make the most of comfortable furnishing, a relatively quiet environment and ready access to a diverse and rich array of reading resources.

Reading aloud

As a social practice, reading can be a meaningful and influential experience when it is shared. Having children read aloud is a valuable educative practice, but children also gain a lot from being read to or sharing the reading.

When people reflect on their earliest memories of reading, it is often shared reading aloud that stands out, associated with nostalgic reflections of enjoyment and togetherness. At home, this may be remembered as the warmth of a lap, the shared laughter over the use of character voices, the nodding off to sleep in the safe space created. You may also have been read to by a teacher, an older sibling, a grandparent, a librarian or another social influence. These can be very fun, meaningful and educative experiences that many who were fortunate enough to have them look back upon with fondness.

To some extent, research has captured the transformative possibilities of the shared reading experience. It is not uncommon for avid readers in adulthood to reflect on their childhood and identify opportunities where they were read to as a formative influence on their later identification as an avid reader (Merga, 2017a). In the ISABR,

> Teachers' reading aloud in their classrooms was also positively recalled, with a respondent from the US recalling her fourth-grade teacher reading '*Box Car Children* aloud to our classes,' and remembering 'being excited to find out what happened next!' Another respondent from the US recalled, 'My fifth-grade teacher read my favourite series to the class, just the first book, and encouraged me to finish it, and now I read it every summer'. (p. 12)

Reading aloud has been established over time as a key literacy-supportive practice, particularly in relation to parental reading to children (Schoon et al., 2010), though its value as a classroom practice has also attracted significant research attention (e.g. Merga, 2017c).

Reading aloud with young children

Much of the research on the benefits of reading aloud focuses on the early years of life.

For example, longitudinal research conducted in Australia found that 'children's shared reading experiences at home at 2 to 3 years of age are associated with their level of vocabulary and preacademic skills at kindergarten age and their academic achievement in elementary school' (Shahaeian et al., 2018, p. 497). The practice can mitigate some of the impact of socio-economic disadvantage for children, given that 'shared reading appears to be more strongly associated with the assessed outcomes in lower to middle SES families compared to the higher SES families' (p. 497).

It is also a practice that is typically very much enjoyed by young children, though many young children have limited exposure. The WASRA research with children in primary school found that the vast majority enjoyed being read to. However, we also found that 'most respondents would prefer a greater frequency of being read to at home', and 'over a quarter of respondents claimed that no one read to them in the home' (Ledger & Merga, 2018, p. 131).

Reading aloud beyond the early years

While reading aloud is often seen as a practice most appropriate to young children who are still developing the most basic reading skills, research suggests that opportunities to listen to reading aloud may be appreciated by young people beyond the early years, affording pleasure (Merga, 2022b) as well as strengthening social bonds, building literacy skills and facilitating access to more complex texts (Merga, 2017c).

Enjoyment of reading beyond the early years has been found across many nations. A recent survey of children in China found that many children who had been read to previously before cessation, 'were not ready for it to stop', with 46% of children aged 6–8 and 33% aged 9–11 wanting their 'read-aloud' opportunities to be continued (Scholastic, 2020, p. iii). Similarly, an Australian survey found that across all ages surveyed (6–17 years old), 'the overwhelming majority of children (86%) say they love(d) being read books aloud at home or like(d) it a lot – the main reason being because it is a special time with parents' (Scholastic, 2016a, p. 5).

There may also be significant benefits for continuing to read aloud with older children, particularly for, but not limited to struggling literacy learners. Research in the UK involved 20 English teachers reading 'two whole challenging novels at a faster pace than usual in 12 weeks with their average and poorer readers ages 12–13'. Students 'made 8.5 months' mean progress on standardised tests of reading comprehension, but the poorer readers made a surprising 16 months progress', leading the authors to conclude that 'simply reading challenging, complex novels aloud and at a fast pace in each lesson repositioned "poorer readers" as "good" readers, giving them a more engaged uninterrupted reading experience over a sustained period' (Westbrook et al., 2019, p. 60).

Transforming attitudes towards reading

Reading aloud can enhance young people's attitudes towards reading, and encourage greater engagement in reading practices. A recent Jordanian community-based reading intervention We Love Reading (WLR) successfully used read-aloud sessions with children, finding improvements in their reading attitudes and practices when juxtaposed with a comparison group who were not involved in the intervention (Mahasneh et al., 2021). Children have described being read to as transforming their perceptions of books and reading. For example, a student described how being read to by her teacher inspired her at a young age:

> it was Year 1 and we were reading this book called – it's like, a Dr Seuss book. And she would – like, we'd always laugh and giggle, and every time we laughed and giggled, she would continue reading and she'd put lots of expression. And that's kind of one of the things that made me, I want to read like that and I want to be good at reading.
>
> (Merga, 2016b, p. 265)

Where children are read to and they have the opportunity to share a pleasurable reading experience with others, it can inspire and engage. Furthermore, recent research from Germany found that 'joint book reading predicted students' self-reported time spend in leisure time reading', illustrating how shared reading aloud is positively associated with students' reading frequency (Pfost & Heyne, 2023, p. 12).

Growing understanding of the benefits of reading aloud for building literacy skills and enhancing engagement has led to the adoption of initiatives to extend young people's opportunities for exposure to reading aloud beyond the early years. For example, a relatively recent state government initiative in Western Australia was responsive to the research in this space, actively promoting the practice at school and community levels:

> In 2017, after my project findings about negative effects of early curtailment of reading aloud to young people had received substantial media coverage . . . the DoE (Department of Education) got in touch, wanting me to consult with them on the Never Stop Reading program. In brief, this government-driven initiative was designed by the DoE to improve the reading and broader literacy outcomes for children beyond the early years of schooling, and through this program, I had the DoE driving the translation of my research in classrooms and homes. Former school teacher and Premier's wife Sarah McGowan shared my findings with Australian primary schools throughout the state, and I appeared on television and undertook radio and newspaper interviews to support this initiative. My research is featured prominently in the campaign, reflecting the role I played in consulting with the DoE as they developed their ideas.
>
> (Merga, 2021a, p. 662)

As such, even though reading aloud may seem like a 'fluffy pedagogy' like reading for pleasure (Vanden Dool & Simpson, 2021), the research behind it has informed government-led initiatives and garnered wide interest in the media, suggesting that both the general public and policymakers do, at least to some extent, appreciate its importance. While we have a plethora of research to support its benefits, it also resonates on an intuitive level. Hopefully, this will give schools who have been hesitant about employing this approach, particularly beyond the early years, the courage to experiment with its implementation.

Maintaining the practice and the message

It is vital that the importance of reading aloud with children both in the early years and beyond is effectively communicated. As previously noted, the WASRA research findings suggest that some parents believe that reading with their child is no longer necessary once their child can read independently (Merga & Ledger, 2018). This finding has also been mirrored in international reports, with US data suggesting that

> reading aloud peaks at age five. While a majority of families read aloud 5–7 days a week before a child enters kindergarten (55%), this percentage begins to decline dramatically with each additional year of age. This decrease is closely mirrored

by parents' view on the importance of reading aloud as children grow older . . . When asked why read-aloud decreases or stops, parents most commonly cite the fact that children can read on their own. For many kids, becoming an independent reader corresponds with the first major decline in read-aloud frequency among the 6–8 age group.

(Scholastic, 2019c, p. 8)

Children from lower socio-economic backgrounds are far less likely to be read to than their more advantaged counterparts (Scholastic, 2019c), and not all parents will be able to provide this experience for their children at home due to a wide range of issues they may face, such as long working hours, health conditions or low adult literacy. Adult literacy levels may be lower than typically understood; for example, 43 million US adults have low English literacy skills (National Centre for Education Statistics, 2019). As such, it is vital that schools be responsible for providing enjoyable shared reading experiences, and that they don't assume that all homes are well equipped to take full responsibility for this role.

Many children have very limited exposure to reading aloud at school. Our research on the WASRA project found that around 3% of children reported their teachers reading books to them on a daily basis, with only 23.7% contending that this practice occurred often, and the vast majority (68.1%) reported being read to only sometimes (Ledger & Merga, 2018). When teachers were asked about barriers to reading aloud with children in primary schools, a lack of time and related complex demands of the curriculum inhibited regular opportunities for reading aloud with students (Merga & Ledger, 2019). Schools seeking to create whole school reading cultures would benefit from establishing shared expectations that reading aloud be a regular practice that students are exposed to, both in the early years of schooling and beyond, potentially giving teachers confidence to devote more time to this beneficial practice, by privileging it rather than situating it as a peripheral pedagogy.

Making the most of reading aloud

So what is the best way to read aloud with young people?

As recently noted by Son et al. (2023), there are very few studies that examine 'patterns or components in shared reading engagement', or consider 'various reading behaviours reflecting the components' (p. 47). However, this new US research suggests that incorporating opportunities for an interactive component may be beneficial for literacy scores, and 'children show interactive engagement in shared book reading by asking and answering questions about the story and prints and sharing related experiences' (p. 57). As such, providing some opportunities for interaction during the read-aloud experience could be beneficial, though further research with larger and geographically diverse samples is needed, particularly given that the desire to discuss books during the reading process may be specific to American students, or students from learning contexts where their interaction is expected. In contrast, it could be seen as undesirably interruptive by some students, perhaps particularly when they are from cultures where this kind of contribution from students is not expected.

Furthermore, other research has found nearly identical gains for vocabulary learning where children were read to with either explicit techniques (such as pointing and giving definitions) or a more engaging storytelling approach. In the storytelling approach, the adult reader added contextual information, which enhanced the child's interest and engagement in the story (Vaahtoranta et al., 2018).

Personally, I grew up in Australia and I remember *really* hating it every time the fluid reading aloud of a book by my teacher was interrupted for interaction, and given the mixed findings in this area, we cannot assume it is a given that regular interruptions for interaction will be best practice for *all* children. This is a space where further research is really needed. Indeed, struggling readers may not thank teachers who allow interactive components to become tangential as they struggle to hold onto the tenuous thread of reading comprehension. While we wait for further research in this field, judicious allowance for interaction that does not impede fluidity could be the best approach, and interruptions for interaction should support reading comprehension rather than be tangential.

As such, at this stage, when reading aloud to a child or group of children to promote enjoyment, we can:

- Provide a comfortable space where the children can hear and see you, and you can hear and see them easily. Some students will rely on being able to see your lips to support their understanding of what you are saying (e.g., Bourguignon et al., 2020).
- Read books that reflect their interests, and show that you've taken these interests into account.
- Where reading a sustained book over multiple days, elicit a recap when picking up a story each day for those who may have forgotten the plot progression, and for students who have been absent.
- Don't hesitate to reread the same story more than once (on demand) as this can be beneficial reinforcement while also being enjoyable.

- Read with expression and show an emotional response to what you are reading where appropriate.

(Merga, 2016b)

Professional development and laying the foundation

While literacy is an essential competency that needs to be fostered across the curriculum, by all teachers within a school, not all teachers will have equal confidence and competence when it comes to fostering reading engagement and supporting the whole school reading culture (Merga, 2023b).

For teachers to commit to, and play a key role in supporting the whole school reading culture, they may need extra support in the form of targeted professional development, and in my professional role I have been involved in whole school seminars, and delivering intensive workshops in this area to address this common need. However, while an expert researcher can enhance knowledge and skills in this space through these kinds of opportunities, a *sustained* commitment to ongoing professional development over time, and beyond sporadic or one-off engagements may be necessary to support teachers to be active advocates and educators in this space (Merga, 2023b). This means that *within* your school, you ideally need a literacy leader who is willing to coach and support the ongoing professional learning of staff in this regard.

Building staff knowledge, skills and reading engagement

If every teacher is expected to be a teacher of reading, and a supporter of reading for pleasure, there is an associated knowledge and skill base that may need to be fostered. For example, in their US middle school context, Daniels and Steres (2011) found that

> the teachers repeatedly stated it was difficult to maximize the increased time for school-wide reading because of their lack of knowledge about young adult literature. They wanted to promote reading and to read with their students, but they did not feel comfortable recommending books; nor did they have a clear understanding of how to teach students to choose and interact with books. (p. 10)

In this case, they addressed the issue by making time at the beginning of workdays before students arrived and in meetings to deliver professional development in order to build teachers' knowledge of young adult literature.

As previously explored in the section on teacher modelling, individuals with poor attitudes towards reading certainly exist and undertake teacher training, and these future teachers are less likely than their more engaged counterparts to invest in reading promotion to support the reading engagement of their students (Vansteelandt et al., 2022), so professional development that fosters teachers' reading engagement as well as their knowledge and skills in this area may be vital to ensure uniform implementation of a whole school reading approach.

Some teachers may be particularly resistant, and while in some cases this can be because they are feeling overwhelmed with the current curricular demands they are experiencing in their learning area and/or year group, sometimes it can also be because they have low personal valuing of reading. In worst cases, some teachers may subtly or even openly resist supporting the activities involved in establishing a whole school reading culture, as found in a recent study:

> The issue of inconsistent classroom implementation was raised by a number of teachers. Although it appeared that they were uncomfortable directly stating that some teachers were not consistent in their adherence to the program: 'Some teachers must let students do other things during Just Read, as some students are constantly asking "do we have to read today?"' Some teacher respondents implied that the issue of forgetting books was in part due to the teachers' expectations with regards to reading: 'Students not bringing books to lessons. These issues have only occurred on classes that I have been covering'.
> (Collins et al., 2022, p. 98)

As with the implementation of any new initiative within schools, initial professional development is about upskilling and providing access to research-supported practices, but also about winning over key stakeholders to be fully and knowledgeably supportive of the whole school reading culture vision. I provide clear guidance on how to do this effectively in the subsequent chapter on implementation planning in change management.

Promising emerging possibilities

Fostering reading engagement and reading cultures in schools is a lively and dynamic research space, full of evolving ideas and fuelled by the passion of researchers and educators alike. While more research is needed in these areas, there is a range of emerging possibilities that schools can incorporate into their whole school reading cultures with confidence that there is a promising, though still developing body of research supporting their efficacy. I look forward to monitoring the future research that appears in this space, which we can use to strengthen our understandings and adapt our practices accordingly.

Story dogs

As a 'dog parent' myself, I am intrigued by the potential of story dogs to influence young people's experiences of reading. Story dogs, also often known as reading dogs, are dogs that children can read to, enabling them to practise their reading skills with a non-judgemental listener, building confidence and fluency.

They are already being used in schools. In the 2020 *School libraries promoting wellbeing* project, a dedicated school library manager in a primary school in Australia described the benefits of using a story dog with her young patrons. The story dog (given the pseudonym Katie) was used as a resource to build students' confidence in reading. The Library Manager explained that 'the story dog works with Year 1s and 2s mostly who don't have parents reading with them at home, or who are just a bit nervous, and it's amazing':

> The child without the dog will pick up a book or not say a word. Katie comes in, and they lay on the mat, one hand on Katie, and just read, they'll read out loud to you. Because all of a sudden, it's just taken away . . . like, it seems like that part of their brain that worries about what's going on is taken up with this tactile, beautiful . . . the smell of the dog, the touch of the dog, and so . . . She's a retriever. Oh my gosh, she's beautiful. (p. 95)

While the use of story dogs may not be appropriate in all contexts (for example, where children have allergies to or a phobia of dogs), there is a steadily growing body of research celebrating the powerful impact that they can have. In addition to offering literacy benefits, reading to dogs can enhance young people's wellbeing and reduce their anxiety and stress (Canelo, 2020; Henderson et al., 2020). Steel et al. (2021) found that UK teachers were typically very positive about the potential benefits of reading to dogs, particularly in reference to social, emotional and behavioural benefits, with barriers and challenges to implementation seen as surmountable. Unsurprisingly, the use of story dogs has also had positive media coverage in recent times (e.g. Mikrut, 2023).

One of the most heart-warming recent studies in this area is a small US case study that involved elementary school age children reading to shelter dogs in their shelter environment. The young readers typically had a very positive experience, and were felt to demonstrate greater confidence and motivation due to their involvement in the programme, which was also felt to support the students' social and emotional development (Rodriguez-Meehan et al., 2022).

Parallel audio and print book exposure

Students may enjoy and benefit from consuming literature in a variety of formats. Audiobooks have been growing in popularity in recent times, and UK research found a notable increase in students' engagement with audiobooks during COVID-19 related lockdowns (Best et al., 2020). The potential for audiobooks to enhance reading engagement also emerged in this research, with 52.9% of students indicating that listening to audiobooks has enhanced their interest in reading (Best et al., 2020). There may also be gender-related engagement advantages to promoting audiobook exposure, given that boys who do not enjoy reading are more likely than non-reader girls to indicate that they enjoy listening to audiobooks (Best & Clark, 2021).

Given the recognised benefits of reading aloud to young people already explored in this book, it follows that even while more research is needed in this space, the extant research suggests that audiobook listening can be a great way of extending students' literacy skills, particularly where students read along with the audiobook. In a recent review of the influence that audiobook listening and concurrent print reading can have on comprehension, researchers found that audiobooks may be a useful instructional support, enhancing reading comprehension, and this may particularly be the case for non-native speakers of English, and struggling readers (Singh & Alexander, 2022). I know that many schools are already experimenting with using audiobooks in this manner, as I often speak with teacher librarians at conferences who are using concurrent audiobook and print book opportunities to successfully engage struggling readers.

Some readers of this book may think that this section could easily have been slotted into the section on collection building. However, while this new research does have obvious implications for collection building, facilitating concurrent audio and print book exposure is more complex than making sure this resource is available in our school libraries. If we are working with this approach, we will need to ensure that struggling readers have access to audio and print books both at school and at home. It also has implications for device provisions so that students can access audiobooks with print books during sustained silent reading opportunities, again within and beyond school, without getting distracted by the multiple affordances of these devices that have been reported on in previous research (Merga & Mat Roni, 2017a).

Social media inspiration

Social media platforms host burgeoning populations of young people, so when looking to foster reading engagement in ways that resonate with young people's current interests, exploring how they use and interact on social media platforms can provide valuable insights. We can even use social media to help hook students on books.

Social media platforms such as TikTok are already having an impact on young people's consumption of books and their attitudes towards reading. Questionable controversies aside (e.g. Perrigo, 2023), and while further rigorous research is needed in this area, market research polling of young adults found that 59% agreed that Booktok or book influencers had supported them to discover a love of reading, 55% draw on Booktok for recommendations, and 68% felt that Booktok had influenced them to read a book that they would not have normally considered (Brown, 2022). Similarly, a Dutch student's study found that Booktok could encourage those who are not yet avid readers, but not explicitly avoidant, to read more frequently, potentially having a transformative impact (Welling, 2022). Academic research at postgraduate and professional level is lagging in this area, though studies looking more generally at the influence of technology on young people's leisure reading preferences have also begun to capture reference to the use of TikTok as a valued source of book recommendations (Loh & Sun, 2022).

Intrigued by the possibilities of the subcommunity of Booktok on TikTok generated typically by young content producers (CPs), I conducted research that explored how schools and libraries can draw upon the ways that young people promote books to each other in order to inform how books are promoted to them within libraries. I suggested that those involved in fostering reading engagement in young people could 'use these findings from analysis of Booktok content to build young reader friendly spaces and give greater primacy to current popular commonalities informing recommendations, such as emotional response in readers' advisory services' (Merga, 2021b, p. 8):

> Booktok data suggests that many young people connect with books primarily for the emotional response they will elicit, and millions of views are collectively accrued by CPs' promoting books to give a certain desired emotional reaction, including readers seeking books that will 'destroy' them emotionally. Libraries can consider placing greater emphasis on displaying and recommending books in relation to emotions, such as a display of books that will make you sob until you have no tears left, or kinds of characters that resonate with the current Booktok community, such as strong female leads. Using places as a point of appeal can also be powerful, perhaps asking readers where they would like to go next and showing footage of fiction places such as Middle Earth or Hogwarts. (p. 8)

The possible advantages of drawing on social media to inspire reading cultures and make meaningful and authentic connections between school and home reading practices have also begun to be addressed in other research (e.g. Jerasa & Boffone, 2021).

Author visits

Given the substantial challenges faced by many authors in the current economic climate (Crosby et al., 2022), opportunities to both support the artistic community and promote students' reading engagement offer appeal. If we want our students to enjoy high-quality books, we need to back our writers of books for children and young adults.

There is limited research that quantifies the impact of author visits on students' reading engagement and/or achievement. My research with teacher librarians found that 'author visits were highly valued for their ability to make meaningful connections between the students and literature, and to make real the profession of writer' (Merga, 2019d, p. 161), and teacher librarians described seeing increased engagement and interest in their students, as seen in increased student borrowing numbers of the author's books from the school library. For example, a teacher librarian explained that 'we had Jack Heath here last year, and I don't know if you've ever seen him, he's a young man, and he writes really action-packed books. I've been through our reading stats and his books just flew' (p. 209). As such, while further research is needed, author visits may stimulate student borrowing and interest in reading.

In the UK, Clark and Lant (2019) note that scant evidence 'on the impact of writer visits' may be due to the fact that it is a 'broad area including different models (from assemblies to residencies) with different aims (including increased enjoyment of reading, improved writing skills and many more) and as many different approaches to delivery as there are writers working with schools' (p. 1). While this diverse application highlights the wide range of benefits authors may confer, it can also make it hard to quantify impact across schools and authors. Clark and Lant's (2019) analysis of the limited available data led them to conclude that 'writer visits can be a valuable element of a rich and varied approach to literacy in the most successful schools', and they noted that this is another area where there is a concerning 'disparity between the children who have access to this opportunity, with the most privileged children (those attending independent schools) much more likely to work with a professional writer than their peers in state-run schools' (p. 12). Research that focuses directly on students' experiences, attitudes and gains in direct relation to author visits is needed.

Activities to be subject to measures of effectiveness

I am aware that this chapter presents a somewhat overwhelming range of possibilities for schools looking to enhance their reading culture and promote reading for pleasure to see improved educational and related outcomes in their students. I have been careful to select measures that are associated with research demonstrating their benefits, so that schools know that when they select from the initiatives outlined in this chapter, they are being responsive to research in best practice in this field.

It is certainly not expected that schools will be able to adopt the full range of practices and strategies highlighted in this chapter. As I will discuss further later in this book, the key point is to select those which are feasible, and which can realistically be implemented within current resourcing and structural constraints. Whatever approaches you select to enact your whole school reading culture initiative, they need to be subject to measures of effectiveness so that you can evaluate whether or not they have been implemented with fidelity, and reflective of best practice, which I will explore further in the chapter on evaluation. However, for my purposes here, I simply seek to illustrate that you have freedom to select whatever approaches you want to take that are research responsive, and no one is going to expect you to be able to do everything!

For example, in implementing a culture of reading at a middle school in the US, the following approach was taken, which in parentheses I link to the practices featured in this chapter:

- For 15 minutes per day, everyone at school silently read self-selected reading materials. (*Opportunities for regular silent reading for pleasure of self-selected materials*)
- There was 'school-wide support for teachers and administrators to also read during the school day and to talk about their reading with students'. (*Modelling; Talking about books*)
- 'All teachers, regardless of content area, were expected to have a bookshelf of young adult books and were given financial support to purchase the books'. (*Accessible and visible books; Investment in collection building*)
- 'English teachers provided time to read silently every day in class, during which students were able to read their books of choice'. (*Opportunities for regular silent reading for pleasure of self-selected materials*)
- 'The principal regularly gave book talks in English classes and asked students about their reading when he saw them on campus'. (*Modelling; Talking about books*)

- There were regular staff meetings with teaching faculty that focused on 'how to talk about books with students'. (*Professional development; Talking about books*).

(Daniels & Steres, 2011, p. 4)

This flexibility within the parameters defined by the extant research on best practice means that your school's journey towards the whole school reading culture will be unique, and reflective of what is likely to best work in your given context. As with whole school literacy policies (Merga, 2023b), there is no one size fits all approach. The above model is not perfect, with 15 minutes being a very short time to get absorbed in sustained reading among other limitations, and your school may prefer to track a different course based on the findings detailed in this chapter.

3
Stakeholder Engagement and Resourcing

The success of your journey towards implementation of a whole school reading culture will be very heavily influenced by your ability to secure strong stakeholder engagement and adequate resources to sustain the process. Whether you are leading the process from the school library, the English staffroom or any other area within the school, you will need to garner the support of educators, school leadership, support staff, parents and guardians, and key stakeholders in the broader community. To maximise the opportunities available to the school, you may seek additional funding from external sources. To this end, this chapter focuses on stakeholder engagement and resourcing before we move on to considering change management principles more broadly, though you will notice strong interrelationships with other parts of this book.

Research exploring comprehensive school reform in the US found that stakeholders within the school differed in their understanding of comprehensive school reform components:

> We found five contextual factors to explain the variation among model schools: the challenge of getting buy-in by teachers new to the model, principals' leadership activities supporting the implementation process, the alignment of the model with ongoing programs, the quality of developer support, and policies that influence stakeholders' decisions to implement model components.
>
> (Cotner et al., 2005, p. 1)

While stakeholder engagement is an essential component of effective comprehensive change management within schools, it is useful to consider it independently as a starting point so that its importance is not lost among the competing demands of change management.

Planning for a whole school reading culture is also an opportunity to strengthen relationships with key stakeholders in the broader community, as well as fostering new, productive and mutually beneficial connections. Not all schools are currently making the most of possible literacy and reading resources available to them in their contexts. For example, while many schools in the UK make the most of their public library resource, as indicated in their literacy policies, schools in Australia rarely mention making use of these resources though they are also typically available (Merga, 2022a).

Planning for initial and sustained educator and leader engagement

Even if you are used to working alone, when it comes to embedding a whole school reading culture, this should be a team endeavour, led by a competent and inspired leader. When it comes to successfully implementing a whole school reading culture, you will need to draw on support from within and beyond the school to realise this goal. As my book emphasises, while this transformation may be led from the library, English staffroom or elsewhere in the school, for successful change management to occur, every educator, leader and support worker in the school should be invested in its success.

Collective ownership and distributed responsibilities

If you try to take sole ownership of this initiative, it is unlikely to take root. Boucher (2001) described realising that the literacy initiative she had introduced was not going to be established without her ongoing guidance after she moved on from the school where it was implemented:

> That summer, the whole staff participated in a professional development opportunity at which the presenter asked them to describe their reading program. The audience, the entire staff with whom I had worked, was silent. Not one of them could explain the program, nor could they state the purpose of the four-year reform initiative. I realize now that I broke one of the most important reform rules: we didn't develop the program, I developed the program . . . The purpose of the reform must influence everyone's every decision; everyone should be moving in the same direction and understand why. It would appear that in my case I kept all of that to myself. In sum, my failure to build internal capacity resulted in a multi-year struggle for the school to regain ownership and direction.
>
> If the staff had had collective ownership and understanding of the literacy program reform initiative, then the program would have continued to develop and improve even though I had resigned. (p. 4)

Fostering a whole school reading culture needs to be a shared responsibility with distributed leadership involvement throughout the school so that it is not seen as the vehicle or brainchild of a single individual, but rather as a shared and supported goal. For successful implementation of change management, 'widespread communication, including discussion and decision-sharing between top managers and empowered head teachers and teachers, is needed' (Alkahtani, 2017, p. 218).

Delegation of responsibilities is really important. Leaders of a whole school reading culture should embrace a distributed leadership model that resists previous conceptions of 'the traditional "superhero" leadership model, which holds that leading a school is a one-person business' (Hulpia & Devos, 2010, p. 565):

> Due to the increased complexity in the educational system, and especially in large secondary schools, it becomes probable that no one individual has all the knowledge, skills, and abilities that would enable him/her to accomplish all of the leadership functions, without distributing them among a team. (p. 565)

As I explore further herein, such a model is essential to promoting buy-in from staff, also allowing you to make the most of the strengths of a diverse team.

Stakeholder identification and knowledge exchange

The first step in planning for initial and sustained stakeholder engagement is identifying who the stakeholders are. These will include educators and support staff and leadership within the school, but also key external stakeholders.

This needs to be followed by a committed period of knowledge exchange. While the team driving the whole school reading culture will need to provide information sessions outlining their vision, as explored further in the subsequent chapter, they will also need to be open to listening to and learning from the expertise of the other stakeholders, both internal and external. As such, at the outset, while a clear vision can be articulated, it is important that it not be set in stone prior to this consultative process or stakeholders may believe that their input is not valued or needed, potentially leading them to disengage.

According to the National Library of New Zealand (n.d-b), to create a school reading culture, the leadership team and staff need:

- to understand the impact of reading on student achievement
- a shared vision of the school's reading culture

- to know why a reading culture is important
- to know what an engaged reader looks like
- to fully support the library and its resources, services and programmes. (para. 2)

Engaging robust dialogue and exchange of ideas around these points and other relevant issues can be a good start for fostering committed educator and leader engagement.

Activating motivation

You want your stakeholders to be as passionate about this change as you are. In building their whole school reading culture, Mace and Lean (2021b) described the importance of fostering staff motivation. Some of the strategies they employed to engage staff in being active supporters of the initiative included presenting staff with books as gifts, which demonstrated the school's commitment to investing in the initiative, as well as providing teachers with reading material. Staff were given choice, self-selecting their gift to ensure that it met their interests. A specific staff collection was also developed in the library in order to sustain staff with reading material.

Early opportunities for motivating professional development in this area also played a noteworthy role in encouraging stakeholder buy-in in this school:

> Staff valued the keynote address given by our academic mentor Dr Margaret Merga prior to Just Read starting in January 2020. Dr Merga spoke passionately of the importance of reading for student wellbeing and the improved literacy outcomes daily reading brings. She stressed the critical role our staff have in modelling reading behaviour. Dr Merga's presentation strengthened support for the reading project amongst our staff.
>
> (Mace & Lean, 2021b, para. 11)

As such, this team's plan to foster early engagement in stakeholders was multifaceted, and these are just some of the many initiatives that the team enacted to support the success of the project. However, because you have already read this far, you do not need to engage an external third party to provide professional development in this area unless you want to. The necessary elements of the whole school culture and elucidation of benefits have already been covered in this book, so you are ready to conduct in-house learning in this area, that can be sustained over time.

Material benefits can be enjoyed by staff involved in a whole school reading culture which may not be apparent to staff initially unless they are exposed to these possibilities. For example, Mace & Lean (2022) found that

> the introduction of a daily silent reading program was seen as a gift by the vast majority of teachers, as it allowed a pause on formal teaching and learning while they immersed themselves in a book of their own choosing. A significant number of our staff have reignited their passion for reading. Others have read fiction books for the first time ever and have maintained this habit. Staff have identified reading as assisting with their wellbeing or in making connections with students. It is now very common in our school to overhear staff passionately sharing their latest read with their peers. (para. 18)

Staff may be more motivated to commit to supporting the whole school reading culture if they can see potential benefits for themselves as well as the students.

The importance of leader support

A reading culture is shaped through collaborative effort, supported and strengthened by relationships within the school (Merga & Mason, 2019), and these can be fostered and maintained through a supportive leadership team. Principals and the leadership team play a powerful role in shaping school culture, as we have explored in detail in earlier research (Merga & Mason, 2019). However, school leaders do not always consistently support whole school literacy approaches (e.g. Merga, Mat Roni, et al., 2021b).

In a best-case scenario, you will be blessed with a leader who is also a reader. Where leaders are passionate readers themselves, the school library may see stronger resourcing and support, and such leaders are a supportive and encouraging reading model who can influence staff, students and the broader school community (Merga & Mason, 2019). If your leader is neutral or negative towards establishing a whole school reading culture, you will need to focus your efforts to build and maintain positive support for the initiative.

Parents and guardians

Parents and guardians are key stakeholders in their child's education, whose role should not be neglected, and whose support will enhance students' experience of the whole school reading culture. As illustrated in the previous chapter, parents and guardians are potent social influences who are likely to substantially influence their child's reading engagement, whether this influence is intentional or not. However, the role of parents and guardians in relation to their support of a school reading culture has not been closely explored in the extant research. While there is limited research that looks at how to activate and sustain parental support for the development of a whole school reading culture, there is a growing body of research that looks at fostering parental engagement in school-based learning and initiatives more generally, that can be drawn upon to inform this goal.

Fostering home/school communication

The degree to which schools interact with the parents and guardians of their students varies greatly, and information exchanges can take many forms. Uni-directional forms such as school newsletters can be used to transmit important information (e.g. Merga & Hu, 2016), but they may be seen as didactic or inaccessible depending on the information shared and the language and tone adopted. Being uni-directional, they may not effectively encourage dialogue, investment, and knowledge exchange, though they can be used to communicate research around the benefits of sustained attention on the importance of reading.

For example, in our research, we found that some school leaders used newsletters and articles to build parental support for student reading for pleasure, with a teacher librarian explaining that

> our principal writes articles on reading all the time. She's a good reader. She's always quoting from literature. She's always writing about research. She's done a few articles, just for parents. We have a parent newsletter, and she's put in things like statistics that show kids who read recreationally do so much better after school and all that kind of thing.
>
> (Merga & Mason, 2019, p. 180)

While more research is needed on how parents and guardians receive such missives, it is worth noting that these communications crafted and initiated by the principal were felt to position the school leadership as committed and supportive advocates of reading for recreation within the school community, therefore potentially having a positive impact both within and beyond the school.

Barriers to involvement

Furthermore, schools and parents/guardians may have very different understandings of what parental and guardian involvement actually constitutes, so schools should be explicit in their expectations for parental involvement in supporting a whole school reading culture, and offer training and information to support these expectations. As noted by Antony-Newman (2019), 'while educators value school-based activities (volunteering, attending parent-teacher conferences, serving on parent councils), parents often confine their role to the home environment (setting expectations, monitoring child's progress, helping with homework, discussing schools)' (p. 362), and the misalignment may be most significant where parents/guardians are immigrants: 'coming from different cultural and educational backgrounds, they bring in distinctive sets of expectations, often not corresponding to those of teachers' (p. 363). The depth of the pool of shared understandings and expectations may be far shallower than expected, given that our norms are shaped by our experiences and resultant conditionings.

Communications with culturally diverse homes about supporting children's reading frequency and attitudes must not take for granted shared collective understandings about what this involves and can look like; you will need to be very clear. For example, many parents were never read to as children, so assuming that all parents know how this can be done to optimise enjoyment and learning is a mistake, and opportunities for learning and easy-to-read information providing advice and support should be facilitated through the school (e.g. Merga & Ledger, 2018).

Seeking to elicit or enhance parental and guardian support for a whole school reading culture can also involve reframing understandings of what constitutes involvement, so that both involvement within the school and within the home are explicitly valued, particularly given that in many cases, parents and guardians will not be available for school-based activities for a wide range of reasons, many of which may be beyond their control. Indeed, 'parental capacity to be actively involved in their children's education is not equally distributed with class, race, gender, and immigrant status all playing important roles' (Antony-Newman, 2019, p. 362), along with numerous other factors including, but not limited to, parents' own experiences with schooling, their health and their baseline literacy skills. When reflecting on the building of whole school reading cultures, teacher librarians working to this end have identified 'significant competing pressures that parents may face which can impact upon their ability to encourage reading engagement in their children' (Merga & Mason, 2019, p. 186). Ideally, schools should communicate diverse ways that parents and guardians can support the initiative so that every family can be involved, despite unequal home resources; schools should be active in addressing these differences where possible, such as by ensuring that students have access to books in the home sourced from school, including to large volumes of books over sustained periods of education interruption such as school holidays.

To engage parents and guardians with the goals of the whole school reading culture and to invite the investment of their time and the input of their expertise, the team in charge of leading the initiative needs to be knowledgeable and respectful of the cultural and linguistic backgrounds and strengths of these families. Unfortunately, where schools seek to foster engagement with parents and guardians, it is often parents and guardians from the hegemonic cultural, class and linguistic backgrounds who form these relationships; 'not all families and communities are acknowledged and/or employed by schools' (Stauss et al., 2021, p. 405). Attention must be given to meeting the needs of marginalised groups within the school community. Schools do not typically consciously privilege the participation of voices from parents in higher social classes and advantaged cultural or racial groups, but they often build in barriers to participation for those who fall outside these groups.

Practical solutions for accessibility

To address practical solutions for accessibility, we first need to consider what the barriers actually look like at the most pragmatic level.

For example, Primary School A seeks to engage parent volunteers in the school so that students in Year 2 can get more practice in reading aloud with an adult.

However, in order to participate, parents and guardians need to:

1 understand a complex email pitched at a University level of reading comprehension that leaves parents from linguistically diverse backgrounds stumped;
2 commit to volunteering at the school the same day and time each week, excluding all parents who cannot commit to this kind of schedule, such as shift workers; and
3 agree to a poorly explained preparatory training programme, which inadvertently communicates an expectation that parental ability in this area will be judged and/or evaluated, causing parents who lack confidence in their own reading skills, and those who had negative experiences of being judged at school to withhold commitment to participate.

When very few parents and guardians from marginalised backgrounds agree to take part, those in charge of planning at School A conclude that this is because these individuals lack commitment and interest in their child's education, rather than considering the barriers they have erected to diverse parent and guardian involvement, and exploring how the programme could be reconsidered to be more flexible, better communicated and inclusive.

Showcasing the whole school reading culture initiative and engaging optimal parental and guardian involvement can take many forms where inclusiveness involves a little more effort for a worthy reward. For example, you might invite parents and guardians to information sessions that invite their feedback and active involvement, ensuring that the session is recorded and available, so that parents and guardians can have access to it if they are unable to attend. Where there is a non-English speaking community within the school, the recording can be subtitled, with online feedback submissions invited in any language; thanks to modern technology, affordances for (relatively) accurate subtitling and text translation are easily available.

It is also important to invite parents and guardians into the school's reading-supportive spaces on their own terms where practical. For example, in our interviews with teacher librarians, we found that schools may invite parents to become patrons of the school library, to

> come in and borrow, too. So, there's a community thing of the parents being involved in it as well . . . I think it's important for the kids to see their parents reading. And the parents have come in and looked for books for their kids to encourage their boys to read.
>
> (Merga & Mason, 2019, p. 183)

In some cases, this involved keeping the school library open for extended hours; 'through the provision of long access hours, school libraries could also become a community access point, resourcing parents as well as students' (Merga, 2019d, p. 98), and 'broadening access to the library offers potential gains for the literacy levels of the broader community, also potentially enhancing opportunities for parents to be reading models to inspire their children to read more' (p. 228). By actively involving parents and guardians, positioning them as valued influences and fostering their own commitment to reading, schools can strengthen and deepen these vital educative relationships.

Grants for school-based research initiatives

Given the widely varying resources that schools are equipped with across many nations, you might need to seek external funding to enable you to enact some of your implementation goals. Even if you are fortunate enough to be working at a school where the budget for school-based initiatives is substantial, there is still credibility afforded when you succeed in winning funding, as I explore further herein, and you can use this to garner stakeholder support.

I have a lot of professional experience in the grant-chasing process. As a former academic, like many of my active researcher peers, I spent an alarming amount of time applying for funding (Herbert et al., 2013). This could be a demoralising process. With low success rates, applying for funds feels a lot like gambling, with significant resourcing invested for a very uncertain outcome.

Is it worth the effort? I would argue that if you have sufficient time and resourcing, it certainly can be.

While working as an academic, I experienced sufficient success to ensure a sustainable research trajectory, though it wasn't all luck and chance. I have also been part of school and professional association-led teams that have successfully targeted and secured funding for resources and initiatives. For example, I was involved in the Queenwood *Just Read* whole school reading project (Collins et al., 2022; Mace & Lean, 2021a), which secured substantial funds as an Association of Independent Schools of New South Wales (AISNSW) School Based Research Grant for their planned initiative. I also worked closely with ASLA to identify and successfully apply for research and research-dissemination funding from BUPA (Merga, 2021c).

I have also both led and been part of teams who have won many research grants funded by philanthropic organisations, such as the Ian Potter Foundation Grants among others.

It's worth noting that I have often subsequently won grants with the same funder, having previously delivered on project milestones, so if you put together a good application, win the grant and then exceed expectations in delivery, you are setting your school up for potential further successes. Don't take your foot off the accelerator when you win the grant, because you will need to regularly report your progress in line with the agreed project milestones, and you need to aim to be a little ahead of what you have previously projected to allow for unexpected delays later in the project, such as illness of a team member, or an unforeseeable global pandemic!

It's true that there is usually a lot of competition for these kinds of funding sources (Blanco et al., 2016), so you will need to invest time and effort to craft an application that will be competitive. There are tips that I've learnt through research and through trial and error that I can share here to boost your chances of success in these risky but potentially hugely beneficial activities. While there are many kinds of grants, I will focus here on the kinds of grants where the funder expects to see research or project outputs delivered that offer benefits for educators beyond your school.

Drawing on the breadth of my experience in this area, here are **15** of the **key steps** that can lead to success when you are going for a school-based research grant, as presented by me at the ASLA conference in April 2023 (Merga, 2023c). These are suitable for absolute novices as well as more experienced applicants seeking to further hone their craft:

1. **Find prospective funders and create a list.** Once you have at least a general idea of what you are looking to fund, start by creating a longlist of possible funders. Locate prospective funders in your area(s) of interest and create a list once you have investigated them to determine:

   1 what they fund,
   2 if the funding amount is likely to meet your needs, and
   3 if the timings of funding periods align with your needs.

   If you involve an academic partner in your initiative, they should be able to point you in the right direction to find potential funders of school-based research in your country and region. One approach is to 'scan the landscape of funding agencies for one that is seeking to support projects that might be similar (in one way or another) to a more general idea' (Blanco et al., 2016, p. 114).

2. **Get to know the funder(s).** Read up on their mission and goals, peruse their website to see what they celebrate, read their annual report and access any information you can about prior grant holders and projects to determine whether your project falls within the same priorities and values without repeating prior work (Blanco & Lee, 2012). At this stage, you will eliminate further funders and create a shortlist. Begin to align what you have to offer with what they both explicitly and implicitly want. For example, whether they state this or not, contemporary funders typically want to see a lot of bang for their buck in terms of the production of outputs that will reach professional and general audiences. I'll talk more about this in relation to **step 14**.

3. **Get to know the grant.** It's time to focus in on one grant opportunity. Choose the one that best aligns with your needs. Read the guidelines carefully, and follow the directions; this may sound obvious and a simple tip, but it is 'one that is often missed' (Blanco & Lee, 2012, p. 451). Everyone on the team needs to be across the grant guidelines too:

   > Most granting agencies set precise guidelines for what must be included in a grant proposal, as well as strict format requirements and word/page limits. Reviewers are accustomed to finding information in specific sections of the application. Thus, it is important that the authors read the directions carefully,

follow the guidelines, and organize their application to guide reviewers through it.

(Blanco et al., 2016, p. 115)

While you may have another preferred way of organising your information, it is important to be compliant with the guidelines when writing up your grant application as reviewers may miss important information about your application if you put it in the wrong sections. They are only human, and often very time poor just like you.

4. **Take any opportunity to check alignment with the funder.** Some funders will encourage prospective applicants to contact a key person if they have any questions about their eligibility or the application process, and 'grant writers shouldn't fear e-mailing or calling a grants agency to talk through their potential interest in a project' (Sohn, 2020, p. 133).

    In the past, I've often made use of this, and it has genuinely helped me to better align my project to what the funder was targeting in that funding round. Don't waste their time, so do make sure that before you get in touch you have a brief but informative pitch put together which argues for what you want to do, and why it is a worthy investment that aligns well with their interests. Respecting their time is important, and you also need to be able to demonstrate that you have already familiarised yourself with the funder's strategic goals; they should not have to explain anything to you that is already available online.

5. **Make sure you have a complementary team.** In your application, you may need to show how the expertise of the different team members will be drawn upon to argue for the feasibility of the project. You can consider qualifications, experience, expertise and contributions of each team member, as well as their demonstrable ability to collaborate (Wisdom et al., 2015). It's no coincidence that I have often worked with the same colleagues over and over again. I look for people with complementary skill sets, not people with exactly the same expertise and strengths that I possess.

    On a personal, practical level, take dispositions into account. If the most highly qualified genius in your school is also a terrible team player who gets pleasure out of putting others down, the value their involvement might add to the application will be offset by the barrier they pose to actually completing the grant in a timely and harmonious manner. If you use them, you'll need to be judicious about how you do so, to minimise the impact of their negativity on the whole team.

6. **Stand on the shoulders of giants.** You will probably need to show that what you want to do is research-informed (Malin et al., 2019). This

involves providing evidence that you have deeply intellectually engaged in the academic literature on your topic so you understand the current issues, research findings and methods being used to explore your area of interest. Reviewing related research literature can 'help to better identify the problem or research question related to your project that has not yet been addressed by others and to tailor your project accordingly' (Blanco & Lee, 2012, p. 451). Take the time to familiarise yourself with this literature and make judicious use of it in your application in order to mount a strong, research-supported argument. Even if you can't find research that reflects a similar project, you can use your references to the research literature to inform your methods.

7. **Use a logical method.** You need to clearly describe and explain your methods, including your evaluation methods (i.e. how you will determine if your project was successful) (Blanco & Lee, 2012). If you decide to work with an academic mentor (see **step 10**) they should be able to give good advice about what would be the best approach. Reading the methods sections of other grant applications will help you to understand how the story needs to be relayed so that your methodological choices are clear and logical to reviewers, and well aligned with your research aims.

8. **Know your school.** A study of educators' requests for grant funding concluded that 'the strongest applications are those with explicit theories of action that also incorporate local data and deep contextual understandings' (Malin et al., 2019, p. 14). Local data refers to contextual data from classrooms, year groups, whole school, regions and states/territories (Malin et al., 2019). The reviewers of your grant should be able to get a good understanding of your school, and local data should be used persuasively to give them this insight.

9. **Distinguish yourself.** If previously funded projects are listed on the funder's website (and they often are), you can use this information to make sure that you are not basically repeating what someone else has done. While there will be similarities because you are following similar or the same funder guidelines, you should be offering something novel. Furthermore, you need to sell why your team are the right people, and your school is the right place to conduct this novel project. Funders are fully aware that 'critical to the success of any project is putting together a team that is committed and has the expertise, the passion, and the time to commit to the work' (Blanco et al., 2016, p. 119), so don't be reluctant to sing your own praises in a realistic manner that includes clear evidence for your assertions.

10. **Partner with the right academic mentor.** One way to boost the credibility of your team is to partner with an academic mentor, whose work you will be able to lean on in your efforts to establish that you have the expertise element covered. There are also other advantages if you choose an experienced and knowledgeable mentor, some of which I list here.

    - They can advise on appropriate methods, project management planning and realistic budgeting.
    - You can get free access to some of their data collection tools (e.g. Qualtrics) and data analysis tools (e.g. NVivo).
    - You can boost your data literacy, and learn how to analyse data.
    - You can (and indeed in most cases must, if working with an academic mentor) put the project through institutional ethics approvals, which will allow you to share findings in peer-reviewed literature and ensure that your project is compliant with contemporary ethical expectations.

    Ideally, you need to build in some funds to support the academic mentor's contribution for them to be permitted by their institutional employer to take the time to contribute to your project. If this is not possible due to the small size of the funds on offer, you still may be able to negotiate some involvement from an academic mentor if you co-author research works from the project.

11. **Be realistic.** Gorsevski (2016) notes that 'the most convincing grant proposals answer the question that lurks in the grant reviewer's mind: How risky would it be to fund this project? How bold yet feasible are the ideas and actions being proposed?' (p. 31). Funders are only going to invest in your project if you demonstrate that you have the resources to pull it off successfully and deliver on your promises. To be convincing, you need easy-to-interpret, logical and carefully considered project planning.

    You might be tempted to use this funding opportunity to add budget items to boost your school that are not completely essential to the project. This is not a good idea. You should 'ensure budgets request only essential items and reflect an honest portrayal of the funding that the team needs to successfully carry out the work' (Wisdom et al., 2015, p. 1723), and if you've found ways to save the funder money by using existing resources, you can flag this if relevant within the application as the school's in-kind contribution.

12. **Be clear and audience aligned.** Make sure you get someone outside your team to review what you have written; often planning that makes sense to you will not translate beyond the team, and you may not necessarily have the opportunity to provide clarification if the funders are confused. The person who reviews your grant may have never taught in a school, and they will be busy, so 'write clearly and avoid jargon' (Blanco & Lee, 2012, p. 451). Make sure you signpost your key messages, use topic sentences and graphic elements to highlight key points and make them accessible at a glance. If your reviewers have to guess what you mean, you are very unlikely to progress.

    Remember that the *funder* is your target audience for this application, so you need to get to know them so that you can tailor the content, language and tone of your application accordingly. This may sound obvious, but when you are used to communicating primarily with students, parents and school leadership teams, you might find yourself falling back on writing for these audiences rather than the funder.

13. **Think about the benefits beyond your school.** You will usually need to demonstrate that even if your project is directly and solely focused on your school, it can yield tangible benefits *beyond your school*. So while you have to show how your research project will benefit your school, you need to be very clear on additional benefits for like schools.

    For example, the *AISNSW School Based Research Project Application Form* states that applications are assessed based on the following weighted criteria:

    - Rationale (30%)
    - Research design (25%)
    - Wider contribution (25%)
    - Organisational capacity (10%)
    - Professional response (10%)

    (AISNSW, 2022, p. 2)

    Being able to show 'wider contribution' determines a quarter of the assessment, so it's extremely important in this instance.

14. **Go all out in promoting the findings and funder.** If you want your school to be memorable, plan to strongly promote the connection between the project and the funder in your application, then show gratitude and make sure the funder is mentioned in every output once you've won the grant. Make sure the funder remains across your outputs even outside reporting periods so that they have a chance to share your exciting findings while they are still fresh and current. Include broadening your

consideration of audiences who can benefit from this research. In recent times there has been substantial growth in the available research on knowledge mobilisation (e.g. Merga, 2021a), and you can draw on the more practical of these papers to inform your own approach. Don't be afraid to come up with creative and novel ways to promote the findings and funder; often opportunities will arise from your previous efforts in this area (Merga, 2021a).

15. **Learn from failure.** If your grant application does not get over the line, if possible, try to get some feedback on your application. This can help you to strengthen the application for submission elsewhere.

    Many good applications will not be funded. The reality is that 'the vast majority of proposals will not receive funding; rejection rates for grant proposals of between 80–90% are common' (Blanco et al., 2016, p. 120). Falling short really hurts, but it's not necessarily the end of the project. In the past, I have had applications fail with one funder only to have a revised application accepted by another funder. The key is to make sure you make changes to your application to align with the needs of a new prospective funder, and connect with them as per the steps previously outlined.

4
Implementation Planning and Change Management

Schools are dynamic environments. Change is a given in contemporary schools, and may include 'continuous structural school-wide changes, in terms of curriculum, assessment and leadership' which leaves school leaders and staff 'accustomed to both improbability and uncertainty, in terms of what constitutes as best practice when orchestrating change and leading whole school improvement' (Gear & Sood, 2021, p. 2).

Good schools consistently strive to embrace change where needed, in order to enhance their capacity to meet students' educative, social and emotional needs. As such, regular revision of practice to align with evidence, emerging requirements and issues will always be a part of schools' operational processes. Not all attempted changes within schools are successfully implemented, so this cannot be taken for granted. Given its ubiquity, and in some cases, questionable previous implementation, proposed change in schools is often reasonably met with weariness and apathy (Grant, 2009). Moving towards, or strengthening an existing reading culture is a change that will require careful management to garner optimal stakeholder support, and this chapter will provide guidance to this end.

Change management

Simplistically, *change management* in schools can be viewed as the transformation of a school-based culture, curriculum, system, process and/or environment 'from one status to another in a planned or unplanned manner' (Hoşgörür, 2016, p. 2030). As such, change within schools is not always carefully planned and delivered; it can occur spontaneously, or due to unforeseen events such as the onset of a global pandemic. Ideally, we want major changes that reshape school practices and cultures to be informed by careful implementation planning and close consideration of how to best facilitate change management. As such, across contexts, planned change management involves enacting 'deliberate activities that move an organization from its present state to a desired future state' (Stouten et al., 2018, p. 752).

Having a research supported but also practical understanding of how best to plan for building a reading culture, and facilitate change management successfully within your school, is a transferable skillset that you can draw upon beyond this project. Much has been written on the topic of change management, though this literature is typically focused on change management within corporations and professional workplaces more generally, rather than specifically on schools. Nonetheless, the growing body of literature focused on change management in schools can be expected to burgeon in the near future, given how often schools are expected to accommodate very substantial change; for example, where a new curriculum is introduced, or a new technology is widely adopted. Ideally, some of this future research should focus specifically on change management in relation to the implementation of a whole school reading culture.

Even beyond school-specific literature, as I have demonstrated earlier, there are fundamental and transferable principles that emerge in this literature that lend themselves to application in schools (Merga, 2023b). Regardless of your leadership background and experience, this chapter should be of use in outlining a path to change that can direct or fine-tune the existing approaches you draw upon when supporting change in your school.

Leading change in schools

Competent leadership of change is associated with successful transition. Leaders of change in schools need to be able to build trust and foster buy-in and sustained commitment of stakeholders. They need to be excellent communicators, with research suggesting that 'leaders who acted openly, intentionally and invitingly in their communication with colleagues, governors and communities were most successful in addressing possible sources of turbulence' during change management implementation (Abbott & McGuinness, 2022, p. 588). This is part of a process of 'shared sensemaking' (Sullanmaa et al., 2021, p. 2). The tendency for a leader of change initiatives to exclude the participation of others, and follow an autocratic course, perhaps only paying lip-service to a consultative approach, is associated with poor outcomes (Robertson & Briggs, 1998), highlighting the importance of adopting a *discernibly* genuine approach towards communicating with diverse stakeholders.

While the whole school reading culture may be led by the school leadership team, it is probably more likely to be led by middle leadership within the school. Middle leadership refers to a leadership position for practitioners who have school wide responsibilities in addition to their classroom duties. Such responsibilities can consist of pastoral leadership; curriculum leadership; leadership of additional student support; leadership of a team or phase and leadership of a specific school improvement priority. Educational middle leadership is founded on the notion of bringing together the duty of contributing to a strategic leadership remit whilst remaining firmly within the role of a classroom practitioner. It is argued that this 'space' for middle leadership is due to the increasingly hierarchical organisational structures of schools; consequently, being viewed as the 'middle layer'.

(Gear & Sood, 2021, p. 1)

As such, if you are the intended leader of a whole school reading culture, the degree to which the rest of the school community will accept your leadership could be highly variable, and influenced by the extent to which your previous middle leadership work has established you as a leader within your school (Gear & Sood, 2021). Your leadership skills and credibility may need to be confirmed early so that others can be influenced by you with confidence, as your success will at least to some extent be shaped by your leadership 'autonomy or capacity to act', and you will be subject to 'pressure from the top and bottom' of your school (p. 1). You will need the support of senior leadership 'to orchestrate and nurture the space for distributed leadership to occur, suggesting that it would be difficult to achieve, or even impossible, without the support of these leaders' (Gear & Sood, 2021, p. 9).

In order to effectively support the establishment of a whole school reading culture, leaders of the initiative need to establish an underpinning collaborative culture across the school, and this needs to be visibly supported and promoted by the school leadership team. Not all schools will be equally open to embracing a collaborative approach to change. In recent research, close collaboration is positioned as essential for success in implementing change within schools, and to some extent this involves school leadership commitment to robust and practical planning for change as explored further subsequently (Mestry & Govindasamy, 2021).

Change leader traits and the opportunity for growth

Much has been written about the characteristics of effective leaders of change management, including work focused on schools. For example, Guerrero et al. (2018) identified behaviours and traits associated with being an effective manager of change:

teachers have indicated that they appreciate leaders who are humble, honest, credible, and respected. They also find it ideal when principals motivate and lead, at the same time encourage their participation through coaching and mentoring, while maintaining a positive outlook. These leadership characteristics are indicative of teachers valuing principals as their guide and model for appropriate behaviours during change. (p. 384)

If you are preparing to lead significant change in schools, self-evaluation against these criteria might help you to close any gaps between your current characteristics and strengths, and these valued behaviours and traits. While there is clearly a degree of subjectivity at play, where actions by a leader may be perceived as 'bossy' by one individual and 'persuasive' by another, it is still useful to begin from a position of introspection.

Indeed, when you seek to lead change within your school, the transformation is often both internal and external. For example, recent research on change management in schools in Northern Ireland included consideration of how being part of a change management process influenced leadership style, noting that in the case of leaders, 'for transformation to work, they had to adjust, build trust, demonstrate clarity of vision, show enthusiasm and motivational leadership, as well as capitalising on staff skills. Leading change, however, was deemed highly positive' (Abbott & McGuinness, 2022, p. 586). While there will be barriers to change that are pre-existing and therefore more easily identified for early mitigation, as the reading culture is introduced, unanticipated challenges will present themselves, providing opportunities for you to demonstrate your agility as a leader.

While there are many ways that change management can be framed, this chapter synthesises a range of approaches to outline a possible four-step process for implementing change successfully as explored herein (Merga, 2023b; Stouten et al., 2018).

Step 1. Assess the opportunity for change and empower others to commit

This vital step involves widespread data capture, as well as active and agile knowledge exchange negotiation, to the end of building concrete support and ensuring that pragmatic and informed decisions guide the change. This step can be likened to 'unfreezing', as a 'preparatory stage when it is realised that the existing situation cannot be continued and a change is needed' (Benji-Rabinovitz & Berkovich, 2022, p. 100).

The key purpose of this step is for you to identify and measure what your school is already doing, and whether or not it is working, which will involve collecting and analysing diverse data sources from a wide range of stakeholders. You will need to systematically audit what is both explicitly and tacitly enacted at school and classroom levels. As explored further later in this book, this stage also has very important implications for subsequent evaluation (the topic of the following chapter).

At this step, you need to raise the need for change, highlighting benefits for students and staff that are responsive to targeted stakeholder needs. For example, if you have a leadership team that is primarily concerned with seeing gains in students' literacy scores, you will need to share research linking components of a whole school reading culture with improved literacy performance as outlined earlier in this book in order to secure their buy-in, while not losing sight of the bigger picture of benefits for learning and literacy attainment beyond these narrowed limits.

Barrier mitigation

This is also your opportunity to identify and address pre-existing and foreseeable barriers to implementation, and to build motivation and invite broad support and participation.

Depending on the context, these might include common challenges such as disagreements between factions within the school on implementation or other issues, or apathy from the staff, where 'while not actively resisting change, they had no desire to be involved in the process, did not wish to put any energy into improving themselves or the school, and just wanted to be left alone' (Robertson & Briggs, 1998, p. 51). As noted by Grant (2009),

> practical people that we are, no teacher is going to jump blind into a still lake just because someone suggests it's a refreshing experience. They will want to know why this has to be done, what the benefits might be, how will the change actually happen and who will be its true agents. (p. 21)

Addressing these issues is a core part of empowering others to commit, and respectful dialogue and co-construction of these points are crucial to moving forward together. Both assertive and patient dispositions will need to be modelled by the leaders of the initiative, particularly where the biggest challenges come from staff engagement. Overcoming teacher resistance to change can be one of the greatest challenges, as this often involves 'engraining a change in staff mindset', especially in relation to 'the older staff and overcoming reluctance to explore new teaching and learning programmes' (Mestry & Govindasamy, 2021, p. 555). By inviting and valuing their involvement, and making clear the benefits of the whole school reading culture for both the students and the staff, some of the apathetic and even resistant staff can be won over. You will need to effectively communicate the advantages of the change, and strategically allay fears to show that consideration has been given to reducing any negative impacts on staff. When any substantial changes are being implemented within a school, close attention to the impact on the workload and wellbeing of the staff within the school is important (Alkahtani, 2017).

Educator ownership, contribution and voice

To get everyone on board, you must create opportunities for teachers to make a substantial contribution to the whole school reading culture and its implementation. As noted in the previous chapter, collective ownership and distributed responsibilities are crucial to success, and 'this point is particularly pertinent for those leaders who struggle to delegate, and who prefer to pursue their own vision with the support of others' (Merga, 2023b, p. 197).

You will be seeking to encourage your team as well as all relevant stakeholders to take psychological ownership of the initiative. This refers to promoting a state in which stakeholders see alignment with its goals and their own (Benji-Rabinovitz & Berkovich, 2022). This must be established very early in the change management process, with stakeholders potentially opting in or out of the initiative before the process begins in earnest:

> According to participants' accounts, this type of ownership is established before the change is introduced in the school, with the change agent going through several steps to develop the programme of change. These steps usually include actions that the change agent is involved in, which manifest in gradual development, with the investment of time, thought, and/or funds on the part of the agents. (p. 107)

At this stage, there will be many contributing voices. Schools that succeed in change and reform may be those whose decisions are informed by the widespread involvement of staff, parents, and other stakeholders (Robertson & Briggs, 1998). Where stakeholder contributions inform the decision-making process when planning for a whole school reading culture, highlighting these diverse contributions can be an important step.

At some point in your career, if you are an experienced educator, you have probably been part of a change initiative where your consultation has not been valued; rather, it functioned as an insincere box-ticking performance for the leaders of the initiative. You probably remember how this made you feel, and how it impacted on your willingness to support the initiative.

Unsurprisingly, stakeholders may disengage when they feel that 'their involvement was not very authentic in that their input was not really used in the decisions being made' (Robertson & Briggs, 1998, p. 51); those who contribute to the underlying vision and formulation of goals need to see their inputs valued and used in these early processes and resultant documentation.

Students are stakeholders too

In this vein, when formulating goals and co-creating an underlying vision, the perspectives and voices of the students should not be excluded (Abbott & McGuinness, 2022), and students may have insights into barriers and enablers of reading that are not obvious to the planning team. For example, there may be affordances in a student's home environment that they use to support their reading that are absent in the school context. Simply asking students what the school can do to support them to read more is an important step to take at this initial stage, particularly given that research indicates that children at both primary and secondary level can have great insight into what would make them read more in a general sense (Merga, 2016c; 2017f).

Step 2. Create and support a reading culture team

While to some extent, the reading culture team will need to include every implicated party within and beyond the school, you will also ideally need to have a designated reading culture team that works closely together in order to facilitate the transformation.

What are you looking for?

The composition of this team can be integral to its success. Often school teams and committees evolve through a combination of self-nomination and taps on the shoulder by the leading parties. However, if you are in the fortunate position of being able to influence the composition of your team, you will be seeking to attract team members with most or all of the following qualities.

- Willingness to work collaboratively as part of a cohesive team and sincere support for the whole school reading initiative across the life of the project.
- Ability to work with some independence and agency in implementing and driving allocated responsibilities as applicable.
- Capacity to work with school leadership and engage their support and participation.

- Ability to liaise effectively with diverse implicated stakeholders throughout the school, and listen to and be responsive to their views and concerns.
- Ability to build relationships with existing and new external stakeholders to strengthen the capacity of these supports to contribute to a whole school reading culture.
- Originating from diverse roles, learning areas, year groupings within the school, as well as representing diverse genders and cultural backgrounds where possible.
- Demonstrated commitment to respectful communication with stakeholders at diverse levels within the school.
- Aptitude for goal setting and pragmatic planning.
- Ability to be adaptive and flexible, and responsive to evolving opportunities and issues.
- Understanding of their students' interests and issues, with established rapport with students.
- Demonstrated capacity for advocacy, and comfort with articulating ideas and possibilities that may challenge the status quo.
- Reliability in investing time and sustaining inclination to play an active and ongoing role in the team.
- Willingness to diplomatically offer critical feedback, and to receive feedback and make adjustments accordingly.

(Adapted from Merga, 2023b)

Having a team in place with supportive and conducive characteristics can take you a long way towards meeting your ultimate goal of change management success.

While I have worked with schools that have had a pre-existing or early assembled team in place, I have also worked with schools that come to the planning table still needing to recruit a team given a lack of support within the school. If this is you, don't be discouraged; getting the previous step of assessing the opportunity for change and empowering others to commit should help you to generate the interest of a team. Even if the team is small, size can be offset through cohesion, ambition, energy and commitment.

What will they do?

From this point, the team need clarity around their collective role as a team, but also their individual contributions and expectations of their time and commitment, which may vary considerably. For teachers and support staff across the school to offer initial and sustained support for the initiative, as aforementioned, a distributed leadership model is important (Abbott &

McGuinness, 2022), and at the very least this should involve allocating further distributed leadership roles and related agreed accountabilities to the team members (Merga, 2023b). Once these have been agreed upon, and team members have been appointed, these positions need to be promoted beyond the team so that the broader school community know whom to liaise with in relation to different facets of the whole school reading culture implementation.

While there is a paucity of extant research that looks at what these roles can be, Table 3 offers some suggestions that you might wish to consider.

Table 3 *Some possible distributed leadership roles on a whole school reading culture team*

Role title	Brief description	P/S/W*
Team Leader	Leads the whole school reading culture team.	W
Evaluation Leader	Responsible for evaluation of success of the initiatives embedded in whole school reading culture planning (see Chapter 5).	W
Learning Area Liaison	Responsible for connecting the reading culture initiatives to learning areas (content or subject areas) including but extending beyond English/Language Arts in secondary schools.	S
Early Childhood Liaison	Responsible for tailoring reading culture initiatives to the youngest age groups in primary schools.	P
Parent Liaison	Responsible for liaising with parents, collecting their feedback, communicating expectations and achievements, and providing training opportunities.	W
School Leadership Liaison**	Ideally is a member of the school leadership team, liaising directly with the principal on all key matters relating to the whole school reading culture.	W
Community Liaison	Responsible for liaising with community stakeholders, collecting their feedback, communicating achievements, and strengthening external relationships.	W
Library Liaison	Represents the role of the school library in building and supporting a whole school reading culture.	W
Struggling Literacy Learner (SLL) Advocate (see also below)	Advocates for SLLs, ensuring their diverse needs are accommodated, communicating with support staff.	W

*P: primary school; S: secondary school; W: whole schooling system (includes P & S)
** The School Leadership Liaison will not be needed if the principal is part of the whole school reading team, and they attend any meetings on a regular basis. If the principal is part of the team and attendance becomes patchy, a School Leadership Liaison can be established at this point to ensure that they remain across all developments.

While the exact titles and roles and responsibilities for any positions you seek to appoint within the team can be entirely responsive to your school's unique needs, Table 3 serves as a starting point for considering what these could be, and encompass.

A focus on the Struggling Literacy Learner Advocate

In Table 3, I include a Struggling Literacy Learner (SLL) Advocate, who I have positioned as a staff member who acts as an advocate for students who are experiencing difficulties with literacy learning for typically diverse reasons, being 'typically low achievers with poor engagement in literacy learning' (Merga, 2020a, p. 371). This group will include students who are still struggling to acquire independent reading skills beyond the age at which these are typically established. Given that these students are the most at risk when it comes to reading and literacy learning more generally, extra focus must be given to the potential of this role.

Some further explanation is needed, given the extant controversies in this space:

> I know there has been dissent about using the term 'struggle' in recent times, and I recognise that it can contribute to a homogenising deficit discourse that can obscure the strengths and differences within this group, but I am strategic in my choice of this term. First, like Lupo et al. (2019), I believe that 'struggle is not a bad word, as there are benefits of overcoming the struggle of reading difficult texts with the right type of support' (p. 558). Second, and perhaps most importantly, I am also concerned about more positively naming or framing these students in the literature, because on a pragmatic level it is already very hard to access sufficient support to meet the needs of these students (as we explore in detail in Merga, Mat Roni, et al., 2021a). Any change of nomenclature that downplays the difficulties these students experience could have the effect of further decreasing the likelihood that educators and schools will get adequate resourcing to support their needs, which as I explore herein, are complex and varied.
>
> (Merga, 2022b, p. 57)

As such, I make a considered decision to use the term *struggle* in the title, though other terms may be preferred in your learning context.

As I have noted previously, 'the cognitive and attentional challenges facing struggling readers are significant, and as young people move through the years of schooling and are exposed to texts of increasing complexity, struggling readers can fall further behind' (Merga, 2019c, p. 147), so when building a reading culture, close attention must be given to the needs of these students. An SLL Advocate can ensure that their needs are considered across the range of initiatives proposed and implemented as part of the establishment of a whole school reading culture, with considerations on how to make adjustments that are as unobtrusive as feasible to optimise the learning and participation of this group of students.

For example, in conjunction with school library staff, an SLL Advocate may take responsibility for ensuring that schools provide age- and skill-appropriate materials for struggling readers with diverse interests and literacy barriers (Merga, 2019c). As noted by Moore et al. (1999), 'all adolescents, and especially those who struggle with reading, deserve opportunities to select age-appropriate materials they can manage and topics and genres they prefer' (p. 102). These can be made available within the main collection in libraries. For struggling students to be able to access texts and enjoy reading them beyond the early years of schooling, you will need to be responsive to their literacy skill levels as well as their personal preferences in order to foster enjoyment and related accessibility.

Step 3. Formulate and communicate a powerful vision of the change

Once you have clarified and detailed the baseline picture, and assembled a dynamic team, it is time to formulate and communicate a powerful vision of the change that communicates what your school wants to be doing, and what it wants to be. This requires the team to work closely in 'developing a clear and motivating vision for the reason for change which imagines specific end goals' (Merga, 2023b, p. 196).

Formulating the vision

After identifying your school's priorities and needs, draw on the earlier chapters of this book, and liaise with stakeholders as explored further herein to plan this trajectory to a whole school reading culture, to begin closing the gap between the documented actual, and the aspirational but attainable. It will involve a process that:

- 'demands a tolerance for messiness, ambiguity, and setbacks, an acceptance of the half-step back that usually accompanies every step forward'
- 'evolves through negotiation between the sometimes contrasting needs and roles of stakeholders within the school community'
- results in a vision 'clear in intention, appealing to stakeholders, and ambitious yet attainable', 'focused enough to guide decision making yet flexible enough to accommodate individual initiative and changing circumstances' (Kotter, 1998, p. 30)

- involves 'motivating and inspiring – keeping people moving in the right direction, despite major obstacles to change, by appealing to basic but often un-tapped human needs, values, and emotions'
- imagines the school culture 'in terms of what it should become over the long term' articulating 'a feasible way of achieving this goal' (Kotter, 2001, p. 27).

To this end, change management experts suggest that you allow the process of formulating a vision to be a little bit messy. Rather than following a strictly rational planning process of planning and allocating resources accordingly, 'leading an organization to constructive change begins by setting a direction – developing a vision of the future (often the distant future) along with strategies for producing the changes needed to achieve that vision' (Kotter, 2001, p. 26). At the end of this stage, you will have a shared vision for what you want to ultimately achieve.

Agreeing on strategies

Once this vision is formulated, strategies for achieving the vision will need to be negotiated and agreed upon. This is where you decide how you will arrive at these goals through negotiation, drawing on your previously acquired knowledge of what the school is already doing, and whether or not it is working, and your agreed, shared vision. These strategies need to be those that stakeholders generally believe are realistically attainable within your unique school context, and they can be explored in relation to the research-supported strategies articulated in early sections of this book.

The importance of selling the value of these strategies remains at this stage; justification of allocating learning time and resources to the introduction of new strategies will form part of the negotiation process. In secondary school contexts, when selling the benefits of a whole school reading culture to educators across the learning areas, you may wish to draw on my earlier work that outlines the benefits of reading skills for achievement in learning areas as diverse as science and mathematics (e.g. Merga, 2023b).

Communication of the change

The final important step at this stage is the communication of the change. As noted by Kotter (1998), this will involve using 'every vehicle possible to communicate the new vision and strategies' and ensuring that all stakeholders involved in implementation have the necessary knowledge and skills to play their role (p. 32). Reading culture team members will need to model *keen adopter* attitudes and practices, and demonstrate a willingness to embrace professional development and related upskilling. The team will need to capture the professional development needs of stakeholders across the school in ways that are supportive and do not make educators feel like they are being targeted, or seen as deficient. Embracing a whole school reading culture as an exciting and beneficial learning experience for all, even those who may have some previous experience in this area, can be one way of positively framing the step.

While this stage of communicating the vision is the outcome of consulting and negotiation, resulting in an agreed way forward, it is also important to stress that the vision will evolve through iterative review and evaluation processes, and the window of stakeholder contribution to influencing the vision has not closed for good. Good leaders of change maintain open channels to receive ongoing feedback, and it is important that while communicating the vision, it is also stressed that this ongoing feedback will be warmly received and closely considered.

Furthermore, you may wish to develop 'a communications strategy to ensure that your co-constructed vision reaches all intended stakeholder audiences'; 'if you do not adjust the accessibility of your content, you will only reach the highly educated parents, and not those marginalised parents with lower English literacy, limiting the value and broad applicability of the feedback provided' (Merga, 2023b, p. 197), as briefly touched upon in the previous chapter. Readability is concerned with how accessible a text is to an intended audience, and as a university-educated educator, you may find yourself inadvertently pitching your content to those with a similar level of literacy when in reality, the literacy levels in some aspects of your school community, such as linguistically diverse parents, may be far lower.

Accessible communications

You may wish to consider the following to ensure that this communication is as accessible as possible, some of which have been briefly touched upon in earlier sections:

- The most important step is to identify your audience(s), given that 'without an understanding of who your audience is or how they read, it is difficult to make appropriate adjustments', with features such as 'vocabulary or sentence length' purposefully adjusted to enhance readability (Gaylie, 2023, p. 11).
- Avoid exclusionary jargon and use of terminology the audience will be unfamiliar with.

- Introduce new concepts and explain them using Plain language and clear examples.
- Consider running communications through a free online readability tool such as SHeLL (Sydney Health Literacy Lab) Health Literacy Editor (Ayre et al., 2023; see Chapter 5 for more information) for communicating with lower literacy audiences.
- Use multimodal ways to share your vision to make it more accessible. For instance, 'you might communicate your vision via video with multilingual subtitle options for linguistically diverse communities, and provide opportunities for face to face exchanges of ideas'.
- Consider pre-piloting communications with target communities such as parents from culturally diverse backgrounds to ensure that your vision is accessible to diverse audiences.

(Partly adapted from Merga, 2023b, p. 197)

Step 4. Plan for implementation

It is then time to generate a clear and workable plan. Once the vision has been devised and communicated, plan for implementation as 'once you know what you want to achieve, the next step is to make clear how you will actually achieve it' (Merga, 2023b, p. 84).

The plan for whole school reading culture implementation can take whatever form works best for you, but here are some suggestions that you can draw upon to inform your approach. This plan might be a standalone document, or it might be incorporated in a whole school literacy policy, or feature as a prominent appendix within such a policy (Merga, 2023b).

The importance of short-term goals

Goal setting is a key component of this planning.

Sustaining commitment to implementation of the whole school reading culture despite the challenging environment in contemporary schools can be difficult, and cannot be taken for granted, even if initial enthusiasm is high. In engaging the diverse stakeholders implicated in the whole school reading culture 'to stay the course' on its implementation, 'they need to see some indicators that the ship is headed in the right direction, even if it is not realistic to see land yet' (Merga, 2023b, p. 202). Opportunities for regular successes can play a key role, offsetting some of the negative impacts of tackling ongoing challenges to the success of the programme.

To this end, the team should agree on short-term, midpoint and long-term goals that relate to the strategies agreed upon in the vision-making process.

All of these goals must be realistically attainable and clearly associated with measurable benefits for the school (Stouten et al., 2018). When adequately communicated within and beyond the school community, 'short-term goals can create a sense of accomplishment and progress towards longer term change objectives' (Stouten et al., 2018, p. 766).

When I talk about measurable benefits, I am not purely referring to quantitative evaluation, as I explore later in this book. Goals will not always be associated with improved performance on literacy tests; they may just as likely be associated with measures related to performance, such as gains in students' attitudinal perception of reading, an increase in borrowing data, or externally evaluated increases in students' perceived capacity to apply sustained attention to reading.

While a subsequent chapter focuses on reporting (Chapter 6) in greater detail, identifying short-term wins also involves communicating these successes within and beyond the school. Longitudinal research on change management within schools has found that 'as the reform process proceeded, intentional knowledge sharing promoted views of effective change management over time' (Sullanmaa et al., 2021, p. 17), so these opportunities to communicate successes are also integral to building a perception of successful change management. In addition to short-term goals, you will also need to plan for achievement of midpoint and long-term goals that will take longer to come to fruition, but may also be associated with greater benefits for students.

Viable goal setting

So how should these goals be formulated?
    As I have noted previously,

> the key aim in goal setting at all three time frames is viability. It is essential that you be realistic in your goal setting, and this will involve careful consideration of when it is practical to expect to see change in relation to the strategies you are introducing.
>
> (Merga, 2023b, p. 202)

Herein, I will show on a very practical level how all of these conceptual and theoretical underpinnings from change management literature can be drawn upon to devise and enact very pragmatic planning for a whole school reading culture. However, here it is important to establish that in addition to being across the research on best practice of strategy implementation (outlined earlier in this book), you will also need to consider:

- what timeline is feasible for strategy success,
- what strategy success will look like, and
- how it should be evaluated (explored in Chapter 5).

Each of the strategies highlighted in this book may come to fruition after varying time intervals, and some of them are not appropriate for short-term goal setting, depending on what the goal is. In academic-led educational research, failure of interventions to achieve their expected outcomes is commonly attributed to insufficient length of exposure and/or intensity (Rosenzweig & Wigfield, 2022), and similar issues can reasonably be construed to operate in school-led change initiatives.

For example, if you decide to introduce daily silent reading for pleasure into your school's timetable, and protect its implementation, the first change you might see in the short term could be increased borrowing, which will show that as a school you are heading in the right direction and improving circulation of reading materials. However, it is too soon in the short term to expect to see vast changes in students' performance on reading comprehension: this should be a long-term goal, as it typically takes sustained exposure to increased opportunities for reading to see increases in students' reading comprehension. If you measure your success against this outcome too soon, you might incorrectly conclude that your intervention has been unsuccessful.

For short-, mid- and long-term planning, you need to know what desirable changes you are seeking to capture, how you will detect evidence towards these goals, and if they are suitable as short-term, midpoint and/or long-term goals. While this will be explored in greater depth and detail in the chapter on evaluation, Table 4 opposite shows how this can look; this is by no means definitive, and I only include one way of measuring attainment of the goal where multiple ways often exist. You will note that a thorough collection of baseline data for the purposes of comparison is indicated, and again, this will be explored in greater detail in the subsequent chapter.

Beware of false conflation when planning for projected fruition of goals and evidence of attainment. For example, increases in book borrowing are often incorrectly positioned as increases in student reading volume. Just because books are taken out of the library does not mean that the books were actually read. Book completion surveying is going to be a far more reliable way of measuring attainment of improved student reading volume (see Table 4), even though there will still be the remaining complicating issues around the great variation in book lengths.

Table 4 *Differences in projected fruition of goals and evidence of success*

Goal	One way* of measuring success (and S/M/L**)
Improved student attitudes towards reading	Comparing baseline surveys of students' attitudes to midpoint and long-term measures (M/L)
Improved student reading volume	Comparing baseline data on book completion surveying to midpoint and long-term measures (M/L)
Improved student literacy performance	Comparing baseline scores on reading comprehension evaluations to long-term results (L)
Improved use of the library resource	Comparing baseline data on book borrowing numbers to short-term, midpoint and long-term numbers (S/M/L)
Improved reading stamina	Teacher timing and monitoring of whole class focus periods over time (M/L) compared with baseline
Improved frequency of reading in the home	Student self-report on time spent reading at home (time diary) (S/M/L) compared with baseline
Increasing opportunities for silent reading for pleasure within the school	Teacher self-report on class time spent on silent reading for pleasure (time diary) (S/M/L) compared with baseline

*multiple options for measurement often exist
**short-term, midpoint or long-term

Being realistic in strategy implementation

In a sense, creating a whole school reading culture is a kind of experiment that you will be able to adjust with greater freedom than if it were an experiment being conducted under the more rigorous demands of academic research. It's experimental in that no matter how strong the informing research is, and how faithful you are to using current best practice in implementation, where strategies have never been enacted in a particular context, with a particular set of students, you don't really know what impediments may arise and what unexpected benefits may be gained.

When it comes to planning, it may be hard to determine how long it should take for the strategies outlined in Chapter 2 to yield impacts. This is because there is a paucity of meta-analyses performed in this space, and the inconsistencies and contexts in method where interventions have been attempted can lead to widely varying results. While the success of your reading culture is going to be evaluated to some extent like any experiment, because it isn't happening to reagents in a test tube, there are going to be a lot of factors that impact on its success. You are likely to have multiple strategies to pursue the same goal. However, where you are investing significant time and resourcing, you may wish for more concrete ways of projecting when an effect should be seen as a result of a strategy being employed.

This can be estimated by looking at the previous research. Research suggests that in relation to interventions that foster reading motivation in general, 'effects were larger if the total duration of the intervention was longer' (van der Sande, van Steensel et al., 2023, p. 18). You can draw on research to determine how long a strategy *may* take to reach fruition, if method of implementation is adhered to, and contextual and student factors are similar.

What does this look like on a practical level?

For example, let's imagine that your school has selected a range of strategies from Chapter 2 in this book, and you associate these strategies with your goals and make conservative estimates of their achievement. Use of class time for *reading aloud* is one of your strategies to attain the goal of *improved reading comprehension*. You may then decide what kind of method you might want to use for reading aloud based on the summation in this book.

Alternatively, you may look at this summation but also do further reading, looking at the available research for a model that fits your school. This may be particularly desirable where you are implementing something quite novel, and/or there is actual or anticipated resistance to the strategy, so you want to show how closely you are adhering to an approach that has been documented as successful elsewhere.

You decide to use Westbrook et al. (2019) as a model of an approach to reading aloud. This involved schools reading 'two whole challenging novels at a faster pace than usual in 12 weeks with their average and poorer readers ages 12–13' (p. 60). You read their method closely and consider the implications of doing something similar in your context. You decide that it is feasible to take a similar approach, but apply it across the school, using texts that are challenging for each year group, not just students in ages 12–13.

You don't need to be completely faithful to the previous research, given that the point of you using it is pragmatic, to meet the needs of your school. Your approach can be adjusted for future applications as required based on your experiences, student performance and feedback received. You noted that 12 weeks was needed for this intervention to take effect, so you choose to be conservative and look for changes at the 14-week mark, and this does not include holiday breaks where students will not be exposed to the strategy. You may see effects faster or slower than the original research, particularly given that your school will be employing a *combination* of approaches as part of a reading culture, which may also accelerate goal attainment, as seen in the example from a US middle school cited earlier in the book (Daniels & Steres, 2011).

Writing implementation plans

When it comes to the specifics of writing implementation plans, schools may use a wide range of templates and structures. There is no one way to do this. However, if you take a tabular approach, it is important to make clear what each column relates to so that everyone using the plan is on the same page. For example, you might want to plan under the headings suggested in Table 5.

Table 5 *Possible headings for implementation planning*

Goals	Strategies/ activities for attainment	Launch date (if applicable)	Responsible parties and roles	Resources needed	Measures of success*

(Adapted from Merga, 2023b, p. 212)

In Table 5, *Goals* refer to the goals that you have agreed upon around reading, engagement and literacy. These can relate to changes in literacy performance, but they should also include related attitudes towards reading, successful adoption of new pedagogical approaches and literacy-supportive habits.

For example, if a goal is increasing opportunities for silent reading for pleasure within the school (see Table 3), *strategies/activities for attainment* will detail those in place to support this goal, relating to Chapter 2 of this book, but described in more concrete and applicable terms.

For instance, simply listing an intent for providing *opportunities for regular silent reading for pleasure* is not sufficient. You need to imagine what this is going to entail and be more specific and pragmatic. In brief, you might frame this as daily whole school reading after lunch for 30 minutes, mobile book carts to support book choice on Tuesdays and Thursdays, and timetabling for weekly library visits for every class (Merga, 2023b). In this regard, you have considered four key questions.

1 Who? The whole school
2 When? Daily
3 For how often? 30 minutes
4 How will it be enacted? Reading materials from the library, accessed via mobile book carts and library visits.

Launch date will enable you to keep track of when each of these interventions is enacted; they may begin at the same point, or be rolling initiatives depending on what is feasible in your context. The launch date will also be very important when you come to evaluating the success of the strategies/activities for attainment, as it is surprisingly easy to lose track of when an initiative commenced, particularly in a multifaceted approach to developing a whole school reading culture.

Allocating *responsible parties and roles* allows for the needed distributed leadership I've stressed throughout this book, and increased accountability across the school.

Noting *resources needed* gives you a chance to plan ahead for the specific resources you will need to ensure the success of the strategies/activities for attainment. For instance, in the case of the previous example, you might need to purchase mobile book carts if you do not already have them, or have insufficient numbers.

Measures of success can be seen in Table 4, and a note should be made of whether these are expected to come to fruition at short-term, midpoint and/or long-term, as explored previously, and as will also be explored further in the chapter on evaluation.

Finally, when it comes to fitting implementation planning into an overarching plan for building a whole school reading culture, there are not many exemplars that can be drawn upon. However, here is a possible structure that can be considered (partly adapted from Merga, 2023b).

Title: (Name of your school)'s Whole School Reading Culture Plan
Date of publication/approval: Day/Month/Year
Review cycle/date: (cycle length e.g. every two years), Month/Year (next review due)

Background
- Provide a description of what a whole school reading culture means to your school.
- Why does your school need a whole school reading culture? What are the factors/issues driving this change?
- What is the baseline picture? Include details about historical and current reading engagement initiatives.
- What are the broad relevant reading engagement and literacy goals of the school?

Responsible parties
- Who are the people on the whole school reading culture team? Include the names and titles of the team responsible for planning, and their roles as applicable in:

  — planning,
  — support of implementation, and
  — subsequent evaluation/review.

- Who is the leader of this team, and how will they support their colleagues' efforts to promote reading engagement across the school?
- Provide a clear description of the role of the classroom teacher in fostering a whole school reading culture as well as other key school-

based stakeholders, such as school library professionals, literacy support staff, educational assistants and others as applicable.

Explicit goals and implementation planning
- What are the goals to be attained through plan implementation? What will successfully reaching these targets look like (i.e. how will you evaluate success)? Do not limit this section to improvements in student performance, also consider fostering changes in attitudes towards reading and frequency of reading, and successful adoption of new approaches for building reading engagement.
- Include tabular planning as per Table 5 and related text.

Accommodations for students with specific needs
- Where SLLs may need adaptions in order to participate in the whole school reading culture, this should be closely considered here, with feasible adjustments proposed to optimise participation.

Ongoing professional development for educators
- What are the specific reading engagement-related professional development needs of your staff in relation to building a whole school reading culture? How will you plan to meet them? How will you identify student needs and related teacher knowledge gaps?

Resources and the library
- What resources will you need in order to realise the strategies, environments and activities within this plan? Consider including a list of key resources as an appendix if desirable.
- What is the role of the school library and staff in building and sustaining a whole school reading culture? Are current library staffing and resourcing levels sufficient to enable the library to function as a key reading-supportive facility within the school?
- Are there grants/other funding sources that the school will attempt to win in order to expand resourcing capacity? For schools facing resourcing challenges, or where the credibility of winning a grant is desired, planning for grant applications to expand literacy resourcing capacity can be included as a goal.

Defined roles for parents and external partners
- How will parents and external partners be expected to support the realisation of this plan? How will the school sustain meaningful communication with these stakeholders?

- What kinds of data need to be collected from these partners to ascertain their capacity as external supports and their views towards literacy and reading? You may wish to include outreach and training for external partners in your implementation planning in order to build engagement and capacity.
- If applicable, does your plan include learning opportunities for parents of *both* primary and secondary school aged children to foster early and ongoing reading frequency and engagement within the home?

Evaluation and review planning
- How will you know if this plan was useful? How will you identify areas to address in review and evaluation?
- Who will be responsible for this process? What will plan evaluation and review look like in your school?

Further attention to evaluation is given in the next chapter.

Monitor and strengthen the change process over time

Like most change management efforts in schools, rolling out a whole school reading culture is not a matter of set and forget. Iterative feedback and evaluation measures need to be established to continue to enhance the change process throughout the life of the programme. Indeed, evaluation (covered in the next chapter) forms a key component of monitoring and strengthening the change process over time.

On one hand, strengthening the change process over time is concerned with deeply embedding new strategies and orientations towards reading within a school. It has been likened in change management literature to 'refreezing, or preserving the new state, when the new patterns need to be stabilised and made to become an integral part of the system' (Benji-Rabinovitz & Berkovich, 2022, p. 100). On the other, this can be a problematic image for schools, given that it suggests an inflexible and immutable locking in of an approach to maintaining a whole school reading culture. Schools are in constant states of change, and the whole school reading culture must be responsive to current and evolving needs.

As such, while there will need to be efforts to concretise and sustain aspects of the initiative, there also needs to be an ongoing commitment to flexibility, incorporating new evolutions in best practice, and adjusting to changes in resourcing, student needs and various other triggers typically in flux in schools. This will often involve small adjustments to practices based on feedback from staff, students and/or parents. Strengthening the change process over time involves supporting the new approach, but also adjusting it and including new initiatives as required.

Finally, while I have illustrated that short-term goals are crucial to the success of the project, it is important that while celebrating these achievements, the sense of urgency to sustain effort is not lost. Change management expert Kotter (1998) likens this to 'declaring victory before the war is over' (p. 27):

> When a project is completed or an initial goal met, it is tempting to congratulate all involved and proclaim the advent of a new era. While it is important to celebrate results along the way, kidding yourself or others about the difficulty and duration of organizational transformation can be catastrophic. (p. 27)

Short-term achievements need to be promoted in ways that increase urgency to meet additional goals, rather than communicate the impression that given small successes, no further efforts are needed. While celebrating short-term goals, schools need to keep a close eye on attaining the perhaps more hard-fought long-term goals and sustain their momentum.

5
Evaluation

Whenever you implement a new approach in schools, it is important to build in opportunities to evaluate it. You need to have a planned opportunity to find areas that can be addressed to strengthen the whole school reading culture, as well as identifying successes and strengths. Evaluating initiatives and programmes needs to become a norm in schools, with schools allowing and encouraging this kind of process and permitting the reading culture team to deliberately and critically consider what has been achieved, and where redirection or revision may be appropriate. Freedom needs to be given to (at least internally) consider failures as well as successes so that an iterative process of improvement can take place.

Evaluation plays a key role in improving school performance (Pont et al., 2008) and, as briefly touched upon in the previous chapter, every plan for the development of a whole school reading culture should also include clear planning for evaluation of the plan as a whole, as well as its key components. Evaluation involves the processes, data and scheduling used to monitor, measure and assess progress towards achievement of goals (Merga, 2023b). Evaluation in schools can be an incredibly complex process, and this chapter is not an exhaustive coverage of this important area; rather, it may be a starting point from which further reading and learning may be conducted if you wish.

When we think about evaluation, we may automatically think about seeing changes in quantitative data between Point A at *baseline* (before an initiative) and Point B (after an initiative has been active for a sufficient period of time to realistically expect to see change). However, understanding of how to measure the success of change has evolved over time, with growing recognition of the value of qualitative and mixed-methods approaches. The effectiveness of your plan should not be purely 'determined by quantitative shifts in achievement data'; 'qualitative data in the form of the perspectives of students, staff and parents can also be drawn upon' (Merga, 2023b, p. 117).

Evaluation could and should include multiple forms of data, and capture the perspectives of multiple stakeholders. For example, a school in the UK seeking to analyse the success of a literacy policy was interested in the following data sources.

The impact of the literacy policy will be reviewed by:

- Analysis of reading age data (whole school, case studies and nurture group)
- Analysis of AP (likely to refer to 'alternative provision') progress and achievement data (English, including nurture group)
- Student voice
- Staff voice
- Parent feedback.

(Merga, 2023b, pp. 116–117)

If you are used to seeing evaluation within schools as a purely quantitative project, please keep an open mind while reviewing this chapter, as you may find that it furnishes you with possibilities that are worth embracing.

More about goals

The previous chapter introduced goals in the context of whole school reading culture implementation. It explored the importance of setting short-term, midpoint and long-term goals. In this chapter, we will give further attention to the *kinds* of goals you may set.

The first, most obvious goals that may come to mind will probably be those higher accountability goals; improvements in students' literacy performance as measured in high-stakes testing. In my analysis of literacy policies within schools more broadly, I found that it was common for goals to be solely aligned with

> improving performance on high-stakes testing, and measurement of success featured in the policy has aligned with this goal. This is understandable given the aforementioned accountability demands placed on contemporary schools in relation to high-stakes testing. I accept that it is unrealistic to propose that these demands be ignored or side-lined, as schools 'need to respond to the demands of high stakes testing, while considering socio-economic and geographical contexts' (te Riele et al., 2022, p. 332).

(Merga, 2023b, p. 182)

However, as I have explored previously in this book, it is important that these not be the *only* measurement of success incorporated in the policy. The WASABR research found that

> students were clear that they did not find a purely grades-focused approach to reading encouraging at all. Teachers actively resisting test focus and emphasizing reading for pleasure were perceived as more encouraging. When asked how his teacher felt about reading books, Craig was honest, saying 'we have to do that, we get marked on that, so we have to read a few books, you know, if we want to get good marks for that. It's a part of the grading thing.' Craig viewed his teacher's perception of reading as something that was obligatory and measured.
>
> Craig had never seen his teacher reading a book for pleasure, and his perception was that she did not encourage students to read for pleasure. He described that there was a 'threat' to perform for the purposes of 'our grades and stuff'.
>
> (Merga, 2015c, p. 45)

Simpson and Cremin (2022) critically consider the position of students like Craig, arguing that cultures of high-stakes testing frame 'children's experience of reading', potentially leading to 'young people reading for the system, rather than reading for themselves', enforcing 'conceptions of reading as solitary, not as a social, discursive practice', and 'pressure to improve test scores disconnects the act of reading from critical appreciation and from children's personal experience of literary texts' (p. 10). While your whole school reading culture should yield literacy testing improvements, literacy achievement is more expansive than what is measured in the narrowed set of skills assessed in high-stakes testing, and it is important that you do not inadvertently communicate to students that this is all that matters.

If correctly implemented, you should also have goals that address a broader range of student learning related outcomes as well as other significant goals that can contribute to student learning, and positive student learning experiences. To this end, evaluation is about more than determining whether or not achievement-related goals were reached; you want to improve students' literacy performance, but also foster a related beneficial lifelong reader orientation that will support students to build and maintain their reading skills both within and beyond school.

To this end, in addition to these *literacy testing goals*, we also need to consider *broader performance goals, attitudinal goals, behavioural goals, fidelity goals, staff development goals, wellbeing goals, library resource goals* and *parent engagement goals*. You may of course have many other goals; these are just some examples of likely goals that can be considered for the purpose of evaluation to get schools thinking about goals that may include but also extend beyond what is captured in high-stakes testing.

Broader performance goals are all of those literacy goals that relate to student achievement beyond what is measured in high-stakes testing, and consider cross-curricular literacy. For example, given the aforementioned research in this book, it is realistic to expect to see improvement in performance in mathematics and science skills related to reading comprehension after students have had long-term exposure to substantially greater experiences of sustained silent reading (see Merga, 2023e).

In this context, *attitudinal goals* and *behavioural goals* relate to those underpinning goals fostering positive attitudes in students, and increasing the frequency of exposure to beneficial activities, given the previously explained association between reading engagement and literacy performance (see Chapter 1). The goals of enhancing student attitudes towards reading and enhancing student frequency of engagement in reading should, given the research explored earlier in this book, be the pathways by which we see improvements in measures of commonly tested literacy skills such as reading comprehension and vocabulary. An attitudinal goal might seek to see improvement in students' attitudes towards reading for pleasure compared with a baseline assessment, with a behavioural goal seeking to see an increase in students' self-reported reading for pleasure in the home against baseline reported frequency.

It is also valuable to include goals related to aligning implementation with fidelity to best practice, and specifically consider this in evaluation related to *fidelity goals*. In my experience, fidelity goals are often neglected in evaluation within schools, captured purely on an anecdotal level if at all. This is problematic given the importance of fidelity. If you see little or no improvement in your desired goals, and you have not collected data related to fidelity in implementation, you do not know if the initiative really did fail in your context. Fidelity goals might be particularly useful where a practice is *already* being implemented in schools, such as reading aloud, but the plan seeks to see an improvement in *how* it is implemented, as staff may fall back on old ways of doing things despite agreeing to undertake a revitalised approach.

Poor fidelity to best practice can render efforts towards evaluation worthless.

For example, you roll out a whole school silent reading programme and seek to see an improvement in young people's attitudes towards reading compared with baseline data as a key goal.

However, in practice, students are rarely provided opportunities to actually read silently, as some teachers often use this time for class work where students have fallen behind.

In this case, poor fidelity in implementation will mean that you cannot expect to see a relationship between the silent reading programme and young people's attitudes towards reading. If it is nonetheless found, it is likely due to other factors. However, where attention hasn't been given to fidelity in implementation, schools can incorrectly conclude that sustained opportunities for silent reading do not yield improvements in young people's attitudes towards reading. As such, an example of a fidelity goal might be seeing all classes externally observed to be undertaking sustained silent reading during an agreed daily period, following agreed best-practice elements to be ticked off on a rubric by the observing party. You don't want to go overboard with the surveillance component, but some attention to fidelity goals needs to be given.

Adequate professional development will also need to underpin fidelity goals. It has been contended that researchers can be more effective than educators at rolling out interventions given that 'the former might be better able to deliver the interventions as intended' (van der Sande, van Steensel et al., 2023, p. 6). However, if sufficient attention is given to professional development of staff, to ensure that they are well equipped to deliver the interventions embedded within the whole school reading culture, and attention is given to ensure fidelity to best practice, this is an important step towards addressing this issue.

This leads us to the next kind of goal that we should consider. It can be contended that the best way to ensure that staff who need upskilling in facets relating to implementing a whole school reading approach is to build in *staff development goals*. Without these goals, this imperative can easily fall by the wayside among the competing demands in rolling out a whole school reading culture. As such, goals relating to identifying, targeting and measuring shifts in capacity in relation to staff development can help you to ensure that there is 'tailored and specific planning for ongoing professional learning that is responsive to current and evolving school needs' (Merga, 2023b, p. 147). For example, you might wish to set the goal of seeing an improvement in educators' self-reported levels of self-efficacy before and after sustained staff development opportunities. In relation to staff development goals, it is important not to forget upskilling educators and education support workers who are not classroom-based teachers.

Literacy benefits are not the only advantages offered by a whole school reading culture, and given the association between reading and wellbeing explored earlier in this book, and the growing focus on student wellbeing in contemporary schools, it would be a missed opportunity to omit *wellbeing goals* from consideration for the purposes of evaluation. These goals can also be used to maximise student enjoyment of the reading-supportive opportunities they are exposed to as part of the creation of a whole school reading culture. For example, goals can be set in relation to the school library as a wellbeing supportive reading environment, relating to factors such as availability of resources on key health issues (Merga, 2022b).

In a similar vein, you can plan for the meeting of *library resource goals* that may include but also extend beyond wellbeing. This can help you make the best use of the school library resource which you may direct additional funding to during the implementation of a whole school reading culture. For example, you may seek to improve the volume of students using the library resource voluntarily before and after school and at recess and lunch. This is also a *behavioural goal*.

Finally, given the significance of parents as a key social influence in the reading engagement of their children, setting *parent engagement goals* can maintain and build momentum towards supporting parents to fulfil a reading-supportive role, ideally overcoming barriers in relation to their background or knowledge. This might include setting goals such as seeing an increase in parents' self-reported encouragement of children's reading at home.

Introduction to basic quantitative, qualitative and mixed-methods analysis and data

This section will introduce you to very basic quantitative, qualitative, and mixed-methods approaches to data collection and analysis to give you options, and to support you towards finding the best fit in your approaches to evaluation. In this section I refer to the group of participants/respondents involved as the *sample*, and different stakeholders may constitute different samples within an evaluation plan.

Schools need to collect data in order to shine a light on the effectiveness of an innovation within a learning context. In turn, the kinds of data collected may be perhaps (reciprocally) dictated by the analysis that is going to be employed. This is influenced by consideration of the affordances, strengths and limitations inherent in different approaches which will be touched on here. If you already understand the difference between quantitative, qualitative and mixed-methods approaches in relation to evaluation within schools, feel free to skip this section.

As I am a researcher and educator who is really passionate about research and evaluation methods, it is important for me to underscore that my description of these methods here is in close consideration of the *needs of schools*, which can be very different to the degree of methodological rigour that might be employed in *academic research*, aligning with the intended professional rather than academic audience for this book. As such, I must stress that this is not a methods section written for a research audience, where evaluation is undertaken for different purposes and required levels of scientific rigour.

For example, in this context, the gold standard for evaluation may be seen as randomised controlled trials (RCTs) (Hariton & Locascio, 2018). In brief, these can be understood as

> prospective studies that measure the effectiveness of a new intervention or treatment. Although no study is likely on its own to prove causality, randomization reduces bias and provides a rigorous tool to examine cause-effect relationships between an intervention and outcome. This is because the act of randomization balances participant characteristics (both observed and unobserved) between the groups allowing attribution of any differences in outcome to the study intervention. This is not possible with any other study design.
>
> In designing an RCT, researchers must carefully select the population, the interventions to be compared and the outcomes of interest. Once these are defined, the number of participants needed to reliably determine if such a relationship exists is calculated (power calculation). Participants are then recruited and randomly assigned to either the intervention or the comparator group.
>
> (Hariton & Locascio, 2018, p. 1716)

Obviously, this approach is not typically going to be at all appropriate to the implementation of a whole school reading culture, as it would involve having a control or 'comparator' group excluded from the research-supported strategies outlined in this book.

Furthermore, as you are seeking to build students' reading engagement and enhance their motivation to be lifelong readers, measuring the success of your initiative at the highest academic standard would also be complicated by the fact you will almost invariably, within a school, be combining 'motivational support with skills instruction, which makes it difficult to infer whether effects are caused by investing in student motivation' (van der Sande, van Steensel et al., 2023, p. 6). You are deliberately planning to employ a combination of strategies and practices, rather than a single one.

RCTs can be challenging to get right, and where flaws exist in design, such as in relation to method and sample recruitment, findings can be problematic (see Yeh et al., 2018 for an informative coverage of some of these issues). The research purpose behind an RCT is not the same as your pragmatic purpose in rolling out your plan, so there is no need to aspire to impractical standards.

If you are only using research-supported strategies, and you are working within a school, your overarching aim is unlikely to be testing the efficacy of an approach as a whole in order to continue to build the body of research in this space, which has already been, at least to some extent, tested in the research. Instead, your goal is to improve student outcomes; exploring the efficacy of an approach in your context is an adjunct to this aim.

To this end, you might wonder why I have even bothered to include mention of RCTs in this book. It is because I have seen external stakeholders (often parents) who do not fully understand the level of rigour involved in, and the underpinning purposes behind, an RCT question why schools rolling out a whole school reading culture are not using an RCT approach to measure their success. Hopefully, if this happens to you, this brief section will help you to explain to these stakeholders what an RCT actually is, and why this is not practical or necessary in your context.

Nonetheless, if you want to take a more academic, rather than pragmatic approach to using quantitative data for evaluation in your school, I suggest that you read our book *Conducting Quantitative Research in Education*, which has done very well for an academic publication, given that in addition to being available in paper form, it has been accessed online more than 30,000 times according to the publisher's website (Mat Roni et al., 2020) and cited over 110 times by researchers. If you are an academic researcher, my suggestions here may be too simplistic and pragmatic for you to apply to research contexts, as I am more interested in breaking down complex concepts for the purposes of accessibility and use, and what can be realistically achieved for the local and internal purposes of a school than academic purposes, though I do also include a section herein on boosting quality with academic partnership for those wanting the best of both worlds.

Deductive vs. inductive approaches

From here on in, when I describe the kinds of research methods that can be used for the purposes of an evaluation of a whole school reading culture, I will make mention of two key approaches underpinning the selection of these methods. As such, I will be referring to *deductive* and *inductive* analytical approaches to evaluation that impact on design. These can be conceptualised as follows.

Deductive analysis can be viewed as 'data analyses that set out to test whether data are consistent with *prior assumptions*, theories, or hypotheses identified or constructed by an investigator' (Thomas, 2006, p. 238, my italics). For example, you have the prior research-informed assumption that significantly increasing students' exposure to reading aloud following a best-practice model will enhance their growth in vocabulary learning, and you analyse data specifically looking for evidence of this assumption. This is a deductive approach, as you'll be seeing if your prior assumption turned out to be correct or not within your school. Some schools *only* use a deductive approach to evaluation, and they even conflate evaluation with this deductive orientation, without considering how an inductive approach might complement a deductive approach, though in the research community, it is common for evaluation projects to use both inductive and deductive analysis (Thomas, 2006).

To this end, *inductive analysis* can be viewed as 'approaches that primarily use detailed readings of raw data to derive concepts, themes, or a model through interpretations made from the raw data by an evaluator or researcher' (Thomas, 2006, p. 238). For example, you have 'facilitating needs responsive professional development for staff' as a goal to be evaluated as part of your plan. However, you are not sure what the professional development needs of your diverse body of staff are. You conduct a range of interviews with staff where you ask them what their needs might be in relation to the implementation plan of the whole school reading culture, and focus your planning for professional development on both recurring and urgent needs that become apparent from engaging in this process. Identifying these needs used to be referred to as seeing theories or themes 'emerge from the data' (Strauss & Corbin, 1998, p. 12), but sensibly this way of describing the process has fallen out of favour in recent times, given that the role the interpreters of data play in reaching the findings is not neutral (e.g. Braun et al., 2022), and where you are interpreting data related to your own school community, this is certainly particularly relevant.

Getting quality evaluation data from children

It is likely that your evaluation process will involve collecting some data from your students. Collecting reliable data from minors may have some complications associated with it that are worth considering. Drawing on my experiences of collecting diverse forms of data within schools, I propose that you keep the following in mind.

Data *from* a student (e.g. survey comments), rather than data *about* a student (e.g. test results) are self-reported, and this is noteworthy given that researchers make distinctions between different types of data with related inferences about their reliability. For example, in their recent meta-analysis, van der Sande, van Steensel et al. (2023) note that 'a distinction was made between self-reports, teacher-reports, observations, and tests' (p. 21).

Much has been written about the limitations of self-report (e.g. Howard, 1994), such as where a student reports on their own perceived feelings towards reading for pleasure. While recall and other factors can impact on these data, perhaps the biggest threat to the reliability of your data, given where students sit within the pecking order of a school, relates to satisficing:

> When we ask a survey question, we hope that our respondents will give us an honest answer, and tell us what they really think. Unfortunately, young respondents are particularly susceptible to satisficing, where 'a respondent gives more or less superficial responses that generally appear reasonable or acceptable, but without having gone through all the steps involved in the question-answer process' (Read & MacFarlane, 2006, p. 2). As touched on previously, they seek to 'go-along' (Borgers et al., 2000, p. 4) with the will and expectations of the researcher. This is felt to relate to the respondent's motivation, how difficult the task is, and their cognitive abilities (Borgers & Hox, 2001).
>
> We personally believe that more attention needs to be given to satisficing, because many young people just want to make you happy, instead of sharing what they really think, believe or do. Once we understand and expect satisficing, we can explore how to both identify and mitigate it. Regardless of mitigating measures, satisficing is a limitation that applies to most, if not all studies with young people, to varying degrees.
>
> (Mat Roni et al., 2020, p. 27)

However, I would argue that in your school, there is no one as well equipped to determine students' attitudes towards reading as the *students themselves*, and as long as satisficing is understood and steps are taken to minimise risk of exposure through enabling anonymous data collection where feasible, these kinds of data can ultimately be the most useful.

Another common barrier to students' providing quality self-report data on surveys arises when the language is too complex for the literacy level of the students. It will be important when collecting survey responses from students to ensure that they have sufficient literacy to comprehend what you are asking for. To use Australia as an example, by Year 9 there is a gap of around eight years in literacy attainment between the top 10% of students and the bottom 10% (Goss & Sonnemann, 2016), and where possible, you will need to pitch the survey at the level of this bottom 10% to avoid these students simply guessing what the survey says and thus providing results that do not reflect their actual beliefs/perceptions. If your bottom 10% do not have independent reading skills, you will need to come up with an alternative to ensure they have access, such as reading the items aloud and having a scribe input data if needed. While every nation and school will have different literacy spans to account for in this regard, this kind of diversity in literacy performance is not rare, so readability will typically be an important consideration even in secondary schools.

How will you know if your survey is too hard for your students?

Check readability. As I've described previously, 'this is as simple as accessing a free readability tool such as SMOG online and pasting in the text (in chunks if necessary) to determine how difficult to read' your survey is (Merga, 2023b, p. 220). The free readability tool will tell you how difficult to read your text is. Earlier in the book I suggested also using a readability tool to check any text intended for parent communications too. You may find the new online SHeLL (Sydney Health Literacy Lab) Health Literacy Editor (which uses SMOG to determine readability) useful (Ayre et al., 2023), currently available for free at https://shell.techlab.works. Instructions are very straightforward and this is an easy readability resource to use.

Pre-pilot. This simply involves working 'with a small but diverse group of respondents of the same demographic as our intended recipients to check that what we've written in terms of survey items and instructions is understood as we intended it to be' (Mat Roni et al., 2020, p. 30).

The pre-pilot is also vital as beyond readability, you should also be aware that young people do not always interpret surveys in the manner intended by the survey creator. This is why it is so important to pre-pilot any survey tools with a group of students with diverse abilities, ages and backgrounds before collecting data from your students.

It is hard to predict how students can interpret survey items without this pre-pilot. As a grown adult, you don't see the world the same way as a child, no matter how much time you spend with children.

For example, in one study, we surveyed primary school students in Years 4 and 6 about their use of devices for reading books, and one of the questions was 'How old are you?'. That seems straightforward; most people know how old they are.

However, during the piloting process we found that our 'respondents wanted to round up their age in order to seem older', and we were constantly asked if they could do so, so we changed the wording of the survey item to provide clarity, changing the question to 'How old are you right now?' (Merga & Mat Roni, 2017a, p. 191). As adults, the desire to round up our age was certainly forgotten until we spoke with the children during the piloting process, reminding us of the childhood desire to present ourselves as being as old as possible. While this was hilarious for us, as if we were tempted to fudge the numbers on our age, it certainly wouldn't be to inflate it, it was also a good reminder that even very basic questions can be interpreted differently depending on the target audience.

You also need to be aware that data collection can be negatively perceived by students, and this can impact on the quality of the data you collect.

Be clear that data collection is not a test (unless it is). There is a degree of anxiety associated with being part of a data collection process. Students are having data collected from them all the time, but this is usually in the form of assessment. Thus, it's unsurprising that when you collect data from students to inform your evaluation which is *not* individual student assessment data, students may still be under the impression that they are being assessed.

In some cases, data collection *may* involve assessment, especially where you are collecting data about performance in reading comprehension or vocabulary. However, in many cases it does not, and if your students approach a survey collecting data on their attitudes towards reading as though it is an assessment, this is obviously going to significantly impact on how they represent themselves, potentially leading you to collect useless data.

Where data collection is seen as a test, there can be related anxiety which can influence the quality of data collected:

> no matter how many times that you tell them that the survey is not a test, one or a few periods of data collection are not going to magically erase the years of school conditioning that they have experienced. Margaret's repeated insistence that her study was not a test did not stop one young boy from crying when the internet cut out at his school while he filled out his survey during the piloting phase, leading him to believe that he would subsequently fail the test that he definitely was not sitting. Despite the fact that children are unlikely to believe you, it is still important to explain and re-iterate that the survey is not a test, and you should be aware that your insistence that it is not an assessment may actually contradict what teachers have told their students about the activity in order to ensure good behaviour!
>
> (Mat Roni et al., 2020, p. 28)

It is important to be clear and honest when collecting data, and to provide as safe an environment for data collection as possible.

On a related note, as briefly mentioned in relation to satisficing, students may also be very concerned about sharing information with you that they think will cause you to view them in a negative light. For example, you might seek to collect baseline data about students' attitudes towards reading to compare with midpoint data to see if the initiatives result in improvement. However, this baseline data may be falsely skewed towards the positive if students think that you *want* them to be a reader, and are therefore afraid to share that they do not like reading. You will really need to stress that their honesty is valued, and their anonymity will be preserved. The relationship between educators and students is inherently unequal in terms of power, and while this is obvious, the implications it has for the collection of quality data are often overlooked.

Value student participation and honesty. In this vein, it is important to be clear that you value students' honesty when they are providing evaluation data. Let them know that you have made sure that they can contribute anonymously so that there will be no judgements associated with their responses, and explain how the data will be used. Students need to understand that the data will be used to look at changes over time, and that is why their honesty at baseline is so important, and even young children can understand this if you explain it to them carefully and clearly.

Where children understand the point of the exercise, they may be more likely to enter into contributing their data with a commitment to providing a genuine reflection of their feelings, experiences and perceptions. As we have noted previously,

> in a teacher-centred classroom, students can become accustomed to reproducing teacher expectations in all of their responses, rather than engaging in higher order thinking, or offering their own views and experiences. While contemporary classrooms typically move towards being student-centred, where students' values, attitudes and experiences receive validation to some degree, this is not the norm in all classrooms, and at all times. When we ask young students about their values, attitudes and experiences, this could be the first time an adult has ever shown an interest in more than just a reproduction of educative inputs. The experience can be somewhat bewildering for these young people. It's not safe to expect that students will know that you want to know their views just because you ask for them; you need to make this explicit, and again, you need to reiterate it.
>
> (Mat Roni et al., 2020, p. 28)

Furthermore, 'students need to know that what they share is really important, and that it can help solve problems that we are investigating, but this information needs to be shared in such a way as to avoid prompting certain responses' (Mat Roni et al., 2020, p. 29). This means that when you explain that you want to see if there is a change in attitudes between baseline and midpoint, it may be best not to tell students that you are hoping to observe a *positive* change, as they may just do you a favour and provide this for you, regardless of truth. Instead, you can explain that you want to see what kind of change, if any, occurs as a result of an initiative.

It is important to use accessible language in your explanation, particularly when collecting data from young children. For instance, while collecting data we have 'previously explained that "We don't know what young people think about reading books. Grown-ups might think they know, but we can only guess. If you tell me what you really think, this will help us to know"' (Mat Roni et al., 2020, p. 29).

Back up your data. Academic researchers have a tendency to treat data like gold, given how many hoops we need to jump through to get it, and you should do the same.

Regardless of the approach to evaluation that you take, you will invariably be collecting data of some sort to subject to analysis. It is absolutely crucial, and I cannot state this passionately enough, that you back up all of the data that you collect for your evaluation in a safe space that cannot be readily accessed by external parties. This includes any quantitative data you collect, but also data in the many multimodal forms that may be required by your evaluation, which I explore further later in this chapter. Bear in mind that this may include data with substantial file sizes far exceeding that of a typical pdf document or excel spreadsheet, such as large audio or video files. Depending on the data needs of your evaluation, make sure that wherever you are backing up your data, you have sufficient storage capacity to meet your ongoing needs.

It is honestly one of the most depressing things when data is lost, as it can have really negative impacts on your evaluation process, and it means that the generous contributions of your respondents have not been preserved and may not be regained, given that we lack the technology to move through time. This means that you should also think carefully about who has access to the repository where your data is being stored to prevent accidental deletion or other loss of data. Malicious erasure of data is really rare, but it does happen, so depending on your school context, you may need to be extra careful.

Quantitative analysis and data for schools

Quantitative analysis for the purposes of evaluation of your whole school reading culture will usually be deductive in nature, as you will be looking to see if your prior expectations of improvement are met in relation to the goals you have decided to prioritise. You will commonly use a quantitative approach where you already know what must be tested or measured.

As previously noted, for comprehensive coverage of quantitative analysis and data for schools at a more academic level, you may wish to read our previous book (Mat Roni et al., 2020); my brief coverage here will be very practical and aligned with very basic quantitative analysis and data needs that will be sufficient for the purposes of most schools.

Pre-post design

While a range of approaches could be adopted, as previously explored, your school is unlikely to undertake an RCT for the purpose of evaluating your whole school reading programme.

Instead, for the purposes of evaluation, in most cases you will probably be comparing baseline data with data collected at later times from the *same group* of participants, known as a *pre-post design*. While it is possible and in many cases desirable to look for changes at an individual level, pre-post designs for evaluation in schools more typically look at changes at group level. For example, you might see if there are increases in whole group frequency of choosing to read for pleasure outside school at midpoint compared with baseline data.

Stability of test group

When using a pre-post design, given that changes in student enrolments and staffing are ongoing in schools, it is important to stress that while participation may be anonymous, you need to keep track of who provided data at baseline to ensure that you maintain the *same group of respondents*. As soon as you start collecting data at midpoint or long-term from individuals who did not contribute to the baseline data, changes in the data can be attributed to changes in the composition of the group, rather than any impacts of the programme.

Evaluation questions

The first thing you need to do when planning to collect quantitative data is to decide what your evaluation questions (EQs) are. These will be directly responsive to your goals.

EQs are not the same as your survey questions, though your survey items will reflect the EQs. You can have as many EQs as you like.

For example, let's look at how one goal may be reflected as an EQ, and measured on a related survey item, bearing in mind that it is not uncommon for a goal to have more than one associated EQ and survey item.

Table 6 on the next page illustrates how a more general goal is transformed into something more measurable in the form of an EQ, or series of EQs as applicable, and how this EQ can then inform a survey item.

Scales and survey items

Writing good survey items is an art, and they take time and patience to get

Table 6 Example of goals informing EQs and survey items (quantitative approach)

Goal	EQ*	Measurement points	Survey item*	Item type	Scale (if applicable)
Improvement in students' frequency of voluntary use of the school library (*library resource goal, behavioural goal*)	Do students access the school library more frequently in their own time after implementation of the whole school reading programme?	Baseline (for comparison), midpoint and long-term	How often do you visit the school library during your own time (not during class time)?	Frequency scale	1 At least once a day 2 At least once a week 3 At least once a month 4 At least once a year 5 Never

*can be multiple, this is just one example

right. Every person reading this book will have had some experience of attempting to provide responses on a poorly designed survey, which can be a frustrating and occasionally mystifying experience.

To address EQs on self-designed survey tools, schools often use a Likert-type scale. Students are asked to rate their agreement with a statement '(i.e. 'strongly disagree' to 'strongly agree') or frequency scale (i.e. 'less frequent' to 'always')' (Mat Roni et al., 2020, p. 41). Dichotomous scales, where the choice is between two things such as the common yes/no option, are also often used.

Tools need to stand up to external scrutiny, particularly where you are intending to share your evaluation beyond your school. When I have worked closely with clients on the development of scales and survey items, without fail they have been surprised at how some of these can be completely misunderstood due to issues around clarity. It takes time and close consideration to create high-quality scales and survey items. In fact, if you have ever filled out an academic survey, you may have also found errors in the scales or survey items highlighting how challenging this work can be. When I've been shown surveys that have been designed and implemented with students, there are some common issues that I have observed.

First, where there is any possible ambiguity over what is meant by a survey item, you need to rework it until this ambiguity is addressed. You may also have to provide all staff collecting the data instructions on how to do so without shaping students' responses, while ensuring clarity.

For example, drawing on the survey item in Table 6, depending on the age and reading comprehension levels of your students, you may need to explain that 'during your own time' means before school, after school, at breaks and at lunch. You may also need to stress that this does not include going to the library during class time, even though it is *literally* stated in the survey item. You may also need to reinforce that it is fine for students who have other things to do during their own time to share that they never visit the library, and that all responses will be anonymous, otherwise you may find that students fall back on satisficing. You need to avoid taking comprehension for granted.

Second, avoid limiting options in scale items and drawing questionable conclusions. Where practicable, allow for multiple selections, and include an 'other' option with a related open field that allows respondents to enter text where appropriate. For example, let's say you collect data about where your students prefer to sit while reading in the library. You include the options 'chair', 'floor' and 'sofa', leaving off beanbags, which are also available. You allow them to select one response only. Most students select sofa (95%). If you then write up your report which states that students prefer to read on the sofa over any other seating option within the library, this is false reporting, because you've omitted to include a key seating option (the beanbags). In addition, there are some students who were *equally* positively disposed towards sofa and floor, but only one option was permitted. In some cases, multiple options are clearly desirable rather than forcing a single response.

Third, denying neutrality and forcing an opinion can be problematic, and one of the biggest reasons that I rage-quit customer surveys, even if it means I sadly miss out on a prize. If a survey forces me to take a positive or negative position on something I hold a neutral position on, this feels dishonest and frustrates me. A whole school reading programme that shifts students from a neutral position towards reading for pleasure into a positive position, or from a slightly positive position to a very positive position is still achieving something great; students don't need to start out with a negative orientation. Consider allowing neutrality wherever possible.

Fourth, you want to make your surveys as easy to use as possible, so where feasible, skip logics should be used. These are where students are directed by the survey platform to subsequent items based on their response to a prior item.

For example, let's say that you ask students to rank their enjoyment of listening to their teacher read aloud to them on a scale allowing a strong positive, moderate positive, neutral, moderate negative and strong negative response. You might then *only* direct students who selected moderate negative or strong negative responses to an item which asks respondents to select why they do not like being read to by their teacher (allowing multiple selections). Obviously, exposing the students who hold a strong positive, moderate positive or neutral stance to this item is not appropriate, as the question does not apply to them.

Fifth, make sure your scales and survey items do in fact reflect your goals and EQs. You need to be able to draw reasonable conclusions in analysis, and there is often poor alignment between scales and survey items and what is supposed to be tested. For example, as mentioned earlier in this book, you cannot claim that students are reading more when what was measured was an increase in borrowing data from the school library, not reading volume.

Sixth, make sure your frequency scales in particular don't have gaps in them. For example, consider the following item on a survey for unusual teachers.

Question 10. I go to work in an inflatable fish costume:

- Never
- Less than once a month
- Once a month
- 2–3 times a month
- Once a week
- 2–3 times a week
- Daily.

What are teachers who go to work in an inflatable fish costume 4–6 times per week, or 4–6 times per month supposed to select?

On the bright side, we can learn from our novice errors. When it comes to evaluation methods, we can be lifelong learners, constantly improving our skills and updating them as improved methods and related techniques evolve, and acknowledging our limitations.

In my experience, flaws are almost inevitable, even in survey tools designed by experts if they are not *carefully tested* through piloting, and ideally also reviewed by someone with good knowledge of scale design, so you need to rigorously pilot your tools before implementation, and if possible, have an expert cast their eye over them.

Work with clean data

When I talk about working with clean data I am not referring to the removal of unfavourable responses! Rather, once the data are ready for analysis, you usually need to remove the partially completed responses (Mat Roni et al., 2020).

The logic behind this is simple. Let's say you have 124 staff members and you are surveying them at the beginning of the whole school reading programme to capture their baseline attitudes, practices and areas needing further professional development in relation to the goals of the programme.

You find yourself in the very implausible situation of having 136 responses. When you look at the data, you will probably find that one of the staff members might be behind three or four of the incomplete responses if they started the survey, but it cut out due to poor connection, or timed out because they got distracted by other tasks. You may even be told this by a few of the staff members. Regardless of whether you have more responses or fewer responses than you expected, you need to go through and delete all of the incomplete responses, even if this means that you fall short of your desired sample size.

Platform choices

Quantitative data collected in schools take so many different forms and these will not be exhaustively listed here. For example, borrowing data from the library and testing performance data are two common forms of data I see drawn upon in evaluation of a whole school reading programme. Schools also often commonly create their own tools for measuring changes in other areas, not captured by other mechanisms within the school.

Often, before I do consulting within a school, I have data sent to me that captures students' reading preferences as well as their attitudes towards reading and their frequency of reading for pleasure. I see a range of platforms being used to collect and report on these data, and I encourage you to use whatever suits your school.

Many schools use the free affordances available online, while well-resourced schools may invest in more advanced but more expensive platform choices that offer a range of comparative advantages. That said, I see little point in paying for bells and whistles that you are never going to use. While I want to avoid promoting a particular platform in this book, and I believe the most basic, free options can often be fit for purpose, if you do have some extra cash to throw at a platform, here are some of the features you might be looking for:

- **Generous respondent limits.** This is the obvious one. If you choose a platform that has a limit of 200 respondents and your school has 800 students to collect data from, this is going to be a bad fit. Always check for any respondent limits even if these are not clearly stated, as they may apply to platforms and you certainly don't want to find out midway through data collection that your collection has been cut off due to exceeding the respondent limit.
- **Skip logics.** As aforementioned, use of skip logics to move students between items based on responses to prior items without exposing them

to irrelevant content is important. I would always opt for a platform that allows you to easily program skip logics without needing to be an IT genius. Simply, skip logics are incredibly valuable for drilling down into the specifics related to subgroups within your data.

- **Allow multiple logins with moderated user levels.** If you are conducting evaluation in a team (and this should usually be the case), and/or you want to allow some parties access to the data while limiting their ability to edit survey content, you may wish to pay extra for a platform that will allow multiple logins that can be controlled by an overseer/administrator who decides on the level of access granted to each subsequent user. This may be particularly important if you have members of the leadership team who want to be able to keep an eye on the data, but you have concerns that they may accidentally delete responses or otherwise impede the evaluation process. Giving them 'look but don't touch' access can keep everyone happy.
- **Analytical functions.** Generally, the more expensive the platform, the more advanced the analytical functions available within the platform. This isn't going to be relevant for you if you're not intending to do anything particularly sophisticated with your data. However, if you're intending to do some analysis beyond the most basic levels, you can save money that you would spend on paying for a licence for statistics software or applications by choosing a survey platform that will perform the functions that you desire. For example, some of the more expensive platforms will also grant you unlimited filtering and comparison functions, and I can pretty much guarantee that if you have these functions, you will use them. For example, if you collect data about gender on one item, and data about reading frequency on another item, and you want to look at the reading frequency data of boys only, this is easily done.

The final comment I would make about platform choices is to take the time to really get to know the affordances of the platform before collecting data with it. While these platforms are typically very user-friendly, and you don't need a great deal of technical expertise to be able to use them efficiently, doing a mock test run of a survey on why unicorns prefer skateboarding over surfing within your team can help you to familiarise yourselves with how the platform works. It will also enable you to play with possibilities for analysis that are facilitated within the platform.

Basic analysis

There is a lot you can do with data that does not require advanced knowledge of statistical analysis. In many cases, a basic analysis will fit your purposes as long as you are working with a clean data set and understand the basics, and this approach is suitable even for absolute beginners, as long as it is sufficient to meet your needs. I've even published academic papers with only basic analysis where this has been sufficient to meet my research goals.

For example, one of my papers from my PhD project used the following approach to analysis.

> Basic analysis was performed in (name of survey platform), generating frequency, percent, mean, variance and standard deviation for data. Analysis of volume, frequency and attitude toward recreational book reading was carried out according to gender. Each of these data sets was cross tabulated and then analysed for significance.
>
> (Merga, 2014b, p. 164)

So what does very basic analysis entail, and how might you use it with evaluation data on a whole school reading culture?

Let's look at an example. You want to collect some data on students' experiences with a story dog that you recently began using within the school as part of implementing a whole school reading culture. You collect data from 433 students (the total number of respondents, and the sample, also known as the N).

These students are in Years/Grades 5 and 6, and they have all read aloud to the dog at least three times (you've confirmed this at a prior survey item, with a skip logic programmed to make sure that no students with zero experience of reading to the dog see this subsequent item).

There are some struggling readers in your survey group, so you decide to use smiley face images to support your scale, and you make sure there are support staff available to help students to complete the survey.

Question. Do you like reading aloud to Alex the story dog?

The survey platform you are using will treat each scale item as though it represents a number, rather than words. As you can see below, 5= strong positive and 1= strong negative.

Scale.

- I really like reading to Alex (5)
- I like reading to Alex (4)
- I don't feel anything about reading to Alex (3)

- I don't like reading to Alex (2)
- I really don't like reading to Alex (1)

To support the lower literacy students, you could even have a face next to each worded scale item such as in Figure 1.

Figure 1 *Smiley face rating scale*

This image is freely available from 'File:Children's pain scale-ar.jpg' by Robert Weis, licensed under CC BY-SA 4.0. You could source an alternative, but avoid using emojis, as these can be misinterpreted, hold an additional meaning that you are unfamiliar with, and/or be represented differently across devices, leading to differing perceptions of their meaning.

Here are your results:

- 245 (strong positive)
- 146 (moderate positive)
- 32 (neutral)
- 2 (moderate negative)
- 8 (strong negative)

It is worth keeping in mind that whatever survey platform you are using will understand these data as 245 5s, 146 4s and so on.

What can we learn from these data (after cleaning) at a basic level?

Skew. The most obvious thing that might jump out at you when you look at these data is that the data are *skewed* towards the positive. At a glance, you can see that most enjoyed reading to Alex. When it comes to skew, data can take many different shapes. For example, it can also be skewed towards the negative, or show a *bi-modal distribution* where on a line graph, you will see two humps instead of the line trending strongly in one direction. This happens when you have very few respondents taking a neutral position.

Frequency vs percentage. The numbers in the results section indicate *frequency*, which refers to the exact count of responses to each item on the scale. In contrast, *percentage* will show you your responses in relation to how they sit as a proportion of the overall responses. Percentages will be calculated by your survey platform, which simply involves dividing a frequency by the total and then multiplying the result by 100.

For example, let's say you want to know what percentage of respondents really liked reading to Alex. To do this manually, take the 245 strong positives, divide by the N (433), and then multiply the result by 100. Rounded to one decimal place, 56.6% of students really liked reading to Alex.

If you want to be able to report on the percentage of students who enjoyed reading to Alex, add your strong positive (245) to your moderate positive (146), divide by the N (433), and then multiply the result by 100. Rounded to one decimal place, you can reasonably contend that 90% of students enjoyed reading to Alex.

Mean. Along with mode and median, mean is a measure of central tendency in data (Marshall & Jonker, 2010, p. e6). But what does that mean?

You might want to know what the *average* student felt about the dog, and one way to do this is to look at the mean. Basically, mean is calculated 'by adding all the values in the data set and dividing by the number of observations' (Khorana et al., 2023, p. 12). So in our example, we would do the following: 245 x 5 + 146 x 4 + 32 x 3 + 2 x 2 + 8 x 1, which equals 1917, then divide this by N=433. The result (rounded to one decimal place) is 4.4, which means that your average student sits between strong positive (5) and moderate positive (4) in their orientation.

While the mean is clearly not hard to calculate yourself, again, you'll probably never need to as your survey platform will give you this information, but you still need to understand its limitations; mean is the 'most commonly used measure of central tendency' (Khorana et al., 2023, p. 12) but that doesn't make it the most useful option for all data.

Trimmed mean. Some survey platforms will offer you the option of calculating a trimmed mean, which is basically 'a recalculated *mean* with the bottom 2.5% and the top 2.5% of the recorded values left out (hence the word 'trimmed')' (Mat Roni et al., 2020, p. 51). People sometimes like to compare the trimmed mean with the actual mean as when a large difference exists, this strongly suggests that there are *outliers* in your data, respondents whose views were very different from the rest of the group (Mat Roni et al., 2020). Given that you can literally see the skew and the small group of negative respondents, this probably won't be that useful to you in this example.

Median and mode. Like mean, median and mode are also measures of central tendency, but we use them for slightly different purposes. While the mean gives us the average, mode will give us 'the numerical value with the greatest frequency' and median will give us 'the middle score of a rank-ordered distribution' (Marshall & Jonker, 2010, p. e6). So when will we use them?

Median is helpful when you want to find the middle point in the data, which is particularly useful when you have outliers confusing the picture. For example, let's imagine that you ask parents to rate their satisfaction with a particular intervention run by the school, such as a parent education seminar, on a scale from 1 to 10. Finding the median here will give you a sense of parents' rating of the experience. If the median score is 7, this means that half of the parents rated the experience 7 or higher, and the other half rated it 6 or lower. It is worth noting that 'while the mean is still the most commonly used measure of central tendency, the median is normally the more accurate metric' for research projects, and 'median-based approaches are more accurate than a mean-based approach especially when applied to skewed data and data with a high variance' (Khorana et al., 2023, p. 15). As such, you might find the median more useful to you than the mean, depending on the data.

Mode could be handy when you want to understand which response was most common. This information is obscured in a mean. For example, you might ask a question and the most commonly selected response (60%) will be the *neutral* response, while all of the remaining responses are to the positive sections (40%), with no respondents selecting negative choices. While looking at a mean, your data will be looking positive, but such a high number of neutral responses could mean that this position is genuinely held by the students, or 60% of the students just didn't understand your question so they opted for a neutral position. This would be unlikely (but not impossible) if your survey went through an adequate piloting process, but it might warrant further investigation. Mode is the *least* commonly used measure of central tendency, partly due to its limitations, such as its questionable value for small sample sizes (Khorana et al., 2023).

Standard deviation. Finding out the standard deviation is useful, as it can help you to determine whether your responses were pretty uniform, or whether you have a lot of outliers:

> Standard deviation is a measure of how spread out the data is, the variance of it. The narrower the standard deviation the closer to the midpoint of the data all results will be. Without quoting the mathematical formula behind it, the standard deviation allows for expressing variance using the same units as those used for the observations or measurements.
>
> (Marshall & Jonker, 2010, p. e3)

Returning to this example, if you ask parents to rate their satisfaction with a particular intervention run by the school, such as a parent education seminar, on a scale from 1 to 10 and the standard deviation is low, it means that most of the parents had a similar level of satisfaction, while a high standard deviation suggests that the level of satisfaction varied a lot more. This is obviously handy for when you had a small group of parents attend the intervention in a combative/unreceptive mood, as you can use standard deviation to argue that their negative experiences were not typical. However, always consider these data carefully, as it may mean that you are failing to meet the needs of a particular subgroup within your school community. I return to the importance of considering outliers shortly.

Cross tabs. Many survey platforms facilitate cross tabs, and you will almost certainly want to use cross tabs in your analysis. In addition to items relating to your evaluation objectives, your surveys will probably have items that collect demographic data. For example, in the instance of student surveys, these demographic data may relate to students' age, gender, year group, whether English is an additional or first language, or any other key distinguishing factor that you are interested in considering in relation to the results.

Returning to the example of asking students how they feel about reading aloud to Alex the story dog, while you survey all students at once (a reading aloud question), you might want to know if there is a difference in the experience between students in Years/Grades 5 and 6. Early in the survey, you will ask students to select whether they are in Year 5 or Year 6 (a year group question).

Following the directions on your survey platform, you will be able to easily generate a cross tab report, which will show the results of the reading aloud question by subgroup in relation to the year group question. You might find that more students in Year 6 enjoyed the experience than students in Year 5, and these findings may trigger greater exploration to better understand the difference if it is marked, such as through qualitative data collection.

More on outliers. As you advance in your knowledge of quantitative data analysis, you will find that how outliers are dealt with in different statistical analytic techniques varies. However, don't get lost in the numbers and forget that your data are representative of actual human students. If we ignore the students who really don't like to read to Alex simply because they are outliers, we are failing to recognise the needs of these students. We should find out more about this demographic where possible. We need to know whether the students are afraid of dogs, allergic to dogs, or whether there was something in the method of delivery that could be adjusted to enhance students' enjoyment of working with Alex. Our outliers are important too.

Some limitations. Adopting a purely quantitative approach can fit your purpose; however, in many cases, it will be insufficient as a sole approach to evaluation of a whole school reading culture, and there are many limitations to the use of quantitative data only for the purposes of evaluation within schools.

For example, while quantitative data are popular given the advantages for aggregation, summary and certain kinds of analysis, and even potential for generalisability where sample sizes are sufficient, it is not possible to create quantitative tools for areas of interest that are not preconceivable, so quantitative data are always dependent 'on the availability of prior theories and hypotheses' (Jacobs et al., 1999, p. 718). Furthermore, numbers may not resonate as meaningfully as detailed insights from key stakeholders impacted by the programme. Where there is any ambiguity around the applicability of pre-existing theories and suppositions, building in adjunct qualitative or mixed-methods affordances can be advantageous, as I explore further herein.

Qualitative analysis and data for schools

Despite the emphasis on numerical representation of attainment in schools, sometimes numbers are simply not enough to really understand the impact of an initiative within a school community.

This is where we turn to qualitative data to better understand the impact of a programme where potential impacts cannot be preconceived for survey measurement. The 'major advantage of the qualitative approach is that it more easily allows for the discovery of new ideas and unanticipated occurrences' (Jacobs et al., 1999, p. 718). This is why qualitative data are increasingly recognised as important for establishing a case for school performance (e.g. NSW Department of Education, 2023). If you are struggling to come up with a scale that will fully capture what has been experienced by respondents within your school community, step away from the scale and consider some qualitative data collection.

Qualitative methodology is a huge and diverse field of knowledge, and in this section, I will severely limit my exploration of this field to a very small subset, concerned with a few commonly adopted pragmatic applications within a whole school reading culture evaluation. You may wish to embrace the application of qualitative methods that fall outside the scope of what is discussed here, depending on the needs of your school, so further reading may be needed. Be warned; even the most methods-savvy readers may find the literature in this space very difficult to engage with, given the complex underlying theories and the proliferation of technical language (Thomas, 2006). I will keep this section succinct and closely linked to real-world implications to fit the needs of my audience. Qualitative data can be explored using a deductive or inductive approach (e.g. Merga, 2021b), but an inductive approach is far more common, and will be the focus of this section.

The biggest advantage of using a qualitative approach relates to the fact that we do not know what we do not know. While quantitative data tools often force a selection from a preconceived number of possibilities, qualitative data opens up the field to capturing what has not yet been conceived. It enables a breadth of responses and invites the voices of those directly impacted by a whole school reading programme, importantly including those of marginalised groups (Chen et al., 2023). It can be contended that qualitative analysis enables 'a detailed examination of the thoughts, feelings, opinions and/or experiences of individuals, groups or communities. By taking into account the local context, qualitative analysis can assist in developing solutions that are tailored to the particular context', and it 'can also be useful for providing a narrative around quantitative data' (NSW Department of Education, 2023, p. 3).

For example, in one instance when I worked with a school, they were interested in capturing qualitative data as part of a mixed-methods approach (see next section for more on mixed methods). Among many other areas, they sought to capture how their teachers perceived the benefits of a whole school Reading for Pleasure programme for students, as well as the challenges teachers observed in the implementation of this programme. This included opportunities for teachers to add text in open fields to explain their perception of the programme's benefits and describe the issues that they observed (Collins et al., 2022), which would enable them to better understand the responses given on the quantitative items.

While possible issues could be stipulated based on prior research in this area, due to the paucity of research evaluating elements of a whole school reading culture, and the possibility of unique, unforeseeable and valuable responses, a qualitative approach was needed as an adjunct to the quantitative approach. A small team of three educators involved in programme implementation (with some initial guidance from me as their academic mentor) identified key recurring themes in the data which they were then able to draw upon to better understand teacher perceptions of the process, with the exact method they used described subsequently herein in relation to thematic analysis.

What kinds of data?

Qualitative data are typically available in a text, image or video form (or combination), whether written, spoken or multimodal, though they can also take other less common forms. Qualitative data are also often represented in an alternative mode. For example, when they include audio, they may be transcribed in text form, with both the original sources and transcription, or just the transcription, subject to analysis. Similarly, where data are captured in video form, you may create an accompanying written description of the video content (e.g. Merga, 2021b). There are many possibilities for these kinds of transformations that are used for the purposes of data analysis and reporting.

For your purposes, here are some types of qualitative data that may be used in the evaluation of a whole school reading culture, with an example of how they might be used. To deal with these possibilities in depth would take a book in itself, but the taste I provide here should be sufficient to give you a feel for whether or not this data source may appeal to you and warrant further exploration.

Text from surveys. These are typically data entered in text boxes and open text fields in survey tools. While this is not one of the favoured methods within the qualitative methods community, I have found that it enables schools and researchers to make the most of a survey tool, and my own research has contended that 'addition of qualitative fields allowed this survey to be exploratory, enabling respondents to raise new issues potentially extending beyond the anticipated scope of responses as defined by the existing literature' (Merga 2016a, p. 16). Where qualitative data can be entered into a survey that also contains quantitative items, this is known as a 'single-tool, single-stage mixed-methods approach' (Merga, Malpique et al., 2021, p. 1141), which I will return to in the section on mixed methods. One possible use of qualitative items with text fields in surveys could include asking students who indicate that they do not enjoy silent reading at school to explain why this is the case in an open text field, enabling deeper probing of the issue, as well preserving the anonymity of respondents in a way not often available in qualitative approaches.

In addition, sometimes respondents can be frustrated with a survey when they expect to have the opportunity to share feedback related to their own experience, but the limitations of the survey do not allow them to do so. In previous research I did in the health professions, I added an item with an open text field that asked, 'Were there any other gaps not addressed in previous questions that could be addressed in pre-service training to improve your work-readiness? Please explain' (p. 16). If you are surveying your staff as part of your whole school reading culture evaluation, consider including these kinds of open text fields to provide an anonymous feedback mechanism for staff who may be otherwise reticent to share their views for whatever reason.

Interview data. This relates to data collected during interviews with respondents. The recording of interviews is typically done with digital voice or video recording technology. Devices specific to these recording purposes may be used, though the use of multifunctional devices, such as iPhones or other mobile phones can often be more than sufficient.

While there are many varied approaches that can be taken to interviewing within schools, interviews may typically be done using a *semi-structured* or *structured* interview tool if some continuity of questioning is desirable. Here is the difference between these two common options.

- **Structured tool**. Contains questions that are all predetermined and asked in order, so that there is uniformity in questioning.
- **Semi-structured tool**. There is a schedule of questions that can be put to respondents, and where responses raise a need to ask additional questions outside the tool, these tangents can be pursued. This approach is thus far more exploratory. Questions can also be asked out of order.

I've always preferred the second approach, as it allows the interviewer freedom while still ensuring the content has general relevance to the key inquiry underpinning the approach. For example, when interviewing students, I found that while the semi-structured interviews were supported by a uniform schedule, 'frequent departures occurred to allow the students' viewpoints to be foregrounded' (Merga, 2014c, p. 152). This gives respondents greater ownership over their contributions and frees them up to talk about relevant issues that sit outside or parallel to the structured questions.

Whichever approach is taken, interviews will typically be transcribed, with the text then analysed with reference to the audio or video data.

For example, you might conduct semi-structured interviews with parents about the perceived barriers to their support of building their child's reading engagement within the home.

Documents. Documents may be produced by educators, the school or other relevant entities, and analysed to give insights needed to justify the programme or during evaluation. To provide a simple and practical example, you might analyse lesson plans produced *before* the implementation of the whole school reading culture, and then compare these with those produced *during* implementation to uncover how the programme has influenced planning and pedagogy if this relates to your goals.

Student-produced drawings and interviews. Students create a drawing in reaction to a prompt, and are then interviewed to provide further feedback and explanation. For example, this could involve asking children in the early years of schooling to draw a picture of themselves reading. In interviews, these children can provide explanations of the elements that they have drawn, and you can ask them about the factors that can make them enjoy reading and support them to be comfortable during the reading process. This is an ideal method to use with very young children who are not able to write independently, but it is also a useful method to use with older children who might be more confident to speak about an issue where they have a drawing to help them to articulate their thoughts.

Student reading logs. As part of their participation in the whole school reading culture, students may create reading logs reflecting the reading that they have done, and providing insights into their reading experiences.

These logs can record quantitative data about student reading volume when produced in a spreadsheet form or other numerical form.

However, there may be greater power in the production of student reading logs that take a qualitative, rather than quantitative approach, such as when the reading log takes the form of a *visual diary*, which allows for visual and textual representation of reading experiences. While the same data on reading volume may not be as easily extrapolated from these works, they can speak to young people's changing perceptions of their experiences and provide key insights into their attitudes towards different works.

Why this can be beneficial, and what this can look like, was described by a teacher librarian in my earlier book:

> Requiring students to keep a record of their reading that can be made available for external review communicates an expectation that children develop and maintain a regular reading practice, and it can also provide both students and teacher librarians with an additional indicator about reading practices which can be used for the purposes of regulating or increasing these practices. In Liana's case, this also involved creating of an aesthetically appealing piece, examples of which were shown to me during the interview process.
>
> Liana described the creative way that this was enacted in her reading program:
>
> — we keep visual diaries as well. You know how when you read a book and you don't want to have to do something at the end of it? I really want them to just enjoy the book. But I also needed to record somehow what they were doing, which is why we have a reading log, but I also got them to do visual diaries so that they could record their reading journey, I guess. (Shows example). This is an example of one where . . . they can either do it visually, they can write, whatever floats their boat, really, about the books that they've read, what they thought about it, who they might recommend it to, all those sorts of things. So, it was just a record of their reading journey through school . . .
>
> Rather than write a dry summative paragraph, Liana encouraged her students to reflect on the book that they read using words or images of their choice, in as abstract or literal a form as desired, with high student control and choice. She also kept a reading journal herself which she was able to show the students as a model.
>
> (Merga, 2019d, pp. 116–117)

We might expect to see a change in students' attitudes towards reading for pleasure during the programme that could be reflected in students' visual and textual representations in such qualitative logs, an interesting way to allow students to give us rich insights into their experiences, and perhaps shifting perceptions.

Video recordings of activities. Videos are texts that can be subject to qualitative data analysis, and researchers have contended that video recording may be particularly useful for creating a multimodal record, and enabling this detailed data to be examined by multiple analysers, which can enhance 'reliability, trust and wealth in the production and analysis of empirical data' (Garcez et al., 2011, p. 259).

For example, if you wanted to evaluate increasing fidelity to best practice in reading aloud, videos of early implementation could be compared to videos of later implementation for evidence of improvement. Once data are collected, the subsequent process can involve 'watching, coding, and analysing the data, with the goal of transforming the video images into objective and verifiable information' (Jacobs et al., 1999, p. 718) that are useful to your school. I cover this coding in more detail in the upcoming section on thematic analysis.

While this could also involve quantitative data analysis where a lesson could be subject to a check-box audit to determine if a group of preconceived best-practice indicators for reading aloud are enacted, a qualitative exploratory approach can be taken. Children's reactions in forms not previously delimited can be drawn upon to gauge the effectiveness of the approach to reading aloud. Both quantitative and qualitative approaches could be explored concurrently as mixed methods.

Focus groups. These typically consist of a small group of participants led by a moderator, and focus on in-depth discussion of one key topic or issue:

> The term focus group refers to the role of the group members who are focused on a particular discussion topic. Certainly, such groups can provide you with information about people's opinions and feelings concerning the topic. But the real strength of focus groups is that you will also gain insight into their reasons for those opinions. In other words, you will understand the 'Why?' behind their responses.
>
> (Jayanthi & Nelson, 2002, p. 2)

For the purposes of evaluation of your programme, you might use a focus group at the outset to determine what form community stakeholder contributions might take, which might be subject to subsequent quantitative evaluation. Focus groups at the outset of the programme will have the added advantage of allowing the voice of key community stakeholders, thus encouraging early stakeholder ownership and buy-in.

Observation notes and feedback. In this context, observation notes and feedback relate to written descriptions of key aspects, such as activities or environments in education-related spaces.

For example, while recognisable barriers to implementation of whole school silent reading initiatives may be collected on a quantitative scale, unforeseen events that disrupt the activity (impacting upon fidelity of implementation) may be captured as qualitative data in the form of observation notes, which can offer much-needed insights into these impediments.

Teachers could be directed to record observation notes that could then be analysed to:

- mitigate these barriers,
- develop a richer and deeper understanding of what barriers can look like, and
- potentially expand future iterations of the quantitative scale.

Thematic analysis

The most common (though certainly not the only) approach to qualitative data analysis is thematic analysis, which can be approached in many different ways (e.g. Braun & Clarke, 2014). In very simple terms, thematic analysis will typically be an inductive process by which themes and patterns are identified in qualitative data through an iterative process of analysis.

Many researchers have defined and clearly articulated specific approaches that can be used to this end, so if you are intending to use thematic analysis to make meaning of your data sources during your evaluation, you will have a range of approaches to choose from.

For example, the implementing team at a school I worked with previously reviewed a number of approaches before deciding to follow a process outlined by Braun and Clarke (2006). In basic terms, this involves doing the following, as adapted from Clarke & Braun (2013):

- **Familiarisation with the data**: Read/listen to/view (as applicable) the data through many times and not just in transcription form if data have been transcribed. Jot down anything interesting that occurs to you at this stage.
- **Coding**: Start applying labels (codes) for important aspects of the data that have relevance to your goals and EQs that underpin your analysis. Collect relevant parts of the data which articulate these codes.

- **Look for themes**: Themes are

    a coherent and meaningful pattern in the data relevant to the research question. If codes are the bricks and tiles in a brick and tile house, then themes are the walls and roof panels. Searching for themes is a bit like coding your codes to identify similarity in the data. This 'searching' is an active process; themes are not hidden in the data waiting to be discovered by the intrepid researcher, rather the researcher constructs themes.

    (Clarke & Braun, 2013, p. 120)

    Bring together all of the coded data relevant to each of the themes.
- **Review the themes**: Once you have allocated your codes so that they sit under the umbrella of themes, check them again. On review, not all of your codes will work well with the themes they have been grouped under, which will see you creating new themes or splitting existing themes. You may also delete themes that are ultimately redundant, such as where they overlap with other themes and are not of sufficient interest on their own. Check that 'the themes tell a convincing and compelling story about the data, and begin to define the nature of each individual theme, and the relationship between the themes' (Clarke & Braun, 2013, p. 120).
- **Finalise themes**: Once you've finished the shuffling, rebranding and deleting process in the previous step, you are ready to write a detailed analysis of each theme. This might involve you asking yourself '"what story does this theme tell?" and "how does this theme fit into the overall story about the data?"), identifying the "essence" of each theme and constructing a concise, punchy and informative name for each theme' (Clarke & Braun, 2013, p. 120).
- **Reporting**: Write up your explanation of your findings, situating them within your overarching evaluation, and relating them back to your goals and EQs (as outlined previously in relation to Table 6). Your write-up will incorporate extracts from the data to inform the reader by constructing a cogent story about the data (Clarke & Braun, 2013) in relation to the driving purposes of your evaluation, allowing for the voices of your participants to be heard where applicable.

But what might this look like in practice? To give you a sense of what this might look like when applied by educators to research within schools, it was enacted as follows:

> The data were coded using Braun and Clarke's (2006) six-phase framework for thematic analysis. As a first step, a group of three of the authors read through the

data individually and developed initial codes for the first research question. The group then worked collaboratively to code the data. The researchers then worked to individually code the other two data sets. The group then collaboratively coded these data sets to ensure inter-coder reliability.

A list of all codes was then compiled for each research question on a whiteboard and the group worked collaboratively to group the codes into themes. The group then followed step 4 of Braun and Clarke's (2006) six-phase framework and re-read the data to ensure that the data matched the themes that had been developed.

The data analysis team conferred regularly with the academic mentor to clarify the process and seek her input on the process. The academic mentor did not take part in the coding process, nor did she offer any themes. This ensured that the generation of themes was iterative and inductive as the data analysis team were not as familiar with the research literature as the academic mentor and did not commence the analysis with preconceptions about the themes that could exist within the data.

(Collins et al., 2022, p. 93)

An unexpected side-effect of working on thematic analysis together could be building collegiality within the group, as negotiating and contesting the themes as part of the analytical process is a shared effort towards a common goal.

Conflict-of-interest and satisficing

Both qualitative and quantitative data will always be influenced to some extent by the person creating the data collection tools and analysing the data. At the more egregious end of the scale, this could be a school administrator who creates a survey about parent satisfaction with a whole school reading culture implemented within a school, only allowing for positive responses on the associated scales. There are many more subtle ways that conflict of interest can impact on data collection and analysis, and many of these can be unpremeditated.

Quantitative data can be just as problematic as qualitative data when it comes to conflict of interest. The idea that quantitative data are somehow more objectively truthful than qualitative data is not something that those of us who work commonly with quantitative data would always universally subscribe to. The questions asked on surveys, and the limited set of responses our respondents can select from, are too easily manipulated to meet sometimes very questionable organisational, government or industry needs.

While this reservation is noted, we should consider the unique issues related to conflict-of-interest, satisficing and data collection methods commonly used in qualitative analysis.

For example, when you are interviewing your own students who you are involved in the assessment of, and have a pre-existing and ongoing relationship with, the power imbalance cannot be ignored. The implications of the relationship on shaping how you ask the questions, and how the questions are understood, needs to be taken into account. This is particularly important if you want to collect data that are actually useful to you, and not simply a reflection of what students think you want to hear, and what will keep them safe and garner your approval to protect their relationship with you going forward.

Where possible, it's great to be able to have a staff member who is not the direct teacher of students handling any interviews with students. Again, students will need to be assured that their contributions will be protected, and will not be able to be ascertained through *deductive disclosure*, which is particularly pertinent in qualitative data collection and analysis (Kaiser, 2009). Put simply, avoiding deductive disclosure involves avoiding the publication or sharing of 'any data that was too specific to an individual case, and therefore could conceivably lead to identity being revealed' (Merga & Mason, 2021b, p. 309).

However, in some cases respondents might be a bit ambivalent about having their anonymity assured, as they sometimes wish to find themselves within the subsequent reporting of the data. Taking this into account, in my more recent projects where possible, I have allowed interview respondents to select their own pseudonyms so that they can track their voices easily in any outputs (e.g. Merga, 2019d; Merga & Mason, 2021b).

Dealing with subjectivity

Perhaps the biggest issue, given your relationship with your school, and your vested interest in seeing the success of your whole school reading culture, will be the subjectivity that you will inadvertently bring to data analysis.

In the previous example I gave of an inductive approach, I posed the scenario where interview data were collected, transcribed and analysed to determine staff professional development needs in relation to the implementation plan of the whole school reading culture. On one hand, your close knowledge of your school, the available resources and the staff in question is an asset, but on the other, your close proximity means that you may have already made assumptions about the likely findings, and you may read the data looking for confirmation of these assumptions, rather than with an open mind. You might have exploratory intent, but in reality, your approach might be confirmatory. Furthermore, as I have noted previously, 'given the tensions between conflict of interest, professional achievement, accountability and external expectations', evaluating your own whole school reading culture can be problematic (Merga, 2023b, p. 222), and where there is greater scope for subjectivity in analysis, as in the case of the use of qualitative methods, these issues may get in the way of making the most of your data.

However, there are things you can do in order to minimise some of these risks. While again there is a wealth of literature in this area, it is typically designed to meet the rigour demanded by academic research to secure peer-reviewed publication. Though there are many approaches that can be taken, here are two simple and practical steps you can take to enhance the trustworthiness of your qualitative processes:

1 **Independent parallel coding**. Where resources permit, while you're coding the data, have someone (or multiple others) also go through the process without seeing what you come up with. Compare the two (or multiple) and negotiate to create a combined set of codes that you all agree on (Thomas, 2006). I have done this in the past, such as in analysis of the content of school newsletters, where 'two coders independently coded the responses, and then discussed discrepancies, negotiating modifications until a final dataset was created' (Merga & Hu, 2016, p. 78), and it is a really interesting, eye-opening process that helps you to understand the limitations of your own worldview and subjective understanding.

2 **Stakeholder checks**. Qualitative data is not always accurately construed. Some of the biggest issues in using qualitative data are that:

   a. respondents do not always clearly communicate
   b. researchers misunderstand what they have been told, or what they have seen or heard
   c. technology malfunctions or underperforms, impacting on data quality and retention
   d. the time lapse between data collection and analysis can mean that important contextual factors that shaped meaning may be forgotten if not recorded at the time of data collection
   e. in the heat of the moment, such as in an interview or focus group, respondents may say things that in retrospect they wish to step back from, sometimes because they are not completely truthful or accurate representations.

Stakeholder checking can be a boon for the trustworthiness of your research as they

> enhance the credibility of findings by allowing participants and other people who may have specific interests in the evaluation to comment on or assess the research findings, interpretations, and conclusions. Such checks may be important in establishing the credibility of the findings. For example, participants in the settings studied are given a chance to comment on whether the categories and outcomes described in the findings relate to their personal experiences. Stakeholder checks may be carried out on the initial documents (e.g. interview transcriptions and summaries) and on the data interpretations and findings.
> (Thomas, 2006, p. 244)

For example, when we did a study involving the interviewing of 30 early-career academics in Australia and Japan, 'interviewees were offered the opportunity to review the transcripts and redact or add content prior to analysis', and 'two respondents (one Australia based, one Japan based) availed themselves of this opportunity' (Merga & Mason, 2021a, p. 2).

Resourcing

On a pragmatic level, it is important to note that qualitative analysis and data collection are best managed as a group rather than by an individual, and not just for the issues raised in relation to dealing with subjectivity. If you are in the rare position of 'soloing' your evaluation, you need to be aware that building in a qualitative component to your process will involve a significant investment of time that may be untenable for one person.

The fact that it can be incredibly time consuming to collect, transcribe and analyse qualitative data could be why some schools seem to underutilise qualitative data in evaluation processes. This noted, aspects from the relatively recent innovation of 'rapid' approaches to qualitative data collection and analysis could be drawn on to minimise resourcing commitments 'to speed up data collection and analysis', though teams are still typically needed to ensure the rigour and success of such approaches, and many of these approaches have not been comprehensively evaluated (Vindrola-Padros & Johnson, 2020, p. 1596).

When deciding which kinds of data to collect, you need to take into account what is feasible both in the short and longer term. When data are not in a textual form and transcription is desirable, despite advances in dictation technology, this can be time consuming to ensure accuracy if undertaken by staff. This can be outsourced to a transcription service if adequate funds exist.

However, you will need to ensure that confidentiality is respected, so a professional service needs to be employed that includes such confidentiality clauses in their contracts.

Mixed-methods analysis and data for schools

As you've probably gleaned by this point, I honestly feel that, in most cases, evaluation in schools will be best achieved using a mixed-methods approach. This will allow you to get the best of both worlds and present a rich and detailed picture of how the implementation of a whole school reading culture has transformed your school, advancing a potentially diverse array of goals relevant to stakeholders both within and beyond your school. I just really love using mixed methods because the approach is pragmatic and makes sense, especially where one method helps you to balance out the limitations of the other, as I've touched on previously.

The mixed-methods approach is defined in many different ways, but for our purposes it can be simplistically conceptualised as where quantitative data and qualitative data are both drawn upon, and analysed, for the purposes of enhancing understanding of the impact of the implementation of a whole school reading culture. In this instance, both qualitative and quantitative methods of analysis are utilised and thoughtfully integrated (e.g. Creswell & Plano Clark, 2018).

To this end, the mixed-methods approach involves more than lumping together two different approaches. For example,

> the qualitative data can be used to assess the validity of quantitative findings. Quantitative data can also be used to help generate the qualitative sample or explain findings from the qualitative data. Qualitative inquiry can inform development or refinement of quantitative instruments or interventions, or generate hypotheses in the qualitative component for testing in the quantitative component.
> (Fetters et al., 2013, p. 2135)

Qualitative and quantitative methods can bring out the best in each other when used judiciously and in ways that are complementary. Meaningful integration across methods may be the key to making mixed methods work effectively for you, and I'll return to this point in detail subsequently.

Perhaps the most powerful reason to use a mixed-methods approach is the opportunity to use qualitative data analysis to *explain* quantitative findings. But what does this look like in practice?

For example, let's imagine that improving young people's attitudes towards reading books for pleasure is one of your goals. To measure your attainment of this goal, during the process of evaluation, you survey students to capture changes in their attitudes towards reading as measured on Likert-type scales, as explained previously.

Strangely, when you look at how these quantitative data change from baseline results, there is strong improvement across all classrooms when compared to the baseline, apart from one classroom where there is no significant shift at all. You can stare at these numbers until the cows come home and they will tell you nothing about the reasons for this apparent discrepancy.

Luckily, you have knowledge of mixed methods that you can use to your advantage. You decide to follow up this quantitative data collection and analysis phase with a qualitative phase to try to find out what was going on. You interview students from this classroom about their experiences in silent reading, and you discover that the broken air-conditioning unit in the classroom meant that many students literally fell asleep during silent reading time due to the warm and stuffy conditions, so their attitude towards the practice didn't change.

Without adding a qualitative component to explain the quantitative results, you would never have known about the impact of this resourcing issue on students' reading attitudes, and you would not have had the data you needed to advocate for repairs to the air-conditioning unit in this classroom. Both kinds of data collection and analysis can be built in to complement each other, or they can be adopted as the evaluation progresses where feasible in response to the unique needs of your school. In the next section, I will look at pre-planning for mixed methods in relation to stages and designs.

Stages and designs

When deciding to adopt a mixed-methods approach to evaluation in your school, you need to think about how this will look in terms of sequencing and design to maximise the value of the approach. Qualitative and quantitative approaches can be adopted simultaneously, such as through the use of a 'single-tool, single-stage mixed-methods approach' (Merga, Malpique et al., 2021, p. 1141). They may also be used in *stages*. For example, 'qualitative research can be used to generate new questions and theories, which are then tested through quantitative means, and later revised or expanded through further qualitative study' (Jacobs et al., 1999, p. 718).

How might this be applied to the project of evaluation of a whole school reading culture?

For example, you might specifically seek to mitigate barriers to parent support of their child's reading engagement in the home. Qualitative methods could be used to develop quantitative methods, and then we return to a qualitative approach to better understand quantitative findings (Creswell & Plano Clark, 2018). This may work as follows.

- In Stage 1 (qualitative), a focus group with a diverse set of parents might seek to encourage robust discussion and capture recurring barriers to inform a set of interventions designed to optimise parental participation in building children's reading engagement.
- In Stage 2, a survey (primarily quantitative) might seek to determine if interventions established by the school to minimise the barriers identified in Stage 1 were successful or not by measuring parent agreement with items seeking to determine if the school had enhanced their capacity in these areas.
- In Stage 3 (qualitative), interviews with parents who provided negative responses to the survey may be undertaken to find out how the school can do a better job of addressing the barriers going forward.

As you can see, both qualitative and quantitative approaches inform each other in this instance.

As another example, let's say that as part of your implementation of a whole school reading culture you made a substantial investment in refurbishing and resourcing your school library. You then need to determine if this investment yielded positive outcomes to secure ongoing funding injections and demonstrate accountability and value for money.

While there are many potential ways of capturing the impact of this investment, you might potentially draw on a *convergent design* to capture students' perceptions of the value added by the changes you've implemented. As implied by the name, a convergent design 'occurs when the researcher intends to bring together the results of the quantitative and qualitative data analysis so they can be compared or combined', and this is desirable where you are looking for a more comprehensive understanding of the impact of a facet of your evaluation, and 'to validate one set of findings with the other' (Creswell & Plano Clark, 2018, p. 65). In this case, you might collect and analyse survey data on students' perceptions of the value added by the changes you've implemented in your school library, also collecting and analysing data from student interviews on the same topic. Findings are then merged, compared and interpreted (Creswell & Plano Clark, 2018).

Clearly, both these approaches make sense and are responsive to real-world scenarios and needs, and the methods of collecting data associated with a stage or stages complement each other, while serving a unique individual purpose. Mixed-methods approaches are very practical and can be ideal where there is time and resourcing available to make the most of them, and where their strengths and limitations are well-understood. You can literally use any design that suits your purposes once you understand the strengths and limitations of qualitative and quantitative approaches.

Integration. As briefly aforementioned, in mixed-methods approaches, integration is key. While mixed methods is often seen simplistically as some kind of blending or co-occurrence of quantitative and qualitative methods, in the research community, there is considerable stress on the importance of *integration* between quantitative and qualitative methods. There are whole books written on integration in mixed methods (e.g. Creamer, 2018); however, for your purpose we can understand integration as relating to 'the explicit conversation between (or interrelating of) the quantitative and qualitative components' of a mixed-methods investigation or evaluation (Plano Clark, 2019, p. 108). Clearly, this has relevance beyond academia for evaluation undertaken in schools, as it is another way of considering how these methods are strengthened together, rather than consistently presenting them as separate.

One way of showing this integration is through the use of a *joint display*:

> When integrating through joint displays, researchers integrate the data by bringing the data together through a visual means to draw out new insights beyond the information gained from the separate quantitative and qualitative results. This can occur through organizing related data in a figure, table, matrix, or graph.
>
> (Fetters et al., 2013, p. 2143)

I have often used joint displays in my work as they enable qualitative and quantitative data to be presented in ways that explain each other.

For example, in Table 7, I include a joint display that we created and published in our previous research. In this instance, we wanted to explore whether it is easy for secondary English teachers in the mainstream classroom to find time to support struggling literacy learners, and in terms of design, we used a single-stage, mixed-methods survey tool to collect both quantitative and qualitative data that would enable us to investigate this in some detail. We chose this approach as while quantitative data could tell us how many people agreed that it is easy to find time to support struggling literacy learners, we also needed qualitative questions that enabled our respondents to explain the reasons behind their response.

As you can see, Table 7 includes the quantitative findings, and the analysis of qualitative findings into themes using a similar method to the thematic analysis described earlier in this book. Finally, we presented a text example of each theme. I hope you find that the text examples in Table 7 provide interesting illustrative insight into the themes. Personally, I also like how the text examples remind the reader of the actual humans behind the data, which can be important in triggering an appropriate response where data indicate a need for change. Joint displays can take many forms, but I have personally used a similar structure with relative consistency across my work because I find that it works for me.

While Table 7 shows an example from a research paper, how might you use a joint display in the evaluation of a whole school reading culture?

While this can include data on the same topic from any number of stages, let's imagine that you want your evaluation to include data from a single-stage mixed-methods survey tool administered to students eight months after the implementation of a whole school reading culture. You've asked students if their participation in a whole school reading culture has influenced their enjoyment of reading on a five-point scale, as in Item A.

Item A: How has the new whole school reading culture changed your enjoyment of reading?

1 Strong positive change (you enjoy reading a lot more)
2 Slight positive change (you enjoy reading a bit more)
3 No influence (no change)
4 Slight negative change (you enjoy reading a bit less)
5 Strong negative change (you enjoy reading a lot less)

Whatever the results on this item, you will definitely want greater insight into the responses than what can be captured on a 5-point scale. However, the questions you might ask the positive respondents might be different to what you would ask the negative respondents. Given the limitations of a survey, how can you get more information?

With modern survey platforms, it's easy to use the aforementioned skip logics to direct the respondents to appropriate qualitative data fields with targeted questioning. While you can't be as responsive as you would be asking questions in person, this approach at least allows for some basic differentiation.

How would this work?

Students who choose 1 or 2 (positive responses) will be directed by skip logics in the survey (revisit the section *scales and survey items* if you've forgotten what skip logics are) to Item B.

Item B: What parts of the new whole school reading culture made you enjoy reading more? Please write your ideas in the box below.

Table 7 *Joint display of reasons for agreement/disagreement on sufficient time*

Agreement	in sample (%)	Theme	Text example
Agreement (strong/somewhat)	8.88	Group work	'Group work with rotation'
		One-to-one support	'Have plenty of allocated time to help them specifically'
		Scaffolding	'Scaffolding and chunking to assist all year levels'
		Support staff	'Student support teachers, counsellors, Indigenous support teachers'
Disagreement (strong/somewhat)	86.35	Administrative demands	'Documentation procedures and demands at the College severely limit time to focus on teaching practice and mastery'
		Behaviour management	'Poor behaviour means I can rarely support students on an individual basis'
		Class size and individual support	'Class size – regardless of 'expert' opinions, class size DOES matter, that is, the smaller the class, the easier it is to individually attend to learning issues in the classroom'
		Competing demands	'Abandoning the flock for the lost sheep – difficult to balance how much focus to give them so that it is not at the expense of the majority who are more capable'
		Curriculum	'Pressures of the curriculum. By the time students are in the senior years of secondary school there is very little time to spend on developing literacy skills. The focus has to be on getting through the course which means that many struggle to meet requirements'
		Extent of differentiation needed	'Despite differentiating learning it can be very difficult to meet all the needs of the struggling learners in a class with such diversity. I have one class with two students with reading ages three or more years below their age with a student doing extended studies at a college level'
		Knowledge and training	'Often my colleagues and I don't feel supported in identifying and addressing all literacy problems due to our training being so limited'
		School support	'I'm flat out planning lessons without differentiating across seven achievement levels. And it's all on me to do it, no support from the school'
		Resourcing	'For students that need proper targeted intervention, a lack of resources is the main issue'
		Support staff	'Often it is due to a lack of support staff as I have low level classes and many students with disabilities/learning disabilities and no additional support. I can be in a room with 29 kids and I sit one-on-one with kids who need the support, and I look over at the others who need support, and I just can't be in two places at once. So lack of support staff (which I think stems from lack of funding)'

(Merga, Mat Roni et al., 2021a, p. 358)

Students who choose 4 or 5 (negative responses) will skip this section and be directed by skip logics to Item C.

Item C: What parts of the new whole school reading culture made you enjoy reading less? Please write your ideas in the box below.

Once you've collected the data from Item A and cleaned your data set, and you have analysed the data from Items B and C to find your themes (with supporting examples from the text), you are ready to report your findings in a joint display. See Table 8 for one way this could look.

Table 8 *Joint display of influence of whole school reading culture implementation on students' enjoyment of reading*

Enjoyment	in sample (%)	Theme*	Text example
Increased (enjoys reading more)	#	Theme 1 Theme 2 Theme 3 Theme 4	'Text example' 'Text example' 'Text example' 'Text example'
Neutral (no change)	#	Theme 1 Theme 2 Theme 3 Theme 4	'Text example' 'Text example' 'Text example' 'Text example'
Decreased (enjoys reading less)	#	Theme 1 Theme 2 Theme 3 Theme 4	'Text example' 'Text example' 'Text example' 'Text example'

*you may have many more or fewer themes than indicated in this example; I've just selected four as an arbitrary number for the purposes of providing an example.

Determining baseline data needs and evaluation planning

Now that you know what some of your possible choices are when it comes to data collection and analysis, you can lock in your planning for evaluation, deciding on your data sources and related analysis. You might want to finalise this in an evaluation plan, which may overlap in some places with your implementation planning, as will become obvious herein.

What are some things to include in evaluation planning?

- **Goals.** These are the goals that already feature in your implementation planning (see previous section for more about goals). For example, increasing students' enjoyment of reading for pleasure.
- **Activities.** These are the actual ways that you are going to measure attainment of your goals. For example, you might undertake a mixed-methods survey with students. Specify the kinds of data (qualitative, quantitative, mixed methods), kinds of activities and related tool(s), and

who the respondents are. You may have multiple activities associated with a goal.
- **Proposed analysis of activity**. This should include your proposed analysis and integration (if applicable). For example, you might state quantitative data (basic), or qualitative data (thematic analysis).
- **Intervals of activity**. For example, baseline, midpoint and end of year are common intervals used for activities in schools. If data are collected at a single collection only, such as after a seminar or single-session intervention, you would specify single collection (midpoint) or whatever is applicable. If data from multiple activities are going to be integrated, this would be specified here. If there is a key event triggering the data collection, this would also be noted here.
- **Leader(s) of activity**. As you no doubt already know from experience, allocating accountabilities helps to get things done. Who is in charge of each activity? The importance of distributed leadership was already covered earlier in this book, and the higher accountability associated with evaluation provides a great opportunity for different team members to step up and take responsibility. If you want to, you can specify team members and responsibilities here too. For example, if the person leading the activity is different from the person leading the reporting of the activity, this distinction may be useful.
- **Resources needed for activity**. This is where you add any transcription costs, survey platform licensing costs, access tools, costs to visit and run a focus group with external stakeholders, which might include items like pizza if you are providing catering and making a party of it! Resources will widely vary depending on what you do.
- **Reporting form(s) and date(s) for activity**. Decide how you'll show the results of your evaluation, and when this will happen. I cover reporting in the next chapter, so don't worry if you're not sure how you want to approach this at this stage. Also include the purpose of the reporting if necessary.

How might this look in action?

Table 9 on the next page covers how one goal might be addressed in terms of evaluation. For the purposes of this example, I have randomly chosen to focus on a *parent engagement goal* articulated earlier in this book: seeing an increase in parents' self-reported encouragement of children's reading at home.

Table 9 Possible headings for evaluation planning in Year 1 of implementation

Goals	Activities	Proposed analysis of activity	Intervals of activity	Leader(s) of activity	Resources needed for activity	Reporting form(s) and date(s) for activity
Increasing parents' self-reported encouragement of children's reading at home.	Hold a focus group with a diverse set of parents (qualitative) to identify current practices, training needs and barriers to the encouragement of children's reading at home.	Thematic analysis.	Baseline (two weeks prior to parent information night).	Nam Haeng-seon and Tom Hiddleston.	Coffee and tea, cakes and biscuits, water and serviettes, voice recorder (x2) and batteries, consent to participate form, external transcription fee.	- To the reading culture team and then the leadership team prior to the parent information night in (report) - On parent information night to show parents that parent education seminar planned in responses to these data are end-user indicated (presentation) - In the final evaluation report - Brief summation in the school newsletter
	Short paper feedback forms (mixed methods) to evaluate the success of parent education seminars in building parents' capacity to encourage children to read within the home.	Thematic analysis (qualitative), basic analysis (quantitative).	After each parent education seminar.	Robert Galbraith.	Printouts of paper forms and pencils.	- To the reading culture team and then the leadership team after each parent education seminar - In the final evaluation report - Brief summation in the school newsletter
	Survey parents about their confidence in and knowledge of applying best-practice strategies for supporting reading for pleasure in the home, using a mixed-methods survey tool.	Thematic analysis (qualitative), basic analysis, compare baseline with end of year data (quantitative).	Baseline, and end of year.	Tana French and Dylan Wang.	Survey platform licence fee, paper copies of the survey available on request.	- To the reading culture team and then the leadership team - In the final evaluation report - Brief summation in the school newsletter

Whichever approach you take, I want to reiterate that piloting your data collection tools is absolutely essential, particularly where you are using surveys. Make sure you always build this into your planning. This two-step process will help you to capture any issues prior to implementation:

1. As previously covered, you should check your tools with a small but diverse group of participants of the same demographic as your targeted recipients to check that any questions, scales or features are understood as you intended them to be (Mat Roni et al., 2020). You will need to sit in with these respondents and ask them questions during this process.
2. Run the pilot with a small group of participants of the same demographic as your targeted recipients using the same conditions under which you are intending to implement the tool. You will need to be hands-off for this part, which is particularly important if you will be absent during the survey delivery process.

Boosting quality with academic partnership

In many cases, the implementation of a whole school reading culture will be solely motivated by the needs of the school. However, I know from experience that, in some cases, programme implementation is also aligned with strategic individual goals of the leader and/or team members.

As such, there is a chance that the person reading this book may be hoping to use the programme as a platform or stepping stone to achieve *individual* vocational or academic goals, while also acting in the interests of their schools. These might include (but are not limited to) launching a whole school reading culture:

- as part of a higher degree by research (HDR) e.g. Honours, Masters, EdD or PhD,
- to constitute submission materials for an internal promotional opportunity, and/or
- to raise their profile beyond their immediate school community, perhaps to seek external employment opportunities.

For example, in the past, I have worked with schools where members of the school community intended to go on to do an HDR. They also wanted to increase their opportunities for dissemination to increase recognition of the programme, to propitiate school leadership and potentially enhance local enrolments by promoting quality and innovation within the learning environment. They were looking to promote their programme beyond the school, and produce high-quality reporting materials, such as peer-reviewed publications, to increase the chances of being accepted into an HDR programme. I have also worked with schools where members needed to report on in-school research initiatives as part of promotional opportunities, and schools where the production of *research* outputs was tied to promises for dissemination that were made when the school won external funding to support the implementation of the programme.

If you are involved in launching this programme as part of an HDR, you will already be in an academic partnership via your supervisory team and institution. However, sometimes those who are *not* doing an HDR may seek to adopt the extra rigour afforded by these relationships due to their own goals, particularly where high-level opportunities for dissemination are desirable.

If you are not currently completing an HDR and some of these reasons have potential relevance for you, read on, but if none of them resonate with you, feel free to skip this section. I do want to stress that you do not *need* an academic partnership, unless you and/or team members have specific professional or related academic goals that would be advanced by such a partnership. Working with academics may offer benefits, but can also entail challenges and pitfalls and make the processes lengthy, as you must meet institutional ethics requirements and sometimes dramatically upskill in your research knowledge.

Fostering an academic partnership is not something that should be just added lightly, without understanding what this is going to mean in terms of time and resourcing commitments. As I have covered previously, in my extensive research on research communications (e.g. Merga, Mason et al., 2018), working with an academic partner on producing outputs for academic and professional audiences can be incredibly challenging, and to meet the high-level of rigour demanded to move successfully through peer review, partnership with an academic who has *demonstrated capacity* to negotiate these tricky spaces may offer value.

Some of the pros of working with an academic partner can also be cons.

Methods and theories. Working with an academic partner can help you to fine-tune your understanding of some of the research methods outlined in this book, and also work with methods at a higher level of rigour than typically needed for school-based evaluation or research done for the internal purposes of a school. Your methodological choices will also need to be underpinned by theory (and I don't go into theory in this book), and if you lack a strong and recent background in educational theory, this knowledge can be challenging to acquire. If you don't need this extra level of rigour, it may be a waste of time and resources to apply it.

Ethics. To be able to publish any research that involves collecting data from humans, your work will need to go through a rigorous ethics approval process, which can take months and numerous iterations of revisions. You may be forced to make substantial revisions to your plans that can result in collection of data that is less useful for the school. While this process will enhance your capacity to share your research findings, and be a valuable learning experience if you are hoping to move into a research role, broadly, the requirements to meet institutional-level ethics approvals may impose counterproductive limitations on creating your whole school reading culture.

Tools. Working with an academic partner can give you access to analytical tools and software that you would otherwise need to pay substantial sums in order to license. However, at the end of the partnership period, you may lose access to these tools, and you may even lose access to the data, if it is being stored on a survey platform that your school does not have ongoing access to. Not all universities have a university-wide licence to high-quality tools, and there can be differences in access levels both across universities, and at faculty, department and school levels (as applicable) within them.

Ownership. Once you enter into an agreement with an academic partner, ownership of the data that you co-create does not necessarily lie with you anymore. You will need to make sure that your school has the final say on any external publication of the data, and any external uses of the data, and that the data remains the intellectual property of the school as far as possible in your negotiations with an academic partner.

A different approach. Your academic partner, if carefully selected, should have a wealth of expertise to contribute to your school. You will be able to use this expertise to build your own knowledge and understanding of identified areas. However, academics come from a different world, which privileges different things. This means your priorities will not be the same, and you will need to communicate effectively to get onto the same page.

Time and workload. While working with an academic partner may help save time in areas, such as analysis, any such benefits are likely to be offset by the significant amount of time needed for the proposed approach to move through ethics approvals. While academics will enter into partnership with you in good faith in most cases, they are incredibly vulnerable to changes in their workload, such as the burgeoning administrative requirements they grapple with in modern institutions (e.g. Miller, 2019). Many will be also constantly in the process of sourcing external funds, and somewhat unanticipated and unpredictable grant success can cut into their time.

It is important to note that not all academics have the same capacity to mentor schools through these often contentious and challenging processes. If you have decided that you want to work with an academic partner, do a bit of due diligence and come up with a shortlist, considering the following.

What are your mentoring needs?

It's important to take the time to closely consider exactly what you are looking for in the partnership before you look for an academic partner. While your position may change, as you enter into discussions with prospective academic partners and learn more about what they can bring to your programme, it's important to have some idea of the strengths you are looking for that align with current knowledge and skill gaps.

Ask yourself whichever of these questions are applicable:

- What is the specialist knowledge base we need them to bring?
- What is the specialist skillset we need them to impart?
- What are the specific research tools we need support with designing?
- What are the specific outputs we need help with creating?

Who are the possible partners?

Once you have identified your mentoring needs, you will be looking for a partner who is:

- **Relevant.** Their areas of expertise need to align well with your areas of need.
- **Feasible.** Determine how much you are willing to financially invest in the academic partnership. Very few academics will be able to enter into a partnership with your school without some kind of remuneration, whether it be cash or in-kind. An example of an in-kind contribution can be agreeing to co-author papers on the data, which can help them to build their publication track record, though very few senior academics will be able to justify entering into a relationship with schools on these terms only, and they are required to constantly justify their workload decisions. Ideally, you will be able to invest some funds to support consultancy in addition to in-kind agreements. Do you have funds to bring someone over from another region or country? If not, you need to find someone local, so look at the staffing profiles of universities or colleges in your area.
- **Available.** The most amazing person in your areas of need may be a high flyer with no spare time. An academic juggling a lot of grants and a lot of publications is unlikely to have time to work with you in a sustained manner, so you can still approach them, but be realistic in your expectations.
- **Accessible.** They will need to be able to communicate complex ideas and foster new skills in accessible ways, and they will need to listen to you.

They need to be able to communicate effectively, persuasively and responsively. If it takes more than a week to hear back from them, they are unlikely to be the right partner.

Do they have a strong track record in peer-reviewed publication?

This is only very relevant if one of the major reasons that you are working with an academic partner is to support you to disseminate your work to both academic and professional audiences. If this is relevant to you, you will need to check that your prospective partner knows how to do this. If this is not one of your needs, you can be less concerned with the publication expertise indicators that I discuss herein.

In my experience, length of academic career is not a good indicator of expertise in publication. This may sound bizarre and counterintuitive, but the reality is that many university professors have had long careers with minimal publications, though the neoliberal forces driving promotion opportunities mean that the younger generations of academics may lack the same possibilities for academic ascent without a strong track record in publishing (as explored further in Merga, Mat Roni et al., 2020).

So who has a good track record in publishing? Go to the research profiles of possible candidates. Google Scholar isn't always well-curated, and there are other issues with its accuracy (some of which are surprisingly funny; see Merga, Mat Roni et al., 2020 for further details, and for more about how Google Scholar works), but it's an okay place to start due to a lack of a strong alternative. You need to consider the following indicators.

- **Frequent and recent.** You're looking for someone who publishes peer-reviewed articles or books on a relatively regular basis, so look at the publication years. If they haven't published anything for several years, they may no longer be particularly research active.
- **Quality.** Google Scholar is not limited to *peer-reviewed* academic outputs, so if you want your mentor to be able to guide you through the process of publishing in this space, you need to check that they have some experience of leading publications in quality peer-reviewed journals. One way to check this is to enter the journal name into Scimago Journal and Country rank here: https://www.scimagojr.com.
If none or very few of the journals where your prospective mentor has published are listed, this would be a red flag for me, as it could mean that they are only publishing with poorly recognised outlets which may have lower publication standards, or even be predatory publications (if

you want to learn more about this, you can read an article such as Perlin et al., 2018 for an overview of predatory publications).
- **Leader as well as passenger.** There are some academics who are primarily passengers in the research publication journey, very rarely doing the bulk of the work on a paper, but often getting their name tacked onto the end or near end of the listed order of authors thanks to their seniority and by adding what is sometimes a very small contribution to a paper. You want someone who has led some of this research, and who has done the bulk of the labour on at least some of their publications. They should be the first-named author of the listed order of authors on at least some of their publications. If they are never the first author, and always near the end of the author list, and they have been working for many years, they are possibly a passenger rather than an innovator. It's important not to judge junior academics by the same standards, as they are sometimes relegated down the author order listings even though they have made substantial contributions, due to exploitation within academia (e.g. Macfarlane, 2017).
- **Relevant in the real world.** If all of the outputs that you discover relate to deeply theoretical, niche and abstract areas that are in the fields you need, but you struggle to see how the findings contribute to real-world practice in schools, this might not be the right person for you.

Do they work well with schools?

Just because an academic is a prolific researcher, this does not necessarily mean that they will work effectively with schools, and that they will even be interested in working with you. You'll be looking for someone who is a good listener, and who does not just assert their expertise without closely considering what *your needs* are. This is where word-of-mouth comes in handy. When you see that other schools have had a really supportive and effective academic partnership, you might wish to reach out and engage this person, or get recommendations from this person if they are not personally available.

Involving external parties in evaluation

While you do not necessarily need an academic partnership at all, one place where it may be particularly useful would be for evaluation. As I have explored elsewhere, 'given the tensions between conflict of interest, professional achievement, accountability and external expectations', evaluating your own whole school reading culture can be problematic, particularly if you want to externally promote what you've achieved (Merga, 2023b, p. 222). Again, you do not need to involve external parties in evaluation unless you want to position independent evaluation as a key selling point in relation to the rigour of your project when you promote it in external spaces, given that 'being able to say that it has been externally evaluated and found to have delivered student benefit will confer credibility', and 'the consultant may also be able to spot something in the data that was hidden from you due to your close proximity' (p. 223) with both the establishment of a whole school reading culture and your school.

If you engage a consultant or academic partner to facilitate evaluation, you will ideally need to reach out to them before implementation so that they can maintain a (relatively) independent and stringent approach, and you can agree on the approach to evaluation and the timeline for evaluation activities, analysis and reporting. In many schools, *the additional expense will not be warranted*, so you do not necessarily need to do this at all! It all depends on what you are planning to do with your programme.

6
Reporting

Reporting can be a very satisfying opportunity to reflect on and showcase what you have achieved as a school.

You put in the time and effort to implement a whole school reading culture, and the school's achievements should be celebrated. You will need to ensure that your stakeholders remain abreast of what you have achieved, so you will be reporting to diverse audiences. To this end, this chapter is primarily concerned with determining avenues and audiences for reporting for impact across the project, with the argument for the importance of early stakeholder communication already articulated in Chapter 3. I will not be going into detail on internal reporting, because every educator has some knowledge of reporting to the 'usual' parties (e.g. school leadership). I'm sure you will establish and maintain reporting to these stakeholders without needing any guidance from me.

Instead, I focus on external reporting, and encourage you to consider how you might expand the scope of your reporting so that what you achieved, and how you achieved it, can contribute to the body of knowledge related to creating a whole school reading culture beyond your immediate school community. I know that this may push some of you outside your comfort zones, but it is definitely worth considering, for the reasons I will delve into in-depth herein.

Ethical reporting

Before we look at different mechanisms for reporting, we need to place the need for ethical reporting front and centre. We need to ensure that our reporting does no harm, particularly given that research conducted in schools, by schools, does not typically collect student consent for participation.

The first priority in reporting is to adhere to ethical standards. We can do this by considering the following.

Remove identifying information before reporting

Where students have contributed their thoughts, experiences and views, we have an obligation to protect this contribution from being associated with them, particularly when accessible by external parties, and where there could be foreseeable negative consequences for these participants. Research suggests that 'children and adolescents are most willing to participate in research when they feel safe' (Crane & Broome, 2017, p. 205), and removing identifying information before reporting is one way that protection from exposure to external scrutiny for individual participants can be managed. This may involve using pseudonyms or 'blinding' the work by adding (student's name) in parentheses. Pseudonyms are definitely preferred for readability.

There is a flip side to this. As noted earlier in the book, students might not want to be invisible in the findings, and in particular, they might want to track what you do with their lengthy contributions in qualitative data collections such as interviews. You can allow students to select their own pseudonyms so that they can track their voices easily if feasible.

You might expect this to be standard, but while collecting data for my recent book, I found data of named students that should not have been available. In this egregious example that I encountered when collecting data on whole school literacy policies, a school in the UK had (hopefully mistakenly) externally published

> a policy that identified (by name) twelve underachieving children ... along with their literacy scores and comments on their learning trajectory. While the included data is important internal information to support communication around student achievement, as a complete stranger outside the school, I should not be able to access specific literacy scores of named students from the UK. This information should never be made publicly available.
>
> (Merga, 2023b, p. 178)

It is important to note that simply using pseudonyms is not sufficient to protect your contributors. Closely read the data as it is presented in the report, and consider if it is easy to use basic deduction to figure out the contributions of certain students, such as where you reference the contribution of a student in relation to their cultural background in a way that can be identifying. As aforementioned, when it is possible to accurately guess which student contributed data this is referred to as *deductive disclosure*, so you need to consider both explicit and tacit identifying of students in your reporting.

Use students' images with care

Using students' images can be very appealing during reporting, as they can help to ground the story you are telling in reporting in context, and show students engaged in the behaviours that your whole school reading programme sought to promote. However, if you do this, you need to make sure that you are operating within the constraints of relevant privacy laws in your region, as well as considering other ethical principles as outlined further herein.

Different regions have differing laws that must be considered when it comes to schools' use of students' images. For example, in Australia, privacy laws dictate practice as follows.

> There are Commonwealth privacy laws relevant to the unauthorised production and publication of a person's image through the *Privacy Act 1988* (Cth). These laws regulate the publication of personal information that conveys the identity of a person or allows their identity to be determined. Under the *Privacy Act 1988* (Cth) section 6, 'personal information' refers to:
>
> > Information or an opinion (including information or an opinion forming part of a database), whether true or not, and whether recorded in a material form or not, about an individual whose identity is apparent, or can reasonably be ascertained, from the information or opinion.
>
> This means images of children that would enable them to be identified – for example, in a school uniform, outside their house, or showing their name – should not be published on the Internet without the consent of both the child and their parent or guardian. Establishing protocols for obtaining parental/guardian and child consent is good practice regardless of whether or not images contain identifying information about the child or young person.
>
> (Australian Institute of Family Studies, 2015, para. 6)

Similar laws exist in the UK:

> Data protection law is likely to apply if photos or videos are taken for official school use, such as for inclusion in a prospectus or other promotional material. Pupils or a parent or guardian, depending on the pupil's age, must be informed how the photos or videos will be used.
> Data protection law doesn't specify an age at which a child is considered capable to exercise their own rights, although 12 years old is typically given as a guideline. However, this should be considered on a case-by-case basis.
> The school will also need to have a valid reason to publish photos or videos.

> These are referred to in data protection law as 'lawful bases'.
>
> Consent offers one possible lawful basis that allows an organisation to use your personal data. However, it will not be appropriate to rely on consent in all circumstances and another lawful basis could instead be relevant. The school should explain which lawful basis they are relying on at the outset, so that pupils and their parent or guardian know what to expect.
>
> Regardless of the lawful basis relied upon, we recommend that the school allows pupils the opportunity to opt-out from their image being used.
>
> (Information Commissioner's Office, n.d., paras. 9–14)

If your region operates under these laws or similar, you can use students' images in your reporting. However, it is best (and indeed, may be a legal requirement) to make sure you have the consent of the students as well as their parents/guardians. You also need to make sure that any images used in your reporting do not identify students in ways that can be harmful to their present lives, or their lives when older, as whatever is posted online can remain there indefinitely and have serious subsequent repercussions. There are also immediate implications for child safety concerning online publication of children's images (see Australian Federal Police, 2023 for a brief overview).

Where you use images of students, it is ideal to briefly include a statement that indicates that their consent was granted. This shows that you have adhered to relevant laws as well as ethical standards, and could also contribute to changing the culture around use of students' images in regions where consent is not routinely collected, by making this a protective norm.

Acknowledge limitations of the data (and programme)

While you may initially baulk at the thought of pointing out deficiencies and limitations in your programme, and its evaluation, doing so is a massive green flag that shows you are likely to be trustworthy, and that you understand that limitations (either preconceived or those that emerged during the process) are par for the course. If you don't want to call them limitations, you can call them 'challenges', 'considerations' or 'food for thought'.

When I read a report issued by a school on an intervention or programme, and no limitations are identified and acknowledged, it honestly just seems like a public relations exercise, and I don't trust the level of rigour behind it. You don't have to write reams and reams on this, but limitations cannot be absent from any work conducted in reality on Earth as we know it.

Professional outputs

Your experience establishing a whole school reading culture can be shared with the broader professional community so that they can learn from what worked for you, and what didn't.

While the philanthropic benefits of this kind of sharing should be obvious, there may also be individual benefits for you. You will be able to develop your profile in your space, establishing yourself as a school-based expert in this area. This can lead to internal and external promotional opportunities. Internally, if you can demonstrate to your school leadership team that the work you have done within your school has resonated and influenced practice beyond your school, you can stand out as an asset worth preserving and promoting. Where your employment is precarious due to funding cuts or contract status, distinguishing yourself as an innovative and committed leader of this kind of initiative can make a positive difference in your vocational trajectory.

You may also find engaging in professional discussions around your implementation of the whole school reading culture offers insights for your benefit, where you open up multidirectional conversations about your process and findings. For example, you may enjoy generous input from schools who have also implemented similar programmes, and who adopted different workarounds for challenges you have identified that you will be able to draw upon to enhance your planning and implementation moving forward.

So how can you start this conversation?

Social media posts. Depending on the social media policy of your school, you may be able to start a conversation through posts on a social networking platform such as Twitter or LinkedIn.

Research on social media has found that professional learning communities can flourish in these online spaces, where educators can seek to draw on a communal knowledge base to foster 'new understandings, new ideas, and new practices' (Goodyear et al., 2019, p. 429), with researchers contending that social media offers 'a contemporary form of professional development that can address the clear challenges associated with teacher learning and, in turn, enhance the quality of teaching and improve student learning outcomes' (p. 432). Research suggests that using social media posts can help you to enter into 'supportive conversations' with peers about challenges you may encounter, fostering a collaborative approach to reflection on your practices (Ab Rashid, 2018, p. 105). I already see this space being used successfully by members of the professional education and library communities (as applicable) to troubleshoot problems and get advice during programme planning and implementation, drawing on the professional insights and expertise of others.

The international nature of social media also means that the pool of respondents is far broader than what might be accessed at a local level, allowing contributors to build professional relationships and seek advice from classroom- and library-based educators across the world. Social media can also be used as a space in which to share reports and circulate other professional publications such as blog entries.

Blogging. Blogging can be a great way of sharing a journey with a professional audience.

While traditionally this might take a written form, and be hosted on one of the many free sites used by content producers, such as *Medium*, video or multimedia blogging may also hold appeal, particularly if you have already established a platform in a video sharing space such as YouTube.

Whereas social media posts can be scattershot, the longitudinal nature of blogging invites the content consumer to track progress over time. As contended by Kietzmann et al. (2011), 'Twitter, then, is more about conversation than identity', whereas 'blogs, on the other hand, are less about staying connected synchronously than about facilitating rich, often lengthy conversations that can be traced back on the blog itself' (p. 245). As such, blogs can be a great way of building and sustaining relationships and knowledge exchange. For example, you can use a blog for keeping parents in the loop in relation to the implementation of the programme, and as a useful space to enable reporting to key stakeholders.

Conferences. Where feasible, conferences may be the ultimate space in which to engage in face-to-face knowledge exchanges with like-minded professionals.

They are a dynamic opportunity to collect feedback and insights from professionals in your field that may lead you to reshaping or reconsidering aspects of your whole school reading culture. In this regard, conferences act as a kind of peer-review opportunity without the demands of the peer-reviewed publication process.

Like all of the other mechanisms discussed in the section, presenting at conferences is also a great opportunity for you to increase your visibility as an expert in implementing a whole school reading culture. While there is a paucity of research that looks at the benefits for educational professionals of sharing experiences and findings at professional conferences, research that looks at the benefits of these activities for academics suggests that establishing a professional network is a key benefit of attendance at conferences (Hauss, 2021). With this opportunity substantially interrupted in recent times due to the pandemic, using your whole school reading programme reporting opportunity to build networks in professional spaces can offer rewards both for your school and your own professional identity. In some contexts such as

Australia, even if the conference fees cannot be covered by your school, you may claim a tax deduction related to this expense as it constitutes a professional learning opportunity.

Professional journal articles. Contributing to professional journal articles can be a great way of generating interest in and conversation around a whole school reading culture.

While I will discuss writing for peer-reviewed journals in a subsequent section, and some professional journals *do* require that authors go through a peer review process, professional journals in education are often not peer-reviewed, and content is often sourced by editors through a combination of editor solicitation and external submission. Here I will focus on this kind of professional journal.

Your presentation at a professional conference may lead to a professional journal's editor reaching out to you in order to solicit a related journal piece. However, even if you do not have your work solicited by an editor, you can contact the editor in many cases and outline a prospective piece for their interest.

To do this, simply go to the website of the professional journal, identify the editor and contact email, and then write a short abstract or overview (a pitch) that briefly covers:

- why you did it (your motivation for change: the drivers behind your whole school reading culture implementation),
- what you did,
- what you found/learnt from engaging in the experience, and
- what about what you did/learnt is innovative, original and relevant to the professional community.

Articles for professional journals are often much shorter than those produced for academic journals, and it is expected that you will use an accessible rather than staunchly academic tone, and focus on the pragmatic implications of your programme, with the professional community's needs clearly in mind. Reaching out to a journal that you already subscribe to, and regularly read will help you to use the appropriate written voice suited to the journal, increasing your chances of having your pitch and final article accepted.

Media outputs

To showcase innovations within the school, such as the intended or successful implementation of a whole school reading culture, some schools seek to promote themselves through mainstream media. This kind of promotion can increase public awareness of the relative merits of your school, potentially playing a role in arresting dwindling student numbers if applicable.

This may involve you reaching out to small-scale local media, such as the community newspaper, if this is available in your school's area. However, I have also worked with schools that have successfully grabbed the attention of larger-scale regional or national media. For example, Queenwood's whole school reading culture plans were covered twice by the *Sydney Morning Herald* (Baker, 2020; White, 2022). This was a significant achievement by the school, given that near the end of 2022 this newspaper reported that it had 'held its lead as the country's most-read masthead, with more than 8.4 million readers across digital and print over the past 12 months' (Sydney Morning Herald, 2022, para. 1). This shows that establishing a whole school reading culture can be topical, warranting media attention, and that this media attention can be from the most competitive outlets if the right angle to foster media engagement is found.

Exposing the school to media scrutiny is not without its risks, as your control over the ultimate message is limited, given that the media outlet does not work for you, and will pursue whatever coverage of your school they feel will be most newsworthy. If your school is interested in garnering media interest, ideally you need to move into this space with some media training, as it is very easy for your message to be misunderstood or distorted, particularly when you are providing comment on your programme in a high-pressure context, such as on live radio, television or streaming. Decide on your key messages in advance while also being responsive and personable in your responses. Stay as calm as possible, and if the interviewer asks you a question and you do not know the answer, obfuscation is a risky course. It is fine to admit that you don't have all the answers at this point in time, and certainly less risky than trying to bluff your way through, given that there is often no opportunity to edit or restrict publication of your comment if it is going out live.

In some cases, media coverage can lead to a snowball effect begetting further media coverage, which can be good for your school depending on the quality and focus of the coverage, but also potentially time consuming if you are regularly needing to provide comment (as I explore in Merga, 2021a).

Academic outputs

As I have previously mentioned, in the past I have worked with staff who wanted to write an academic journal article to promote their school's achievements and report on their findings. This can be a great way to get high-level recognition for the quality of your programme, and to contribute to the evidence-base around best practice, but there is no need to go down this very challenging path unless it fits your ultimate goals. It is important to emphasise that publishing an academic peer-reviewed paper can be incredibly challenging, especially if you have limited knowledge of how this process works, and if you lack a knowledgeable person to help you to navigate this space (Merga, Mason, et al., 2018), so there is no point in undertaking this arduous journey unless you need to (though I would love to see more research from educators published with the credibility associated with quality peer-reviewed journals so that I can cite you).

If you do not go through the institutional ethics approval processes and practices that will allow you to publish data from human subjects, there will be significant limitations on the kinds of approaches you can take to such an article. Therefore, if this is a desired output for your programme, this decision needs to be made *very early*, before there is any data collection from any human respondents. The required approvals can be sought at the outset of your initiative, just after the necessary relationship has been fostered with an academic partner if needed. Please revisit the section on boosting quality with an academic partner if you think you would like to do this.

Getting articles published through the peer-review process involves significant time and labour. To date, I have authored or co-authored 89 peer-reviewed journal articles, some of which did not get accepted at the first place I submitted them. As noted by Harris et al. (2019), your experiences in this space may remind you of Goldilocks, as you struggle to find a fit that's 'just right' (p. 1).

Based on my experiences and the research, here are some further tips for finding the best fit sooner rather than later. For each possible journal, you will need to:

- Read the author guidelines and consider if you can easily meet the requirements (e.g. word count).
- Scrutinise all the guidelines to check that your journal article will be published sometime this century, as lag times can be considerable. Guidelines often include important details such as estimated length of peer review, acceptance rate and whether the required manuscript word length is firm or sometimes negotiable.
- Look at the interests of the editorial board members; if none of them have interests overlapping your own, this may be a red flag, as they may not see your work as relevant.
- Read a selection of recent articles on topics with relevance to your own. If there are no articles that fall into this category, you are unlikely to be

able to cite the journal and join an existing conversation, potentially reducing the likelihood of acceptance.
- Check that data from your country will even be considered. Journals can be shamefully parochial (e.g. Mason et al., 2021). If they never publish work from your country, this can be a red flag.
- Check that the journal publishes methods similar to your own. There is no point in submitting a paper that reports primarily on qualitative data to a journal that exclusively publishes quantitative data. It will simply waste everybody's time. Some journals will explicitly indicate the kinds of methods they will publish in their guidelines. For other journals, this expectation will be tacit, rather than explicit, which means you will need to review the work they publish to determine what is likely to be permissible.
- Check that small-scale (single-school) studies are published by the journal. No matter how big your school is, your findings are still only from one school, and for some journals, this will be a dealbreaker.
- Check that there are no publication fees (unless you have the means to pay them). While at this stage, it is still relatively uncommon for reputable academic journal articles in the discipline of education to charge article processing fees, most journals will charge to make your paper available via open access. There are legal workarounds that you can use to ensure that people can still access your journal article without paying the substantial sums required to make the article available via open access. In many cases, a pre-print of the paper can be shared without breaking your licensing agreement with the journal. You need to closely read the licensing information available to determine if this is the case in relation to your journal, and if any embargo periods or other sanctions on pre-print sharing apply. Sherpa Romeo can be a useful tool for this (https://v2.sherpa.ac.uk/romeo).
- Depending on your reasons for publishing an academic journal article, you may need to pay attention to metric indicators of journal quality. For example, if you intend to use your article as part of a submission to secure a PhD scholarship, it will be useful to be able to demonstrate that the journal is well-regarded. Furthermore, if you are publishing with an academic partner, there may be a minimum impact level requirement associated with their participation that is stipulated by their institution. In education, it is relatively common to use the impact measures indicated at Scimago SJR to determine impact, as I've previously outlined in the section on boosting quality with academic partnership. One alarming thing to note about these impact measures is that they change over time, and you have no control over this. You might publish

in a Q1 (highest quartile for impact) journal, but when you seek to apply for a PhD scholarship two years later, it has dropped down to a Q2 or Q3 status. That's why it's useful to look on SJR at impact stability over time if you think metrics will matter for you, though there's no guarantee that even relatively stable journals will remain so.

If this is your first academic publication, and you're going to be authoring it with others, it's worth understanding that author order matters in this context, particularly if you are using the paper to apply for an HDR.

The first step is determining *if* someone should be listed as an author on the paper. While what constitutes authorship is contested, it can be contended that

> each author should have participated sufficiently in the work to take responsibility for the content. Authorship credit should be based only on substantial contributions to (a) conception and design, or analysis and interpretation of data; and to (b) drafting the article or revising it critically for important intellectual content; and on (c) final revision of the version to be published.
>
> (Bhattacharya, 2010, p. 233)

All three of these conditions must be met (Bhattacharya, 2010).

Once you have your list of authors, you must order the list ethically, given the implications of author order in this context. Again, if you look more deeply at this topic, you will find many different ways that author order can be determined, and while in the discipline of education, the first author has made the greatest contribution to the article, in other disciplines, it can be the last author. We might contend that 'the first author should be that person who contributed most to the work, including writing of the manuscript', and that 'the sequence of authors should be determined by the relative overall contributions to the manuscript' (Bhattacharya, 2010, p. 233), so all authors will need to keep a record of their contributions across the life of the programme, as early contributions to finalising research method have weight along with later contributions such as writing up a section.

Some journals will expect you to provide an 'author contributions statement' to justify the author inclusion and order as it will appear on your article. Here is an example from a recent article to give you a sense of what this can look like.

Author contributions statement
Jennifer Stiegler-Balfour: Conceptualization, methodology, software, analyses, manuscript writing, supervision; **Zoe Roberts:** conceptualization, methodology,

data collection, data organization, draft of manuscript section, reviewing and editing; **Abby LaChance:** Software, draft of manuscript section, reviewing and editing. **Aubrey Sahouria:** data collection, revision of Introduction; **Emily Newborough:** data collection, references and APA formatting.

(Stiegler-Balfour et al., 2023, p. 10)

As you can see, there are clear differences in the degree of contribution which have shaped the author order.

Seniority should not dictate authorship. If your school principal or an academic partner is on the team, and they make a smaller contribution than an early career teacher, the early career teacher's name comes first. If the school principal or academic partner makes no contribution to the paper, they are not listed as an author on the paper, though you may wish to acknowledge their support in the acknowledgement section.

One final comment relates to remuneration. After you have put in all the hard work and have had your journal article accepted, you might expect to be paid for your efforts. Sadly, academic journal articles will not pay you for your content, though you may have to pay them.

Final points

Given the involved nature of some of the mechanisms of reporting that I've outlined here, it should be clear that consideration of reporting and outputs needs to be made at the outset of your planning. For example, the two *Sydney Morning Herald* articles that I mentioned previously that reported on one school's whole school reading culture were published at the beginning, and around the end of the initiative. Once you have decided on which avenues of reporting are appropriate to your needs and approach, you can build interest in your programme, establish your expertise and invite feedback from professionals in your field to enhance the programme going forward.

Conclusions

I hope that by the time you reach this stage of the book, you arrive with strengthened confidence in your ability to roll out or rejuvenate a whole school reading culture in your context.

While I have presented a vast array of options and pathways with research support that you might pursue, please use this book as a tool to inform rather than dictate your choices. Please seek to establish a whole school reading culture that reflects the unique needs of *your* school, following the process that resonates with you and your team, and aligns with your current resourcing constraints.

Literacy proponents and policymakers often fall into the trap of proposing that a single solution can be the answer to all students' literacy problems. As I have explored extensively elsewhere, this is almost always problematic given that learners have diverse strengths, needs and backgrounds (Merga, 2020a). While building students' motivation and opportunities to read in a reading-supportive culture can make a big difference to students' literacy attainment, specific targeted interventions that address students' literacy gaps, as well as cover the required literacy curriculum, will be needed too.

While not the only essential literacy initiative for schools, increasing reading engagement by fostering a whole school reading culture using research-supported strategies can transform students' literacy learning, as well as their attitudes towards reading and related literacy-supportive activities. It will probably not independently solve *all* issues concerned with literacy that your students face, and 'integration of direct skills instruction and motivation interventions might produce synergistic effects and optimize gains in reading performance over time' (Toste et al., 2020, p. 446). To this end, you go a long way towards enhancing student literacy when you pay close attention to making gains in motivation and opportunities to read, while also offering a range of additional targeted literacy interventions as explored in my previous book (Merga, 2023b) and through the work of many other researchers. Many of the strategies that underpin a whole school reading culture yield significant gains for SLLs in particular (e.g. reading aloud to SLLs as explored by Westbrook et al., 2019), so a whole school reading culture can play a key role in closing the gap for these students as part of a multifaceted strategy.

We need more research

A limitation of this book is that the evidence in this field is constantly evolving, with notable gains between my 2018 work (Merga, 2018a) and this offering. This limitation is also a large part of what makes working in this space so interesting. I've presented the strongest possible findings here, but the body of evidence will continue to grow and potentially challenge and reshape what I have contended herein.

Despite the growth in research interest in recent times, we still need a higher volume of research studies in reading engagement to be funded, supported and published in credible peer-reviewed outlets in a far wider range of geographic and socio-economic contexts. While I have endeavoured to include research from many locations, there is limited inclusion of data, voices and experiences from some geographic contexts such as Africa. The extant scope of the research is a further limitation at present, and one that badly needs to be addressed if we want to be able to contend that the research findings in this space truly have internationality.

Furthermore, while I make reference to high-stakes testing scores, including PISA and PIRLS data in this book, as I have published previously, I have great reservations about these data (Merga, 2023b), and much has been written by education experts about the ethical and functional issues with assessment design and reporting of high-stakes testing data (e.g. see Forzani et al., 2022). For more about the limitations of PISA data, I recommend reading Zhao's (2020) detailed review of these issues. There are also a number of significant limitations in PIRLS data, some of which are outlined in the recent PIRLS report, including but not limited to widely different assessment times across the sample, such as the inclusion of fifth-grade students in what is supposed to be a study of fourth-grade performance: 'some Northern Hemisphere countries had to delay assessing the cohort of fourth grade students until the beginning of the fifth grade (September to December 2021) and some countries assessed their fourth grade students one year later than originally scheduled', meaning that students who took part in the 2021 assessment programme 'were 6 months older on average than their PIRLS 2016 counterparts' (Mullis et al., 2023, p. 14).

It is also worth noting that while this book aimed to primarily draw on high-quality peer-reviewed research as an informing credible base for its assertions, I have also drawn upon grey literature in many cases. For those unfamiliar with the term, 'grey literature is research that has not been published commercially and is therefore not necessarily searchable via the standard databases and search engines', and while it has not typically been through the rigour of peer review, it can be contended that 'much grey literature is of high quality and can be an excellent source of up to date research in certain subject areas' (University of New South Wales [UNSW], 2023, para. 1), and this will increasingly be the case as peer-reviewed publication lag times continue to burgeon. However, in some cases, I've used reports from surveys by corporations with a potential conflict of interest given their commercial stake in the findings, so as I've observed previously, 'there is always a risk that such reports may not have been conducted with the same degree of rigour as academic research, and they may have been funded by bodies with a potential conflict of interest' (Merga, 2019d, p. 14). Where this is the case, findings need to be considered with acknowledgement that commercial interest 'could potentially shape their collection and interpretation of the data' (p. 14). This is yet another reason why we need a greater body of peer-reviewed research to be undertaken in this area, meaning that reliance on grey literature will be lessened.

As I continue to work in a consultancy capacity with schools, professional associations, philanthropic organisations and government departments, subsequent iterations of this work will incorporate what I learn in these dynamic environments without identifying clients, unless they have openly published on or promoted my participation with them. While there is much to learn from the research on fostering a whole school reading culture, there is no substitute for the experiences of practitioners in schools and in real-world contexts, which is why I strongly encourage you to share your journey both within your school community, but also with external professionals and researchers as far as possible.

In addition to contributing your practical findings, think about contributing to the research knowledge. This book has explored promising emerging possibilities for fostering reading engagement and creating supportive whole school reading cultures. However, for many of these areas, we are still at the tip of the iceberg in relation to research evidence. I have absolutely no interest in acting as a gatekeeper in this research space, and I would love for you to consider undertaking some peer-reviewed research in this area to help advance the body of knowledge that schools can draw upon when seeking to improve literacy outcomes for their students. For example, if you are already working with a story dog, you could consider designing some research, perhaps with an academic partner, so that you can make a valued and credible research contribution.

I look forward to hearing about how you have used this book to support your approach and to advocate for the creation of a dynamic and creative whole school reading culture in your school, so please shoot me a message on Twitter if you'd like to share your experiences with me: @MKMerga, or find me on LinkedIn where I am a relative newbie.

References

Ab Rashid, R. (2018). Dialogic reflection for professional development through conversations on a social networking site. *Reflective Practice, 19*(1), 105–117.

Abbott, L., & McGuinness, S. (2022). Change management in Northern Ireland's transformed integrated schools: What we want is a school where you can be who you are and it's a safe place. *International Journal of Inclusive Education, 26*(6), 576–591.

Alkahtani, A. (2017). Curriculum change management and workload. *Improving Schools, 20*(3), 209–221.

Allington, R. L. (2014). How reading volume affects both reading fluency and reading achievement. *International Electronic Journal of Elementary Education, 7*(1), 13–26.

Allington, R. L., & McGill-Franzen, A. M. (2021). Reading volume and reading achievement: A review of recent research. *Reading Research Quarterly, 56*, S231–S238.

Allington, R. L., McGill-Franzen, A., Camilli, G., Williams, L., Graff, J., Zeig, J., Zmach, C., & Nowak, R. (2010). Addressing summer reading setback among economically disadvantaged elementary students. *Reading Psychology, 31*(5), 411–427.

Al-Musalli, A. (2014). Redefining the reading culture: Overcoming EFL teachers' prejudices against students' reading habits. *Arab World English Journal, 5*(1), 211–223.

Alvermann, D. E., Young, J. P., Green, C., & Wisenbaker, J. M. (1999). Adolescents' perceptions and negotiations of literacy practices in after-school read and talk clubs. *American Educational Research Journal, 36*(2), 221–264.

Antony-Newman, M. (2019). Parental involvement of immigrant parents: A meta-synthesis. *Educational Review, 71*(3), 362–381.

Applegate, A. J., & Applegate, M. D. (2004). The Peter effect: Reading habits and attitudes of preservice teachers. *The Reading Teacher, 57*(6), 554–563.

Aslam, S., Qutab, S., & Ali, N. (2022). Components of reading culture: Insights from bibliometric analysis of 1991–2020 research. *Journal of Information Science*, https://doi.org/10.1177/01655515221118667.

Association of Independent Schools of New South Wales. (2022). *AISNSW School Based Research Project Application Form*. https://www.aisnsw.edu.au/Resources/WAL%204%20[Open%20Access]/School%20Based%20Research%20Project%20Application%20Form.docx

Australian Bureau of Statistics (2023a). *Children spending more hours a week on screen-based activities: Media release*. https://www.abs.gov.au/media-centre/media-releases/children-spending-more-hours-week-screen-based-activities

Australian Bureau of Statistics (2023b). *Cultural and creative activities (2021–2022)*. https://www.abs.gov.au/statistics/people/people-and-communities/cultural-and-creative-activities/2021-22

Australian Federal Police (2023). *Advice for parents on sharing back-to-school images online*. https://www.afp.gov.au/news-media/media-releases/advice-parents-sharing-back-school-images-online

Australian Institute of Family Studies (2015). Images of children and young people online. https://aifs.gov.au/resources/resource-sheets/images-children-and-young-people-online

Australian School Library Association & Australian Library and Information Association (2020). *Recommended minimum information services staffing levels*. https://read.alia.org.au/file/1459/download?token=BGCcMMtu

Ayre, J., Bonner, C., Muscat, D. M., Dunn, A. G., Harrison, E., Dalmazzo, J., Mouwad, D., Aslani, P., Shepherd, H. L., & McCaffery, K. J. (2023). Multiple automated health literacy assessments of written health information: Development of the SHeLL (Sydney Health Literacy Lab) Health Literacy Editor v1. *JMIR Form Res, 7*, e40645.

Baer, J., Baldi, S., Ayotte, K., & Green, P. (2007). *The reading literacy of U.S. fourth-grade students in an international context: Results from the 2001 and 2006 Progress in International Reading Literacy Study (PIRLS)*. Washington, DC: National Center for Education Statistics, Institute of Education Sciences, US Department of Education.

Baker, J. (2020). 'Sense of urgency': One school's bold plan to get teenagers reading. *Sydney Morning Herald*. https://www.smh.com.au/education/sense-of-urgency-one-school-s-bold-plan-to-get-teenagers-reading-20191220-p53lzb.html

Baker, M., & Milligan, K. (2016). Boy-girl differences in parental time investments: Evidence from three countries. *Journal of Human Capital, 10*, 399–441.

Bal, P. M., & Veltkamp, M. (2013). How does fiction reading influence empathy? An experimental investigation on the role of emotional transportation. *PloS One, 8*(1), e55341.

Baldwin, A. G., & Nadelson, L. S. (2022). Gaps in college student reader identity: Issues of reading self-determination and reading self-efficacy. *Journal of College Reading and Learning*, https://doi.org/10.1080/10790195.2022.2155728

Beek, M., Opdenakker, M. C., Deunk, M. I., Strijbos, J. W., & Huijgen, T. (2022). Relationships between adolescent students' reading skills, historical content knowledge and historical reasoning ability. *History Education Research Journal, 19*(1), 1–16.

Benevides, T., & Peterson, S. S. (2010). Literacy attitudes, habits and achievements of future teachers. *Journal of Education for Teaching, 36*(3), 291–302.

Benji-Rabinovitz, S., & Berkovich, I. (2022). The colours of change ownership: A qualitative exploration of types of change agents' psychological ownership during school change. *Journal of Change Management, 22*(2), 99–119.

Ben-Yehudah, G., & Eshet-Alkalai, Y. (2021). Print versus digital reading comprehension tests: Does the congruency of study and test medium matter? *British Journal of Educational Technology, 52*(1), 426–440.

Best, A., & Clark, C. (2021). *The role of audiobooks to engage reluctant readers and underrepresented children and young people*. National Literacy Trust. https://files.eric.ed.gov/fulltext/ED614814.pdf

Best, A., Clark, C., & Picton, I. (2020). *Children, young people and audiobooks before and during lockdown*. National Literacy Trust. https://files.eric.ed.gov/fulltext/ED607856.pdf

Bhattacharya, S. (2010). Authorship issue explained. *Indian Journal of Plastic Surgery, 43*(2), 233–234.

Black, J. E., & Barnes, J. L. (2021). Fiction and morality: Investigating the associations between reading exposure, empathy, morality, and moral judgment. *Psychology of Popular Media, 10*(2), 149–164.

Blanco, M. A., Gruppen, L. D., Artino Jr, A. R., Uijtdehaage, S., Szauter, K., & Durning, S. J. (2016). How to write an educational research grant: AMEE Guide No. 101. *Medical Teacher, 38*(2), 113–122.

Blanco, M. A., & Lee, M. Y. (2012). Twelve tips for writing educational research grant proposals. *Medical Teacher, 34*(6), 450–453.

Borgers, N., de Leeuw, E., & Hox, J. (2000). Children as respondents in survey research: Cognitive development and response quality 1. *Bulletin of Sociological Methodology/Bulletin de Méthodologie Sociologique, 66*(1), 60–75.

Borgers, N., & Hox, J. (2001). Item nonresponse in questionnaire research with children. *Journal of Official Statistics, 17*(2), 321–335.

Boucher, L. C. (2001). Why you can't buy a vegetable garden: Whole-school literacy program reform. *New England Reading Association Journal, 37*(3), 1–9.

Bourguignon, M., Baart, M., Kapnoula, E. C., & Molinaro, N. (2020). Lip-reading enables the brain to synthesize auditory features of unknown silent speech. *Journal of Neuroscience, 40*(5), 1053–1065.

Braun, V., & Clarke, V. (2006). Using thematic analysis in psychology. *Qualitative Research in Psychology, 3*(2), 77–101.

Braun, V., & Clarke, V. (2014). What can 'thematic analysis' offer health and wellbeing researchers? *International Journal of Qualitative Studies on Health and Well-Being, 9*(1), e26152.

Braun, V., Clarke, V., & Hayfield, N. (2022). 'A starting point for your journey, not a map': Nikki Hayfield in conversation with Virginia Braun and Victoria Clarke about thematic analysis. *Qualitative Research in Psychology, 19*(2), 424–445.

Brown, L. (2022). More than half of young readers credit Booktok with sparking passion for reading, PA finds. *Bookseller.* https://www.thebookseller.com/news/more-than-half-of-young-readers-credit-Booktok-with-sparking-passion-for-reading-pa-finds

Canelo, E. (2020). Perceptions of animal assisted reading and its results reported by involved children, parents and teachers of a Portuguese elementary school. *Human-Animal Interaction Bulletin, 8*(3), 92–110.

Centerwall, U. (2022). In plain sight: School librarian practices within infrastructures for learning. *Journal of Librarianship and Information Science.* https://doi.org/10.1177/09610006221140881

Chang, Y. H., Wu, I. C., & Hsiung, C. A. (2021). Reading activity prevents long-term decline in cognitive function in older people: Evidence from a 14-year longitudinal study. *International Psychogeriatrics, 33*(1), 63–74.

Cheema, J. R. (2018). Adolescents' enjoyment of reading as a predictor of reading achievement: New evidence from a cross-country survey. *Journal of Research in Reading, 41*(S1), S149–S162.

Chen, A. T., Ocepek, M. G., & Zhang, Y. (2023). Guest editorial: Research methods in information behavior research. *Library & Information Science Research, 45*(1), e101221.

Clark, C., & Lant, F. (2019). *Writer visits and children and young people's reading and writing engagement.* National Literacy Trust. https://files.eric.ed.gov/fulltext/ED603684.pdf

Clark, C., & Picton, I. (2020). *Children and young people's reading in 2020 before and during the COVID-19 lockdown.* National Literacy Trust. https://files.eric.ed.gov/fulltext/ED607776.pdf

Clark, C., & Teravainen-Goff, A. (2018). *Mental wellbeing, reading and writing: How children and young people's mental wellbeing is related to their reading and writing experiences.* National Literacy Trust.

Clarke, V., & Braun, V. (2013). Teaching thematic analysis: Overcoming challenges and developing strategies for effective learning. *Psychologist, 26*(2), 120–123.

Clavel, J. G., & Mediavilla, M. (2020). The intergenerational effect of parental enthusiasm for reading. *Applied Economic Analysis, 28*(84), 239–259.

Collins, V. J., Dargan, I. W., Walsh, R. L., & Merga, M. K. (2022). Teachers' perceptions of the benefits and challenges of a whole school reading for pleasure program. *Issues in Educational Research, 32*(1), 89–104.

Cotner, B., Herrmann, S., Borman, K. M., Boydston, T., & LeFloch, K. C. (2005). *A deeper look at implementation: School-level stakeholders' perceptions of comprehensive school reform*. American Institute for Research.

Cox, R., & Schaetzel, K. (2007). A preliminary study of pre-service teachers as readers in Singapore: Prolific, functional, or detached? *Language Teaching Research, 11*(3), 301–317.

Crane, S., & Broome, M. E. (2017). Understanding ethical issues of research participation from the perspective of participating children and adolescents: A systematic review. *Worldviews on Evidence-Based Nursing, 14*(3), 200–209.

Creamer, E. G. (2018). *An introduction to fully integrated mixed methods research*. Sage Publications.

Cremin, T., & Hendry, H. (2022). Literacy histories as opportunities for learning: Reflecting, connecting, and learning from Margaret Meek Spencer. *English in Education, 56*(3), 209–221.

Cremin, T., Mottram, M., Collins, F., Powell, S., & Safford, K. (2009). Teachers as readers: Building communities of readers. *Literacy, 43*(1), 11–19.

Creswell, J. W., & Plano Clark, V. L. (2018). *Designing and conducting mixed methods research* (3rd ed.). Sage Publications.

Crosby, P., Throsby, D., & Zwar, J. (2022). *2022 national survey of Australian book authors*. Australia Council for the Arts. https://australiacouncil.gov.au/wp-content/uploads/2022/11/National-Survey-of-Australian-Book-Authors-Summary.pdf

Daniels, E., & Steres, M. (2011). Examining the effects of a school-wide reading culture on the engagement of middle school students. *RMLE Online, 35*(2), 1–13.

Darmawan, I. G. N. (2020). The changes in attitudes of 15-year-old Australian students towards reading, mathematics and science and their impact on student performance. *Australian Journal of Education, 64*(3), 304–327.

Delgado, P., Vargas, C., Ackerman, R., & Salmerón, L. (2018). Don't throw away your printed books: A meta-analysis on the effects of reading media on reading comprehension. *Educational Research Review, 25*, 23–38.

Department for Education (2014). *National curriculum in England: Framework for key stages 1 to 4*. https://www.gov.uk/government/publications/national-curriculum-in-england-framework-for-key-stages-1-to-4/the-national-curriculum-in-england-framework-for-key-stages-1-to-4

Ding, H., & Homer, M. (2020). Interpreting mathematics performance in PISA: Taking account of reading performance. *International Journal of Educational Research, 102*, e101566.

Dix, K., Felgate, R., & Ahmed, S. K., Carslake, T., & Sniedze-Gregory, S. (2020). *School libraries in South Australia. 2019 Census*. Australian Council for Educational Research. https://doi.org/10.37517/978-1-74286-583-6

Dodes, R., & Jurgensen, J. (2012). Gender games. *Wall Street Journal*. https://www.wsj.com/articles/SB10001424052970204603004577267832212316716

Dryden, N. H., & Goldstein, S. (2013). Regional campus learning commons: Assessing to meet student needs. *Journal of Library Administration*, 53(5/6), 293–322.

Federal Bureau of Investigation (FBI) (2022). *Internet Crime Report 2021*. FBI. https://www.ic3.gov/Media/PDF/AnnualReport/2021_IC3Report.pdf

Fetters, M. D., Curry, L. A., & Creswell, J. W. (2013). Achieving integration in mixed methods designs – principles and practices. *Health Services Research*, 48(6), 2134–2156.

Forzani, E., Afflerbach, P., Aguirre, S., Brynelson, N., Cervetti, G., Cho, B. Y., Coiro, J., García, G. E., Guthrie, J. T., Hinchman, K., Lee, C. D., Pacheco, M., Pearson, P. D., Ross, A., Skerrett, A., & Uccelli, P. (2022). Advances and missed opportunities in the development of the 2026 NAEP Reading Framework. *Literacy Research: Theory, Method, and Practice*, 71(1), 153–189.

Garces-Bacsal, R. M., Tupas, R., Kaur, S., Paculdar, A. M., & Baja, E. S. (2018). Reading for pleasure: Whose job is it to build lifelong readers in the classroom? *Literacy*, 52(2), 95–102.

Garcez, A., Duarte, R., & Eisenberg, Z. (2011). Production and analysis of video recordings in qualitative research. *Educação e Pesquisa*, 37, 249–261.

Gaylie, S. (2023). *Clear language description*. https://open.library.ubc.ca/media/download/pdf/52387/1.0427388/9

Gear, R. C., & Sood, K. K. (2021). School middle leaders and change management: Do they need to be more on the 'balcony' than the dance floor? *Education Sciences*, 11(11), e753.

Gelles-Watnick, R., & Perrin, A. (2021). Who doesn't read books in America? *Pew Research Center*. https://www.pewresearch.org/fact-tank/2021/09/21/who-doesnt-read-books-in-america

Goodyear, V. A., Parker, M., & Casey, A. (2019). Social media and teacher professional learning communities. *Physical Education and Sport Pedagogy*, 24(5), 421–433.

Gorsevski, E.W. (2016). *Writing successful grant proposals*. Sense Publishers.

Goss, P., & Sonnemann, J. (2016). *Widening gaps: What NAPLAN tells us about student progress*. Grattan Institute.

Grant, N. (2009). Schools of little thought: Why change management hasn't worked. *Improving Schools*, 12(1), 19–32.

Great School Libraries. (2023). *Equal futures? An imbalance of opportunities*. Great School Libraries.

Griffin, R. A., & Mindrila, D. (2023). Teacher reading motivation: Factors and latent profiles. *Literacy Research and Instruction*, https://doi.org/10.1080/19388071.2022.2153763

Grimm, K. J. (2008). Longitudinal associations between reading and mathematics achievement. *Developmental Neuropsychology, 33*(3), 410–426.

Guerrero, J. M., Teng-Calleja, M., & Hechanova, M. R. M. (2018). Implicit change leadership schemas, perceived effective change management, and teachers' commitment to change in secondary schools in the Philippines. *Asia Pacific Education Review, 19*, 375–387.

Halamish, V., & Elbaz, E. (2020). Children's reading comprehension and meta-comprehension on screen versus on paper. *Computers & Education, 145*, 103737.

Hariton, E., & Locascio, J. J. (2018). Randomised controlled trials – the gold standard for effectiveness research. *BJOG: an International Journal of Obstetrics and Gynaecology, 125*(13), 1716–1720.

Harris, J., Foulger, T. S., Huijser, H., & Phillips, M. (2019). Goldilocks and journal publication: Finding a fit that's 'just right'. *Australasian Journal of Educational Technology, 35*(4), 1–10.

Hauss, K. (2021). What are the social and scientific benefits of participating at academic conferences? Insights from a survey among doctoral students and postdocs in Germany. *Research Evaluation, 30*(1), 1–12.

Henderson, L., Grové, C., Lee, F., Trainer, L., Schena, H., & Prentice, M. (2020). An evaluation of a dog-assisted reading program to support student wellbeing in primary school. *Children and Youth Services Review, 118*, e105449.

Heppt, B., Olczyk, M., & Volodina, A. (2022). Number of books at home as an indicator of socioeconomic status: Examining its extensions and their incremental validity for academic achievement. *Social Psychology of Education, 25*(4), 903–928.

Herbert, D. L., Barnett, A. G., Clarke, P., & Graves, N. (2013). On the time spent preparing grant proposals: An observational study of Australian researchers. *BMJ open, 3*(5), e002800.

Hoşgörür, V. (2016). Views of primary school administrators on change in schools and change management practices. *Educational Sciences: Theory & Practice, 16*(6), 2029–2055.

Howard, G. S. (1994). Why do people say nasty things about self-reports? *Journal of Organizational Behavior, 15*(5), 399–404.

Hu, J., Yan, G., Wen, X., & Wang, Y. (2023). Gender differences in reading medium, time, and text types: Patterns of student reading habits and the relation to reading performance. *Reading and Writing*. https://doi.org/10.1007/s11145-023-10446-y

Hughes, H., Franz, J., Willis, J., Bland, D., & Rolfe, A. (2016). *High school spaces and student transitioning: Designing for student wellbeing. Research report for Queensland Department of Education and Training*. Queensland University of Technology, Australia.

Hulpia, H., & Devos, G. (2010). How distributed leadership can make a difference in teachers' organizational commitment? A qualitative study. *Teaching and Teacher Education, 26*(3), 565–575.

Ikeda, M., & Rech, G. (2022). Does the digital world open up an increasing divide in access to print books? *PISA in Focus*. OECD Publishing. https://doi.org/10.1787/22260919

Information Commissioner's Office (n.d.). Taking photos in schools. https://ico.org.uk/for-the-public/schools/photos

Ivey, G., & Johnston, P. H. (2013). Engagement with young adult literature: Outcomes and processes. *Reading Research Quarterly, 48*(3), 255–275.

Jacobs, J. K., Kawanaka, T., & Stigler, J. W. (1999). Integrating qualitative and quantitative approaches to the analysis of video data on classroom teaching. *International Journal of Educational Research, 31*(8), 717–724.

Jayanthi, M., & Nelson, J. S. (2002). *Savvy decision making: An administrator's guide to using focus groups in schools*. Corwin Press.

Jerasa, S., & Boffone, T. (2021). Booktok 101: TikTok, digital literacies, and out-of-school reading practices. *Journal of Adolescent & Adult Literacy, 65*(3), 219–226.

Jerrim, J., & Moss, G. (2019). The link between fiction and teenagers' reading skills: International evidence from the OECD PISA study. *British Educational Research Journal, 45*(1), 181–200.

Jian, Y. C. (2022). Reading in print versus digital media uses different cognitive strategies: Evidence from eye movements during science-text reading. *Reading and Writing, 35*, 1549–1568.

Kaiser, K. (2009). Protecting respondent confidentiality in qualitative research. *Qualitative Health Research, 19*(11), 1632–1641.

Kanonire, T., Lubenko, J., & Kuzmina, Y. (2022). The effects of intrinsic and extrinsic reading motivation on reading performance in elementary school. *Journal of Research in Childhood Education, 36*(1), 1–13.

Khorana, A., Pareek, A., Ollivier, M., Madjarova, S. J., Kunze, K. N., Nwachukwu, B. U., Karlsson, J., Marigi, E. M., & Williams, R. J. (2023). Choosing the appropriate measure of central tendency: Mean, median, or mode? *Knee Surgery, Sports Traumatology, Arthroscopy, 31*(1), 12–15.

Kietzmann, J. H., Hermkens, K., McCarthy, I. P., & Silvestre, B. S. (2011). Social media? Get serious! Understanding the functional building blocks of social media. *Business Horizons, 54*(3), 241–251.

Kong, Y., Seo, Y. S., & Zhai, L. (2018). Comparison of reading performance on screen and on paper: A meta-analysis. *Computers & Education, 123*, 138–149.

Kotter, J. P. (1998). Winning at change. *Leader to Leader, 10*, 27–33.

Kotter, J. P. (2001). What leaders really do. *Harvard Business Review*, December, 23–34.

Kozak, S., & Recchia, H. (2019). Reading and the development of social understanding: Implications for the literacy classroom. *The Reading Teacher, 72*(5), 569–577.

Kragler, S. (2000). Choosing books for reading: An analysis of three types of readers. *Journal of Research in Childhood Education, 14*(2), 133–141.

Krashen, S. (2011). *Free voluntary reading*. Libraries Unlimited.

Kuzmičová, A., & Cremin, T. (2022). Different fiction genres take children's memories to different places. *Cambridge Journal of Education, 52*(1), 37–53.

Lance, K. C., Kachel, D., & Gerrity, C. (2023). The school librarian equity gap: Inequities associated with race and ethnicity compounded by poverty, locale, and enrolment. *Peabody Journal of Education*, https://doi.org/10.1080/0161956X.2023.2160112

Layton, E., & Love, M. (2021). A happy medium: Academic library noise from the perspectives of students and librarians. *Codex, 6*(1), 32–53.

Ledger, S., & Merga, M. K. (2018). Reading aloud: Children's attitudes toward being read to at home and at school. *Australian Journal of Teacher Education, 43*(3), 124–139.

Lepper, C., Stang, J., & McElvany, N. (2022). Gender differences in text-based interest: Text characteristics as underlying variables. *Reading Research Quarterly, 57*(2), 537–554.

Lerkkanen, M. K., Pakarinen, E., Salminen, J., & Torppa, M. (2022). Reading and math skills development among Finnish primary school children before and after COVID-19 school closure. *Reading and Writing*, https://doi.org/10.1007/s11145-022-10358-3

Levine, S. L., Cherrier, S., Holding, A. C., & Koestner, R. (2022). For the love of reading: Recreational reading reduces psychological distress in college students and autonomous motivation is the key. *Journal of American College Health, 70*(1), 158–164.

Lewis, K., & Kuhfeld, M. (2022). *Progress toward pandemic recovery: Continued signs of rebounding achievement at the start of the 2022–23 school year*. Center for School and Student Progress. https://www.nwea.org/uploads/2022/12/CSSP-Brief_Progress-toward-pandemic-recovery_DEC22_Final.pdf

Loh, C. E., Ellis, M., Paculdar, A. A., & Wan, Z. H. (2017). Building a successful reading culture through the school library: A case study of a Singapore secondary school. *IFLA Journal, 43*(4), 335–347.

Loh, C. E., Gan, S., & Mounsey, S. (2022). What do children want to read? A case study of how one primary school library supported reading for pleasure. *Journal of Library Administration*. https://doi.org/10.1080/01930826.2022.2117955

Loh, C. E., & Sun, B. (2020). Cultural capital, habitus and reading futures: Middle-class adolescent students' cultivation of reading dispositions in Singapore. *British Journal of Sociology of Education, 41*(2), 234–252.

Loh, C. E., & Sun, B. (2022). The impact of technology use on adolescents' leisure reading preferences. *Literacy, 56*(4), 327–339.

Loh, C. E., Tam, A., & Okada, D. (2019). School library perspectives from Asia: Trends, innovations and challenges in Singapore, Hong Kong and Japan. In J. L. Branch-Mueller (Ed.) *Proceedings of the 48th Annual Conference of the International Association of School Librarianship and the 23rd International Forum on Research in School Librarianship.* IASL.

Lupo, S. M., Strong, J. Z., & Conradi Smith, K. (2019). Struggle is not a bad word: Misconceptions and recommendations about readers struggling with difficult texts. *Journal of Adolescent & Adult Literacy, 62*(5), 551–560.

Mace, G., & Lean, M. (2021a). Building a reader for life: A sustained silent reading program for K-11-Just Read. *Access, 35*(1), 32–39.

Mace, G., & Lean, M. (2021b). The time to read. *Connections.* https://www.scisdata.com/connections/issue-117/the-time-to-read

Mace, G., & Lean, M. (2022). Embracing change. *Connections.* https://www.scisdata.com/connections/issue-120/embracing-change

Macfarlane, B. (2017). The ethics of multiple authorship: Power, performativity and the gift economy. *Studies in Higher Education, 42*(7), 1194–1210.

MacNeil, A. J., Prater, D. L., & Busch, S. (2009). The effects of school culture and climate on student achievement. *International Journal of leadership in Education, 12*(1), 73–84.

Mahasneh, R., von Suchodoletz, A., Larsen, R. A., & Dajani, R. (2021). Reading for pleasure among Jordanian children: A community-based reading intervention. *Journal of Research in Reading, 44*(2), 360–378.

Mak, H. W., & Fancourt, D. (2020a). Reading for pleasure in childhood and adolescent healthy behaviours: Longitudinal associations using the Millennium Cohort Study. *Preventive Medicine, 130,* e105889.

Mak, H. W., & Fancourt, D. (2020b). Longitudinal associations between reading for pleasure and child maladjustment: Results from a propensity score matching analysis. *Social Science & Medicine, 253,* e112971.

Malin, J. R., Brown, C., & Saultz, A. (2019). What we want, why we want it: K-12 educators' evidence use to support their grant proposals. *International Journal of Education Policy and Leadership, 15*(3), 1–19.

Mar, R. A., Oatley, K., & Peterson, J. B. (2009). Exploring the link between reading fiction and empathy: Ruling out individual differences and examining outcomes. *Communications, 34,* 407–428.

Mar, R. A., & Rain, M. (2015). Narrative fiction and expository nonfiction differentially predict verbal ability. *Scientific Studies of Reading, 19*(6), 419–433.

Margariti, D. (2022). School libraries in Greece: The teacher view. *New Review of Children's Literature and Librarianship.* https://doi.org/10.1080/13614541.2022.2136598

Marshall, G., & Jonker, L. (2010). An introduction to descriptive statistics: A review and practical guide. *Radiography, 16*(4), e1–e7.

Mason, S., Merga, M. K., Canché, M. S. G., & Roni, S. M. (2021). The internationality of published higher education scholarship: How do the 'top' journals compare? *Journal of Informetrics, 15*(2), e101155.

Massis, B. E. (2012). In the library: Quiet space endures. *New Library World, 113*(7/8), 396–399.

Mat Roni, S., & Merga, M. K. (2019). The influence of extrinsic and intrinsic variables on children's reading frequency and attitudes: An exploration using an artificial neural network. *Australian Journal of Education, 63*(3), 270–291.

Mat Roni, S., Merga, M. K., & Morris, J. E. (2020). *Conducting quantitative research in education*. Springer.

McGeown, S., Goodwin, H., Henderson, N., & Wright, P. (2012). Gender differences in reading motivation: Does sex or gender identity provide a better account? *Journal of Research in Reading, 35*(3), 328–336.

Medina, E., & McGregor, A. (2019). *PISA 2018: Reading in New Zealand*. Ministry of Education.

Merga, M. K. (2013). Should Silent Reading feature in a secondary school English programme? West Australian students' perspectives on Silent Reading. *English in Education, 47*(3), 229–244.

Merga, M. K. (2014a). Are teenagers really keen digital readers? Adolescent engagement in ebook reading and the relevance of paper books today. *English in Australia, 49*(1), 27–37.

Merga, M. K. (2014b). Are Western Australian adolescents keen book readers? *Australian Journal of Language and Literacy, 37*(3), 161–170.

Merga, M. K. (2014c). Exploring the role of parents in supporting recreational book reading beyond primary school. *English in Education, 48*(2), 149–163.

Merga, M. K. (2014d). Peer group and friend influences on the social acceptability of adolescent book reading. *Journal of Adolescent & Adult Literacy, 57*(6), 472–482.

Merga, M. K. (2014e). Western Australian adolescents' reasons for infrequent engagement in recreational book reading. *Literacy Learning: The Middle Years, 22*(2), 60–66.

Merga, M. K. (2015a). Access to books in the home and adolescent engagement in recreational book reading: Considerations for secondary school educators. *English in Education, 49*(3), 197–214.

Merga, M. K. (2015b). Are avid adolescent readers social networking about books? *New Review of Children's Literature and Librarianship, 21*(1), 1–16.

Merga, M. K. (2015c). 'She knows what I like': Student-generated best-practice statements for encouraging recreational book reading in adolescents. *Australian Journal of Education, 59*(1), 35–50.

Merga, M. K. (2016a). Gaps in work readiness of graduate health professionals and impact on early practice: Possibilities for future interprofessional learning. *Focus on Health Professional Education: A Multi-Disciplinary Journal, 17*(3), 14–29.

Merga, M. K. (2016b). 'I don't know if she likes reading': Are teachers perceived to be keen readers, and how is this determined? *English in Education, 50*(3), 255–269.

Merga, M. K. (2016c). What would make them read more? Insights from Western Australian adolescents. *Asia Pacific Journal of Education, 36*(3), 409–424.

Merga, M. K. (2017a). Becoming a reader: Significant social influences on avid book readers. *School Library Research, 20*.

Merga, M. (2017b). Do males really prefer non-fiction, and why does it matter? *English in Australia, 52*(1), 27–35.

Merga, M. K. (2017c). Interactive reading opportunities beyond the early years: What educators need to consider. *Australian Journal of Education, 61*(3), 328–343.

Merga, M. K. (2017d). Meeting the needs of avid book readers: Access, space, concentration support and barrier mitigation. *Journal of Library Administration, 57*(1), 49–68.

Merga, M. K. (2017e). What motivates avid readers to maintain a regular reading habit in adulthood? *Australian Journal of Language and Literacy, 40*(2), 146–156.

Merga, M. K. (2017f). What would make children read for pleasure more frequently? *English in Education, 51*(2), 207–223.

Merga, M. K. (2018a). *Reading engagement for tweens and teens: What would make them read more?* ABC-CLIO.

Merga, M. K. (2018b). Silent reading and discussion of self-selected books in the contemporary classroom. *English in Australia, 53*(1), 70–82.

Merga, M. K. (2019a). 10 ways to get the most out of silent reading in schools. *The Conversation.* https://theconversation.com/10-ways-to-get-the-most-out-of-silent-reading-in-schools-123531

Merga, M. K. (2019b). Do librarians feel that their profession is valued in contemporary schools? *Journal of the Australian Library and Information Association, 68*(1), 18–37.

Merga, M. K. (2019c). How do librarians in schools support struggling readers? *English in Education, 53*(2), 145–160.

Merga, M. K. (2019d). *Librarians in schools as literacy educators: Advocates for reaching beyond the classroom.* Palgrave Macmillan.

Merga, M. K. (2019e). Read aloud to your children to boost their vocabulary. *The Conversation.* https://theconversation.com/read-aloud-to-your-children-to-boost-their-vocabulary-111427

Merga, M. K. (2019f). Ten ways teacher librarians improve literacy in schools. *The Conversation.* https://theconversation.com/ten-ways-teacher-librarians-improve-literacy-in-schools-110026

Merga, M. K. (2020a). 'Fallen through the cracks': Teachers' perceptions of barriers faced by struggling literacy learners in secondary school. *English in Education*, 54(4), 371–395.

Merga, M. K. (2020b). School librarians as literacy educators within a complex role. *Journal of Library Administration*, 60(8), 889–908.

Merga, M. K. (2020c). 'We talk books': Teacher librarians promoting book discussion to foster reading engagement. *English in Australia*, 55(1), 22–33.

Merga, M. K. (2021a). The academic labour of knowledge mobilization: What scholarly publishers need to know. *Learned Publishing*, 34(4), 655–665.

Merga, M. K. (2021b). How can Booktok on TikTok inform readers' advisory services for young people? *Library & Information Science Research*, 43(2), e101091.

Merga, M. K. (2021c). Libraries as wellbeing supportive spaces in contemporary schools. *Journal of Library Administration*, 61(6), 659–675.

Merga, M. K. (2021d). What is the literacy supportive role of the school librarian in the United Kingdom? *Journal of Librarianship and Information Science*, 53(4), 601–614.

Merga, M. K. (2022a). The role of the library within school-level literacy policies and plans in Australia and the United Kingdom. *Journal of Librarianship and Information Science*, 54(3), 469–481.

Merga, M. K. (2022b). *School Libraries Supporting Literacy and Wellbeing*. Facet Publishing.

Merga, M. K. (2023a). 10 ways to help the boys in your life read for enjoyment (not just for school). *The Conversation*. https://theconversation.com/10-ways-to-help-the-boys-in-your-life-read-for-enjoyment-not-just-for-school-205997

Merga, M. K. (2023b). *Creating an Australian school literacy policy*. Hawker Brownlow Education. https://www.hbe.com.au/hb6449.html

Merga, M. K. (2023c, April 20). *Futureproofing: How to win external funding to power initiatives from the library* [Conference presentation]. ASLA Biennial Conference 2023, Gold Coast, Queensland, Australia.

Merga, M. K. (2023d). How school libraries can promote health literacy in challenging times. *Journal of Library Administration*, 63(3), 291–306.

Merga, M. K. (2023e). Why teachers of science and mathematics should value teacher librarians. *Access*, 37(1), 43–46.

Merga, M. K., & Ferguson, C. (2021). School librarians supporting students' reading for pleasure: A job description analysis. *Australian Journal of Education*, 65(2), 153–172.

Merga, M., & Gardiner, V. (2018). The role of whole-school literacy policies supporting reading engagement in Australian schools. *English in Australia*, 53(3), 37–50.

Merga, M. K., & Hu, Q. M. (2016). Health education beyond the school gates: Use of school newsletters to communicate health messages to parents and their families. *Australian Journal of Education*, 60(1), 73–85.

Merga, M. K., & Ledger, S. (2018). Parents' views on reading aloud to their children: Beyond the early years. *Australian Journal of Language and Literacy, 41*(3), 177–189.

Merga, M. K., & Ledger, S. (2019). Teachers' attitudes toward and frequency of engagement in reading aloud in the primary classroom. *Literacy, 53*(3), 134–142.

Merga, M. K., Malpique, A., Mat Roni, S., Valcan, D., & Ledger, S. (2021). Teachers' perceptions of the impact of COVID-19 on writing instruction in Australia. *Issues in Educational Research, 31*(4), 1138–1155.

Merga, M. K., & Mason, S. (2019). Building a school reading culture: Teacher librarians' perceptions of enabling and constraining factors. *Australian Journal of Education, 63*(2), 173–189.

Merga, M. K., & Mason, S. (2021a). Mentor and peer support for early career researchers sharing research with academia and beyond. *Heliyon, 7*(2), e06172.

Merga, M. K., & Mason, S. (2021b). Perspectives on institutional valuing and support for academic and translational outputs in Japan and Australia. *Learned Publishing, 34*(3), 305–314.

Merga, M. K., Mason, S., & Morris, J. (2018). Early career experiences of navigating journal article publication: Lessons learned using an autoethnographic approach. *Learned Publishing, 31*(4), 381–389.

Merga, M. K., & Mat Roni, S. (2017a). The influence of access to eReaders, computers and mobile phones on children's book reading frequency. *Computers & Education, 109*, 187–196.

Merga, M. K., & Mat Roni, S. (2017b). Choosing strategies of children and the impact of age and gender on library use: Insights for librarians. *Journal of Library Administration, 57*(6), 607–630.

Merga, M. K., & Mat Roni, S. (2018a). Children's perceptions of the importance and value of reading. *Australian Journal of Education, 62*(2), 135–153.

Merga, M. K., & Mat Roni, S. (2018b). Empowering parents to encourage children to read beyond the early years. *The Reading Teacher, 72*(2), 213–221.

Merga, M. K., & Mat Roni, S. (2018c). Parents as social influences encouraging book reading: Research directions for librarians' literacy advocacy. *Journal of Library Administration, 58*(7), 674–697.

Merga, M. K., Mat Roni, S., & Malpique, A. (2021a). Do secondary English teachers have adequate time and resourcing to meet the needs of struggling literacy learners? *English in Education, 55*(4), 351–367.

Merga, M. K., Mat Roni, S., & Malpique, A. (2021b). School leadership and whole-school support of struggling literacy learners in secondary schools. *Educational Management Administration & Leadership, 49*(3), 534–550.

Merga, M. K., Mat Roni, S., & Mason, S. (2020). Should Google Scholar be used for benchmarking against the professoriate in education? *Scientometrics, 125*, 2505–2522.

Merga, M. K., & Moon, B. (2016). The impact of social influences on high school students' recreational reading. *The High School Journal, 99*(2), 122–140.

Mestry, R., & Govindasamy, V. (2021). The perceptions of school management teams and teachers of the principal's instructional leadership role in managing curriculum changes. *Interchange, 52*(4), 545–560.

Mikrut, K. (2023). Aptakisic-Tripp School Dist. 102 launching 'pawsitive' program to help students with reading activities. *Chicago Tribune*. https://www.chicagotribune.com/suburbs/buffalo-grove/ct-bgc-school-district-102-therapy-dog-reading-tl-0302-20230225-ot5gfyc6cveztadp3b2yl2uw7e-story.html

Miller, J. (2019). Where does the time go? An academic workload case study at an Australian university. *Journal of Higher Education Policy and Management, 41*(6), 633–645.

Moore, D. W., Bean, T. W., Birdyshaw, D., & Rycik, J. A. (1999). Adolescent literacy: A position statement. *Journal of Adolescent & Adult Literacy, 43*(1), 97–112.

Mullis, I. V. S., von Davier, M., Foy, P., Fishbein, B., Reynolds, K. A., & Wry, E. (2023). *PIRLS 2021 international results in reading*. Boston College, TIMSS & PIRLS International Study Center. https://doi.org/10.6017/lse.tpisc.tr2103.kb5342

Nathanson, S., Pruslow, J., & Levitt, R. (2008). The reading habits and literacy attitudes of inservice and prospective teachers: Results of a questionnaire survey. *Journal of Teacher Education, 59*(4), 313–321.

National Centre for Education Statistics (2019). *Adult literacy in the United States*. US Department of Education. https://files.eric.ed.gov/fulltext/ED596118.pdf

National Library of New Zealand (n.d.-a). Primary school reading culture review. https://natlib.govt.nz/files/schools/primary-school-reading-culture-review.pdf

National Library of New Zealand (n.d.-b). A school-wide reading culture. https://natlib.govt.nz/schools/reading-engagement/understanding-reading-engagement/a-school-wide-reading-culture

National Library of New Zealand (n.d.-c). Secondary school reading culture review. https://natlib.govt.nz/files/schools/secondary-school-reading-culture-review.pdf

Natriello, G. (2009). High stakes testing and teaching to the test. In L. J. Saha & A. G. Dworkin (Eds.) *International Handbook of Research on Teachers and Teaching*. Springer international handbooks of education (pp. 1101–1111). Springer.

Neri, N. C., Guill, K., & Retelsdorf, J. (2021). Language in science performance: Do good readers perform better? *European Journal of Psychology of Education, 36*(1), 45–61.

Neugebauer, S. R., & Gilmour, A. F. (2020). The ups and downs of reading across content areas: The association between instruction and fluctuations in reading motivation. *Journal of Educational Psychology, 112*(2), 344–363.

NSW Department of Education (2023). *Evidence guide for school excellence – qualitative data*.

https://education.nsw.gov.au/content/dam/main-education/teaching-and-learning/school-excellence-and-accountability/media/documents/Qualitative-data.docx

Office of Educational Technology (2016). *Future ready learning*. United States Department of Education. https://tech.ed.gov/files/2015/12/NETP16.pdf

Organisation for Economic Co-operation and Development (n.d.). *FAQ*. https://www.oecd.org/pisa/pisafaq

Organisation for Economic Co-operation and Development (2010). *PISA 2009 results: Executive summary*. OECD Publishing.

Organisation for Economic Co-operation and Development (2011). *Education at a glance*. OECD Publishing.

Organisation for Economic Co-operation and Development (2016). *PISA 2015 results (Volume I): Excellence and equity in education*. OECD Publishing.

Organisation for Economic Co-operation and Development (2019a). *Education at a glance 2019: OECD indicators*. OECD Publishing.

Organisation for Economic Co-operation and Development (2019b). *PISA 2018 results (Volume I): What students know and can do*. OECD Publishing.

Organisation for Economic Co-operation and Development (2021). *21st-century readers: Developing literacy skills in a digital world*. OECD Publishing.

Perlin, M. S., Imasato, T., & Borenstein, D. (2018). Is predatory publishing a real threat? Evidence from a large database study. *Scientometrics, 116*, 255–273.

Perrigo, B. (2023). What to know about the TikTok security concerns. *Time*. https://time.com/6265651/tiktok-security-us

Pfost, M., Dörfler, T., & Artelt, C. (2013). Students' extracurricular reading behavior and the development of vocabulary and reading comprehension. *Learning and Individual Differences, 26*, 89–102.

Pfost, M., & Heyne, N. (2022). Fostering children's reading comprehension: The importance of fiction reading. *Zeitschrift für Bildungsforschung*, https://doi.org/10.1007/s35834-022-00376-0

Pfost, M., & Heyne, N. (2023). Joint book reading, library visits and letter teaching in families: Relations to parent education and children's reading behavior. *Reading and Writing*, https://doi.org/10.1007/s11145-022-10389-w

Picton, I., & Clark, C. (2022). *Seeing yourself in what you read: Diversity and children and young people's reading in 2022*. National Literacy Trust. https://literacytrust.org.uk/research-services/research-reports/seeing-yourself-in-what-you-read-diversity-and-children-and-young-peoples-reading-in-2022

Plano Clark, V. L. (2019). Meaningful integration within mixed methods studies: Identifying why, what, when, and how. *Contemporary Educational Psychology, 57*, 106–111.

Pont, B., Nusche, D., & Moorman, H. (2008). *Improving school leadership: Volume 1 policy and practice*. OECD Publishing.

Queenwood (n.d.). *Just Read final report.* https://www.queenwood.nsw.edu.au/Just-Read-Final-Report

Rasiah, R., Kaur, H., Baharom, A. H., Turner, J. J., Habibullah, M. S., DA, A. M., & Singaram, N. (2022). The sociology of reading among Malaysian youths: Building a culture of reading to enhance environmental awareness and develop pro-environmental behavior. *Educational Sciences: Theory & Practice, 22*(1), 116–128.

Read, J. C., & MacFarlane, S. (2006). Using the fun toolkit and other survey methods to gather opinions in child computer interaction. In *Proceedings of the 2006 conference on interaction design and children*, 81–88. ACM.

Reeves, S., Exley, B., & Dillon-Wallace, J. (2018). Secondary school English teachers caught in the NAPLAN Fray: Effects of the disparate responses. *English in Australia, 53*(1), 24–32.

Retelsdorf, J., Köller, O., & Möller, J. (2011). On the effects of motivation on reading performance growth in secondary school. *Learning and Instruction, 21*(4), 550–559.

Rettig, A., & Schiefele, U. (2023). Relations between reading motivation and reading efficiency – evidence from a longitudinal eye-tracking study. *Reading Research Quarterly.* https://doi.org/10.1002/rrq.502

Robertson, P. J., & Briggs, K. L. (1998). Improving schools through school-based management: An examination of the process of change. *School Effectiveness and School Improvement, 9*(1), 28–57.

Rodriguez-Meehan, M., Irene Brown, K. G., & Turcotte, N. (2022). 'A win-win for all': Supporting literacy in early childhood and bringing awareness to shelter dogs. *Early Childhood Education Journal.* https://doi.org/10.1007/s10643-022-01389-0

Ronconi, A., Veronesi, V., Mason, L., Manzione, L., Florit, E., Anmarkrud, Ø., & Bråten, I. (2022). Effects of reading medium on the processing, comprehension, and calibration of adolescent readers. *Computers & Education, 185*, e104520.

Rosenzweig, E. Q., & Wigfield, A. (2022). Motivational interventions in education: Five big questions to consider when designing effective interventions. In A. O'Donnell, N. C. Barnes & J. Reeve (Eds.), *The Oxford Handbook of Educational Psychology* (pp. 1–25). Oxford University Press.

Schleicher, A. (2019). *PISA 2018 insights and interpretations.* OECD Publishing. https://www.oecd.org/pisa/PISA%202018%20Insights%20and%20Interpretations%20FINAL%20PDF.pdf

Scholastic (2016a). *Kids & family reading report: Australia.* Scholastic. https://www.scholastic.com/content/dam/KFRR/InternationalReports/KFRRAUS.pdf

Scholastic (2016b). *Kids & family reading report: India.* Scholastic.

Scholastic (2016c). *Kids & family reading report: United Kingdom.* Scholastic. https://www.scholastic.com/content/dam/KFRR/InternationalReports/kfrruk.pdf

Scholastic (2017). *Kids & family reading report: Canadian edition.* Scholastic. https://www.scholastic.com/content/dam/KFRR/InternationalReports/KFRR_CAN.pdf

Scholastic (2019a). *Kids & family reading report (7th Ed). Finding their story.* Scholastic. https://www.scholastic.com/content/dam/KFRR/Downloads/KFRReport_Finding%20Their%20Story.pdf

Scholastic (2019b). *Kids & family reading report (7th Ed). Finding their story data appendix.* Scholastic. https://www.scholastic.com/content/dam/KFRR/Downloads/_KFRR_Data%20Appendix_FindingTheirStory.pdf

Scholastic (2019c). *Kids & family reading report (7th Ed). The rise of read aloud.* Scholastic. https://www.scholastic.com/content/dam/KFRR/Downloads/KFRR_The%20Rise%20of%20Read%20Aloud.pdf

Scholastic (2019d). *Kids & family reading report (7th Ed). The summer reading imperative.* Scholastic. https://www.scholastic.com/content/dam/KFRR/Downloads/KFRR_SummerReadingImperative.pdf

Scholastic (2020). *Kids & family reading report: China.* Scholastic. https://www.scholastic.com/content/dam/KFRR/InternationalReports/KFRR_CHINA.pdf

Scholes, L., Spina, N., & Comber, B. (2021). Disrupting the 'boys don't read' discourse: Primary school boys who love reading fiction. *British Educational Research Journal, 47*(1), 163–180.

Schoon, I., Parsons, S., Rush, R., & Law, J. (2010). Childhood language skills and adult literacy: A 29-year follow-up study. *Pediatrics, 125*(3), e459–e466.

Shahaeian, A., Wang, C., Tucker-Drob, E., Geiger, V., Bus, A. G., & Harrison, L. J. (2018). Early shared reading, socioeconomic status, and children's cognitive and school competencies: Six years of longitudinal evidence. *Scientific Studies of Reading, 22*(6), 485–502.

Shearing, H. (2022). Sats results: Standards slip in Year 6 tests. *BBC News.* https://www.bbc.com/news/education-61980677

Shearing, H. (2023). Year 6 Sats: Children 'distraught' after reading paper. *BBC News.* https://www.bbc.com/news/education-65563170

Simpson, A., & Cremin, T. M. (2022). Responsible reading: Children's literature and social justice. *Education Sciences, 12*(4), 1–14.

Singh, A., & Alexander, P. A. (2022). Audiobooks, print, and comprehension: What we know and what we need to know. *Educational Psychology Review, 34*, 677–715.

Skaar, H., Elvebakk, L., & Nilssen, J. H. (2018). Literature in decline? Differences in pre-service and in-service primary school teachers' reading experiences. *Teaching and Teacher Education, 69*, 312–323.

Softlink (2023). *The 2022 Softlink Australian and New Zealand school library survey report.* Softlink.

Sohn, E. (2020). Secrets to writing a winning grant. *Nature, 577*(7788), 133–135.

Son, S. H. C., Baroody, A. E., & Opatz, M. O. (2023). Measuring preschool children's engagement behaviors during classroom shared reading: Construct and concurrent validity of the shared reading engagement rating scale. *Early Childhood Research Quarterly, 64*, 47–60.

Stauss, K., Koh, E., Johnson-Carter, C., & Gonzales-Worthen, D. (2021). OneCommunity reads: A model for Latino parent-community engagement and its effect on grade-level reading proficiency. *Education and Urban Society, 53*(4), 402–424.

Steel, J., Williams, J. M., & McGeown, S. (2021). Reading to dogs in schools: An exploratory study of teacher perspectives. *Educational Research, 63*(3), 279–301.

Stiegler-Balfour, J. J., Roberts, Z. S., LaChance, A. S., Sahouria, A. M., & Newborough, E. D. (2023). Is reading under print and digital conditions really equivalent? Differences in reading and recall of expository text for higher and lower ability comprehenders. *International Journal of Human-Computer Studies, 176*, e103036.

Stouten, J., Rousseau, D. M., & De Cremer, D. (2018). Successful organizational change: Integrating the management practice and scholarly literatures. *Academy of Management Annals, 12*(2), 752–788.

Strauss, A., & Corbin, J. (1998). *Basics of qualitative research* (2nd ed.). Sage Publications.

Sullanmaa, J., Pyhältö, K., Pietarinen, J., & Soini, T. (2021). Relationships between change management, knowledge sharing, curriculum coherence and school impact in national curriculum reform: A longitudinal approach. *International Journal of Leadership in Education*, https://doi.org/10.1080/13603124.2021.1972165

Sullivan, A., & Brown, M. (2013). Social inequalities in cognitive scores at age 16: The role of reading. *CLS Working Papers, 2013*(13/10).

Sullivan, A., & Brown, M. (2015). Reading for pleasure and progress in vocabulary and mathematics. *British Educational Research Journal, 41*(6), 971–991.

Sydney Morning Herald (2022). The Sydney Morning Herald is the most-read masthead in the country. *Sydney Morning Herald*. https://www.smh.com.au/business/companies/the-sydney-morning-herald-is-the-most-read-masthead-in-the-country-20221118-p5bzif.html

Tang, K. S., Lin, S. W., & Kaur, B. (2022). Mapping and extending the theoretical perspectives of reading in science and mathematics education research. *International Journal of Science and Mathematics Education, 20*(S1), 1–15.

te Riele, K., Stewart, S., & Stratford, E. (2022). Whole school change for literacy teaching and learning: Purposes and processes. *Language and Education, 36*(4), 329–345.

Thomas, D. R. (2006). A general inductive approach for analyzing qualitative evaluation data. *American Journal of Evaluation, 27*(2), 237–246.

Torppa, M., Niemi, P., Vasalampi, K., Lerkkanen, M. K., Tolvanen, A., & Poikkeus, A. M. (2020). Leisure reading (but not any kind) and reading comprehension support each other – A longitudinal study across grades 1 and 9. *Child Development, 91*(3), 876–900.

Toste, J. R., Didion, L., Peng, P., Filderman, M. J., & McClelland, A. M. (2020). A meta-analytic review of the relations between motivation and reading achievement for K–12 students. *Review of Educational Research, 90*(3), 420–456.

Tovey, S. (2022). Engaging the reluctant preservice teacher reader: Exploring possible selves with literature featuring teachers. *Action in Teacher Education, 44*(4), 271–289.

Troyer, M., Kim, J. S., Hale, E., Wantchekon, K. A., & Armstrong, C. (2019). Relations among intrinsic and extrinsic reading motivation, reading amount, and comprehension: A conceptual replication. *Reading and Writing, 32*(5), 1197–1218.

Twenge, J. M., Martin, G. N., & Spitzberg, B. H. (2019). Trends in US adolescents' media use, 1976–2016: The rise of digital media, the decline of TV, and the (near) demise of print. *Psychology of Popular Media Culture, 8*(4), 329–345.

United Nations Educational, Scientific and Cultural Organization (2021). *International Literacy Day 2021.* https://en.unesco.org/sites/default/files/ild-2021-fact-sheet.pdf

University of New South Wales (2023). Grey literature. https://www.library.unsw.edu.au/using-the-library/information-resources/grey-literature

Vaahtoranta, E., Suggate, S., Jachmann, C., Lenhart, J., & Lenhard, W. (2018). Can explaining less be more? Enhancing vocabulary through explicit versus elaborative storytelling. *First Language, 38*(2), 198–217.

Vaknin-Nusbaum, V., & Tuckwiller, E. D. (2022). Reading motivation, well-being and reading achievement in second grade students. *Journal of Research in Reading.* https://doi.org/10.1111/1467-9817.12414

Vanden Dool, C., & Simpson, A. (2021). Reading for pleasure: Exploring reading culture in an Australian early years classroom. *Literacy, 55*(2), 113–124.

van der Kleij, S. W., Burgess, A. P., Ricketts, J., & Shapiro, L. R. (2022). From bibliophile to sesquipedalian: Modeling the role of reading experience in vocabulary and reading comprehension. *Scientific Studies of Reading, 26*(6), 514–526.

van der Sande, L., van Steensel, R., Fikrat-Wevers, S., & Arends, L. (2023). Effectiveness of interventions that foster reading motivation: A meta-analysis. *Educational Psychology Review, 35*, 1–38.

van der Sande, L., Wildeman, I., Bus, A. G., & van Steensel, R. (2022). Personalized expert guidance of students' book choices in primary and secondary education. *Reading Psychology*, https://doi.org/10.1080/02702711.2022.2113944

van der Sande, L., Wildeman, I., Bus, A. G., & van Steensel, R. (2023). Nudging to stimulate reading in primary and secondary education. *SAGE Open.* https://doi.org/10.1177/21582440231166357

van der Weel, A., & Mangen, A. (2022). Textual reading in digitised classrooms: Reflections on reading beyond the internet. *International Journal of Educational Research, 115*, e102036.

Vansteelandt, I., Mol, S. E., & van Keer, H. (2022). Pre-service teachers' reader profiles: Stability and change throughout teacher education. *Journal of Research in Reading, 45*(1), 1–19.

Vershbow, S. (2023). Behind the scenes of Barack Obama's reading lists. *Esquire.* https://www.esquire.com/entertainment/books/a43530028/barack-obama-reading-list

Vindrola-Padros, C., & Johnson, G. A. (2020). Rapid techniques in qualitative research: A critical review of the literature. *Qualitative Health Research, 30*(10), 1596–1604.

Welling, A. (2022). *Leesmotivatie door filmpjes over boeken: maakt Booktok lezen weer populair?* [Bachelor's thesis, Radboud University]. Radboud University Educational Repository. https://theses.ubn.ru.nl/bitstream/handle/123456789/13178/Welling%2C_A.H._1.pdf?sequence=1

Westbrook, J., Sutherland, J., Oakhill, J., & Sullivan, S. (2019). 'Just reading': The impact of a faster pace of reading narratives on the comprehension of poorer adolescent readers in English classrooms. *Literacy, 53*(2), 60–68.

Wheater, R., Rose, S., Ager, R., Liht, J., Styles, B., & Twist, L. (2022). *Impact of Covid-19-related school closures in Key Stage 1 on attainment and social skills of pupils in Year 2 and Year 3 in academic year 2021/2022.* Education Endowment Foundation. https://d2tic4wvo1iusb.cloudfront.net/documents/projects/Impact-of-school-closure-in-KS1-on-Y2-and-3-pupils_publication-update.pdf?v=1669325212

White, D. (2022). How one Sydney school got students reading in the social media age. *Sydney Morning Herald.* https://www.smh.com.au/national/nsw/how-one-sydney-school-got-students-reading-in-the-social-media-age-20220517-p5am3e.html

Wilson, B., Kelly, C., & Sherretz, K. L. (2016). Delaware school libraries master plan: Quality school libraries = higher student achievement. http://udspace.udel.edu/handle/19716/21592

Winberg, M., Tegmark, M., Vinterek, M., & Alatalo, T. (2022). Motivational aspects of students' amount of reading and affective reading experiences in a school context: A large-scale study of grades 6 and 9, *Reading Psychology,* https://doi.org/10.1080/02702711.2022.2118914

Wisdom, J. P., Riley, H., & Myers, N. (2015). Recommendations for writing successful grant proposals: An information synthesis. *Academic Medicine, 90*(12), 1720–1725.

World Health Organization (2022). *WHO COVID-19 research database.* https://search.bvsalud.org/global-literature-on-novel-coronavirus-2019-

ncov/?output=site&lang=en&from=0&sort=&format=summary&count=20&fb=&page=1&skfp=&index=au&q=Merga+Margaret&search_form_submit=

Xu, W., Gao, Q., Yu, X., Guo, J., & Wang, R. (2022). Cumulative reading engagement predicts individual sensitivity to moral judgment: The mediating role of social processing tendencies. *Studia Psychologica, 64*(3), 268–282.

Yeh, R. W., Valsdottir, L. R., Yeh, M. W., Shen, C., Kramer, D. B., Strom, J. B., Secemsky, E. A., Healy, J. L., Domeier, R. M., Kazi, D. S., & Nallamothu, B. K. (2018). Parachute use to prevent death and major trauma when jumping from aircraft: Randomized controlled trial. *British Medical Journal, 363*, k5094.

Zare, M., Kozak, S., Rodrigues, M. L., & Martin-Chang, S. (2023). The roots of reading for pleasure: Recollections of reading and current habits. *Literacy*, https://doi.org/10.1111/lit.12315

Zebroff, D., & Kaufman, D. (2016). Texting, reading, and other daily habits associated with adolescents' literacy levels. *Education and Information Technologies, 22*(5), 2197–2216.

Zhao, Y. (2020). Two decades of havoc: A synthesis of criticism against PISA. *Journal of Educational Change, 21*, 245–266.

Zhu, Y. (2022). Reading matters more than mathematics in science learning: An analysis of the relationship between student achievement in reading, mathematics, and science. *International Journal of Science Education, 44*(1), 1–17.

Zucker, T. A., Oh, Y., Conradi Smith, K., & Baker-Finck, J. (2022). Low-income elementary students access to books & reading motivation. *Reading Psychology, 43*(3–4), 250–276.

Index

academic partnership (and academic publication) 83, 86, 120, 139, 146, 159–65, 174–8
Africa 180
Albania 15
Association of Independent Schools of New South Wales (AISNSW) xv, 82, 87
audiobooks 68
Australia xix–xx, 5–6, 14–18, 21, 25, 30, 32, 34, 36, 38, 42–3, 48, 58, 60, 62, 64, 67, 74, 122, 149, 169, 170, 173
Australian Bureau of Statistics (ABS) xv, 17
Australian School Library Association (ASLA) xv, 43, 82–3
author visits 40, 55, 70

bi-modal distribution 134
British United Provident Association Limited (BUPA) xv, xx, 82
Bulgaria 15

Cambodia 16
Canada 14, 17–18
change management 66, 73–5, 89–111
China 3, 15–18, 21, 60
  see also Hong Kong; Macao
collection building 37–40, 55, 68, 71, 76
Colombia 15
conflict of interest 146–8, 164, 181
content-area literacy 9
convergent design 152
COVID-19 xv, 13, 23–4, 42, 68

deductive disclosure 147, 168
Department of Education Western Australia (DoE) xv, 62
digital literacy 9–11
disciplinary literacy 9

eBook(s) 20–2, 36
empathy 11–12, 34
environmental supports for reading xvii, 2–4, 24, 29, 38, 56–9, 95, 118
Estonia 16, 43
evaluation question(s) (EQs) xv, 127–30, 144–5
expired expectations 4, 19
extrinsic motivation (to read) 3, 6–7

Finland 15

gender 12–15, 21–2, 34, 51, 68, 79, 96, 132–3, 137
Germany 34, 61
goal setting 96, 100, 102–5, 114–18
grey literature 181

health literacy 9, 11, 20, 102, 123
higher degree by research (HDR) 159–60, 177
high-stakes literacy testing 4–6, 13, 43, 49, 114–16, 180
Hong Kong (China) 42
Hungary 15

Iceland 15
India xi, 17–18
Indonesia 15

information literacy xviii, 11
integration (in mixed methods analysis) 150, 153, 157
International Study of Avid Book Readers project (ISABR) xv, xix, 3, 41, 43, 56, 59
Italy 15, 21

Japan 15, 42, 149
joint display ix, 153–6
Jordan 83

Kazakhstan 15
Korea (South) 15

Latvia 15
Likert-type scale 128, 151

Macao (China) 15–16
Malaysia 71
mathematics (maths) 9–11, 15–16, 24, 46, 100, 116
Mexico 15
Moldova (Republic of) 15

Netherlands (the) 15, 91
New Zealand 1, 15, 25, 38, 75
Northern Ireland 39, 92
Norway 67

Organisation for Economic Co-operation and Development (OECD) xv, xviii, 10–11, 13, 15–16, 19–21
orphaned responsibility 4, 19, 46

Peru 15
phishing 11
Portugal 15
Program for International Student Assessment (PISA) xv, 13, 15–16, 19, 21, 28, 180
Progress in International Reading Literacy Study (PIRLS) xv, 13, 16, 24, 49, 180
public library 23, 29, 51–2, 74

Qatar 15

Queenwood 30, 82, 174

randomised controlled trial (RCT) xv, 119–20, 127
reading comprehension xviii, 6–11, 19, 21–2, 24, 31, 61, 64, 68, 80, 104–6, 116, 124, 128

satisficing 122, 124, 129, 146–7
school library xi, xiii, xx–xxi, 2, 5, 7, 13, 22–3, 29, 31, 33, 35, 37–43, 46, 52–3, 56–9, 67–70, 73–4, 76–7, 81, 97, 99, 104–5, 107, 109, 115, 118, 128–31, 142, 152, 172
school library professional(s) xxi, 23, 31, 33, 35, 37, 39–43, 46, 53, 109
Scotland 38
Senegal 16
Simple Measure of Gobbledygook (SMOG) xv, 123
Singapore 16, 42
skew 124, 134–6
skip logics 129, 131–3, 154, 156
Slovakia 15
story dogs 67, 133–5, 137
struggling literacy learners (SLLs) xv, 15–16, 24, 31, 33, 41, 56, 61, 64, 68, 97–9, 109, 133, 153, 155, 180
Switzerland 15
Sydney Health Literacy Lab (SHeLL) xv, 102, 123

teacher librarian xv, xx, 31, 40, 42–4, 46, 55, 58, 68, 70, 78–9, 81, 142
Teacher Librarians as Australian Literature Advocates in Schools project (TLALAS) xv, xx
thematic analysis 139, 143–6, 148, 153, 157–8

United Kingdom (UK) xv, 5, 14, 17–18, 24, 38, 61, 67–8, 70, 74, 114, 168–9
United Nations Educational, Scientific and Cultural Organization (UNESCO) xv, xviii
United States of America (US) xv, 6, 8, 11–12, 14, 17–18, 24, 36, 39, 41–2, 49, 51–4, 59, 62–3, 65, 67, 71, 73, 106

University of New South Wales (UNSW) xv, 181

vocabulary 7, 11, 19–20, 52, 60, 64, 101, 116, 121, 124

Wales 38

wellbeing xi, xx, 7, 12–13, 67, 76–7, 94, 115, 117–18

We Love Reading project (WLR) xvi, 61

West Australian Study in Adolescent Book Reading project (WASABR) xv, xix, 3, 18–19, 26, 32, 44, 47, 55, 115

Western Australian Study in Children's Book Reading project (WASCBR) xv, xix, 4, 28, 47

Western Australian Study in Reading Aloud project (WASRA) xv, xix, 7, 50, 60, 62–3

World Health Organization (WHO) xv, 13

Zambia 16